PRAISE FOR *BOYS*

"If 'the future is female,' where does that leave our boys? Rachel Giese brings her talents as a journalist, a refreshing lack of jargon, and her insights as the mother of a charming, ADHD, hockey-loving son to this urgently important matter—of how to raise stronger, kinder boys. As we say 'enough' to the very worst of male behavior—gun violence and sexual assault—we need to imagine and invest in the best of it as well. This book about reinventing the culture of masculinity could not be more timely or wise."

—Marni Jackson, author of *The Mother Zone* and
Home Free: The Myth of the Empty Nest

"With *Boys*, Rachel Giese shows that there is indeed a 'boy crisis,' but it's not the one we keep hearing about, and it's a crisis whose solutions lie in expanding the limits of boyhood and manhood to enable boys and men to be true to themselves and reach their full potential. I loved this book, such an absorbing and inspiring read, and it left me with hope and admiration for today's boys—and the men they're on their way to becoming."

—Kerry Clare, author of *Mitzi Bytes*

BOYS

BOYS

WHAT IT MEANS TO BECOME A MAN

RACHEL GIESE

SEAL PRESS

Seal Press
Hachette Book Group
1290 Avenue of the Americas, New York, NY 10104
www.sealpress.com
@sealpress

First US Edition: December 2018

Printed in the United States of America

Published by Seal Press, an imprint of Perseus Books, LLC, a subsidiary of Hachette Book Group, Inc. The Seal Press name and logo is a trademark of the Hachette Book Group.

The Hachette Speakers Bureau provides a wide range of authors for speaking events. To find out more, go to www.hachettespeakersbureau.com or call (866) 376-6591.

Print book interior design by Six Red Marbles Inc.

Library of Congress Cataloging-in-Publication Data
Names: Giese, Rachel (Journalist), author.
Title: Boys: what it means to become a man / Rachel Giese.
Description: New York: Seal Press, [2018]
Identifiers: LCCN 2018028868| ISBN 9781580058766 (hardcover) |
    ISBN 9781580058759 (ebook)
Subjects: LCSH: Boys—Psychology. | Masculinity.
Classification: LCC HQ775 .G54 2018 | DDC 155.43/2—dc23
LC record available at https://lccn.loc.gov/2018028868

ISBNs: 978-1-58005-876-6 (hardcover), 978-1-58005-875-9 (ebook)

LSC-C

10 9 8 7 6 5 4 3 2 1

For Jenn & Devon

CONTENTS

Contents

PREFACE

On a late spring day a few years back, around the time of my son's tenth birthday, he and I were running errands in our neighborhood when he spotted a friend. The boys shouted each other's names in delight, and as we passed the kid on the sidewalk, he and my son paused and leaned into one another, clasping right hands and pressing right shoulders together while patting each other's back. Then, seamlessly, they released their grip, and each continued on his way.

I'd seen men greet each other like this—or some other hand-slapping, fist-bumping, dap-giving variation—thousands of times. There's even a famous GIF of president Barack Obama meeting the men's Olympic basketball team in 2012: After offering a sober handshake to an older white staff member, he turns with a high-beam smile to star player Kevin Durant. Palms smack; shoulders bump; backs are slapped. The greeting has its roots in African American culture—in his 2014 photography project, *Five on the Black Hand Side*, Chicago artist LaMont Hamilton traces its origins to the late 1960s during the Vietnam War, when black GIs gave dap as a symbol of unity, brotherhood, and survival.[1] But like so many black inventions, the dap has been co-opted and gone mainstream, especially among younger guys of all races. And in these circles it's less often a signifier of political solidarity than of masculine cool and a socially acceptable way for men to express and share affection. It's not a hug. It's a *bro-hug*.

Witnessing the handshake between my son and his friend was a small marvel, one of those sweet and sharp parental moments of realization that your baby has become worldly and less familiar. It was also a curiosity. I had no idea where he picked it up or how often he'd tried out this gesture to make it look so graceful and confident, as though he had been born doing it.

My son's childhood and early adolescence, and his growing mastery of the rituals of manhood, are more an amazement to me than they might be for other parents. My wife and I adopted our son when he was one, so we have no genetic connection for comparison—no *he has your musical talent*, no *he got his dexterity from me*—nor did either one of us have a boyhood of our own. And our son, with his swagger, his inability to sit still, his gross-out humor, and his love of sports, video games, and skateboards, ticks many of the boxes of the traditional boy profile. A family member once joked about the twist in fate that placed such a stereotypical boy in a home with two women. But I don't see it that way. Our son's rough-and-tumble spiritedness didn't appear to me as more male than female (I know a lot of rowdy girls), nor did I think his ample affectionateness and tenderness made him an exception to his sex (I know many gentle men). Our son has had plenty of male role models: uncles and grandfathers, family friends, teachers, mentors, and coaches. When he was around eight, I asked him if he ever wished he had a dad or felt that he was missing out by not having one, and he paused for a moment to consider. "There's one thing," he said. "I think if I had a dad, I'd get to go to McDonald's more often." Not wanting to let this go unchallenged, I told him we knew a lot of dads who didn't go to McDonald's, like a neighbor who was vegetarian and a foodie friend who bought meat only from the organic butcher. My son shrugged, already bored and regretting this conversation. "Okay, fine," he said. "All I know is that you two lesbians never take me to McDonald's."

Aside from making a family joke out of depriving our son of Big Macs, my wife and I didn't dwell on what it meant to be two women raising a boy when he was younger. We figured he could call on his uncles when it was time to learn to shave. But pretty much everything else a kid needs to be taught, qualities like decency, resilience, empathy, honesty, and tenacity, are genderless. A greater consideration for us was race. We're both white, and our son is Oji-Cree and Ojibway. When it came to our son's sense of self, we were far more consumed with ensuring he was connected to his indigenous roots and culture than we were with worrying about whether he'd know how to tie a tie or throw a baseball. (My wife taught him to do both.)

Besides, we have a certain slant on the issue. Just as we had no preference for adopting a boy or a girl, we didn't anticipate that we'd raise a boy or a girl all that differently. Within our own circle of friends and in the larger LGBTQ community, gender isn't a garrison but an amusement park, where rules about masculinity and femininity are questioned, exaggerated, and turned upside down. From the time he was a toddler, our son has been around all manner of men who express all manner of manliness, from macho to fey, including a gay uncle who embraces both—he's a former high school football player who's knockout gorgeous dressed in drag. Masculinity isn't solely a male domain, either. There are butch women in my son's life, most notably my wife, who gets her hair cut at a barbershop, has tattoos snaking down both arms, and even now, in her forties, is regularly mistaken for a teenage boy. When our son was young, we aimed to raise him without a strict gender agenda. Like good feminists, we bought him a toy cooking set as well as Thomas the Tank Engine trains. How much this would inoculate him against gender stereotypes, we didn't know. But at the time, his adulthood felt so distant that it was impossible to imagine what our little boy would be like as a man. Until, one day, it wasn't.

The glimpse I had of my son giving dap to his friend made me stop short. *When had he become such a guy?* I wondered. And now that he was older, how would his transition from boy to man alter him? I began to more seriously consider the ambient noise of the rules of masculinity, the lessons both implicit and overt that my son was absorbing about male culture and manhood. What did he think it meant to be a man? Was manliness for him simply about endearing and benign rituals like handshakes and a fondness for "guy stuff" like basketball and *Call of Duty*? Or was he also picking up on the more troubled and troubling manifestations of masculinity, such as aggression and emotional detachment? What did he think of being a man in relation to women? My son is now in his early teens, and his coming of age coincides with a moment when masculinity is under examination: terms such as *male privilege*, *patriarchy*, *misogyny*, and *toxic masculinity* have made their way from university gender studies departments into the mainstream.

It's also a moment when masculinity is felt by some as being under dire threat, as evidenced by the growing allure of online forums and websites populated by men's rights activists, so-called pickup artists (PUAs), outraged male gamers, and other guys expressing varying degrees of confusion and fury about the changing social order. To many of them, feminism and the achievements of women have emasculated men and upended natural gender roles. "Aggrieved entitlement" is a phrase used by Michael S. Kimmel, a sociologist at Stony Brook University in New York and the author of *Guyland: The Perilous World Where Boys Become Men* and *Angry White Men: American Masculinity at the End of an Era*, to describe the general mood of this subset of predominantly white men who feel they have been usurped by others who appear to be progressing: women, immigrants, and people of color.

An extreme version of aggrieved entitlement was articulated by twenty-two-year-old Elliot Rodger, who killed six others and himself in a rampage in Isla Vista, California, on May 23, 2014. Troubled since he was a little boy, as a teenager Rodger retreated into *World of Warcraft* and online forums like PUAHate, which was created to mock suave pickup artists who boasted about their sexual exploits. It was there that Rodger, resentful of his lack of romantic success, found common cause with fellow "incels"—or "involuntary celibates." In forum posts and in videos he shared on YouTube, he ranted about both the women who turned him down and the men they found attractive ("Stacys" and "Chads," in incel slang): "Men shouldn't have to look and act like big, animalistic beasts to get women. The fact that women still prioritize brute strength just shows that their minds haven't fully evolved."[2]

Hours before his killing spree, he posted a video in which he said, "All you girls who rejected me, looked down upon me, you know, treated me like scum while you gave yourselves to other men. And all of you men for living a better life than me, all of you sexually active men. I hate you. I hate all of you. I can't wait to give you exactly what you deserve, annihilation."[3] He also emailed a 137-page manuscript titled "My Twisted World" to his therapist, acquaintances, and family members. In it he recounted his obsession with status and power, as well as his self-loathing and humiliation at having to "suffer virginity [his] whole life." Rodger began his attack by stabbing three men in his apartment and then, as part of his plan to punish "sluts" for their "crime" of not being attracted to him, drove to a nearby sorority house. There he shot three women walking outside the building, killing two of them, and then he shot and killed another man at a convenience store. Driving away, he exchanged gunfire with police and injured another thirteen pedestrians before turning the gun on himself. He died of a self-inflicted gunshot wound.

Rodger's murders were an extreme but not entirely unforeseen demonstration of a brewing backlash against women. His language echoed much of the content on the forums he frequented, and his actions brought into relief the mounting tension between what boys and men have long been told is their birthright (power, money, status, and female attention) and the present-day social reality in which girls and women increasingly have more agency, independence, power, and choice. Soon after the attack, the #YesAllWomen hashtag went viral on social media to highlight the ubiquity of male aggression directed at women and to suggest that Rodger's actions represented a broader male fury. Writing on Rodger, feminist philosopher Kate Manne observed that "misogyny often stems from the desire to take women down, to put them in their place again. So the higher they climb, the farther they may be made to fall because of it."[4] (On April 23, 2018, in what appeared to be a copycat attack, Alek Minassian, a twenty-five-year-old student in my home city of Toronto, allegedly drove a van onto a sidewalk and into crowds of pedestrians. Ten people were killed and more than a dozen injured—the majority of the victims women. Shortly before the attack, Minassian had written on Facebook: "The Incel Rebellion has already begun! We will overthrow all the Chads and Stacys. All hail the Supreme Gentleman Elliot Rodger!")[5]

My Generation X girlhood and adolescence encompassed a similar clash between progress and retraction. Growing up post sexual revolution and post–Second Wave feminism, my opportunities for education, a career, and personal freedom were far beyond anything afforded to my mother and my grandmothers, but in the broader world women's gains in independence were being spun as both a threat to our happiness and a danger to men's identity and self-esteem. I was a teenager when *Newsweek* published its infamous (and since debunked) 1986 story warning that a single forty-year-old woman was more likely to be killed by a terrorist than get married.[6]

Three years later, on December 6, 1989, in a horrifying assault that presaged Elliot Rodger's attack, a twenty-five-year-old man named Marc Lépine stalked the corridors of École Polytechnique in Montreal,

Canada, armed with a rifle and a hunting knife. He entered an engineering classroom and separated the men and women. Then he turned to the female students and said, "You're all a bunch of feminists, I hate feminists."[7] He killed six women instantly, and then eight more, before he shot himself. In his suicide note, Lépine, who had applied to the school's engineering program and been rejected, said he blamed feminists for destroying his life, and he said he believed women shouldn't become engineers, because they would take jobs from men. (The anniversary of the Montreal Massacre is recognized each year in Canada as a National Day of Remembrance and Action on Violence Against Women.)

Like Rodger, Lépine was a disturbed individual, and his anger at feminists felt familiar. When I attended college myself, the reading list of my women's studies courses included Susan Faludi's *Backlash: The Undeclared War Against American Women*, tracing the mounting hostility toward the movement. As far as women had come since the 1960s, true equality—in the form of pay equity, reproductive rights, racial justice, LGBTQ rights, and safety from violence and harassment—remained elusive. In fact, by the late 1980s, feminism was not only declared "dead" but had become the scapegoat for everything from infertility and a lack of marriageable men to female depression and a spike in eating disorders.

In the thirty years between my son's childhood and my own, gender roles and expectations have continued to evolve and progress. Millennial and postmillennial women have enlivened feminism, reconstituting the movement as more dynamic, inclusive, and intersectional—the last a term coined by US law professor Kimberlé Crenshaw in the 1980s to describe overlapping social identities (such as being black, female, and lesbian).[8] Beyoncé has proudly proclaimed herself a feminist, as have a growing number of young celebrities such as Amandla Stenberg, Rowan Blanchard, Zendaya, and Emma Watson. *Teen Vogue* and *Rookie* run stories about rape culture, reproductive rights, and transgender pride. In popular culture for girls, strong, smart female characters have flourished, in movies and TV series, including *Inside Out*, *Doc McStuffins*, and *Moana*, and in the arrival of a big-screen Wonder Woman and *Star Wars* Jedi heroine Rey. As a culture, we have poked enough holes in assumptions about femininity and femaleness that most of us now celebrate the idea of girl power and female strength. We believe that girls can and should play sports, that they're capable of excelling at science and math, that they can be both vulnerable and strong, that they may grow up to be soldiers, presidents, teachers, doctors, and engineers. There has been a wealth of academic research and media conversations about the impact of gender stereotypes on girls' self-esteem, behaviors, and opportunities. We recognize the value of strong, varied female role models, and we have well-honed critiques about the influence of Barbie and porn on girls' body image and sexuality.

But when it comes to challenging gender stereotypes and their effects on boys, we haven't been nearly as thorough or thoughtful. In her 2004 book, *The Will to Change: Men, Masculinity, and Love*, bell hooks argues that one of the oversights of feminism "has been the lack of a concentrated study of boyhood, one that offers guidelines and strategies for alternative masculinity and ways of thinking about maleness." One reason is that, generally speaking, boys have a higher status than girls in a sexist culture, so it's assumed they only benefit from this inequality. But as hooks points out, "Status and even the rewards of privilege are not the same as being loved."[9] She's correct: we haven't yet cast enough of a critical eye on the demands of masculinity—for instance, the expectations that men be physically aggressive, sexually dominant, emotionally stoic, tough, and in control—and the impact those expectations have on boys who do and don't live up to them. Even when we are cognizant or critical of these rules, it's usually in response to an act of violence (a school shooting, a gang rape, a campaign of online harassment), or it's in reaction to an alarming statistic about boys' dysfunction (their struggles in school, their failure to launch into adulthood, or their escalating rates of depression and suicide). We're afraid for boys or afraid of them. But this fear does little to help or change them. Instead, it pathologizes: they're violent; they're dropping out and abandoning college; they're addicted to their phones and video games and porn; they're wallowing in their parents' basements; they're becoming radicalized in online forums; they're succumbing to drugs or gangs.

In this framing, "boy" is an unquestioned, unchanging, and homogenous identity, and boys themselves are presented as the problem. What's rarely acknowledged is the role adults and the broader culture play in shaping the way boys are perceived and the way they perceive themselves. Nor does it recognize the agency boys use to either conform to or rebel against norms of masculinity at any given time to suit their individual needs. The kid who can't sit still, the one who is forever starting fights, the guy who catcalls his female classmates, the boy who hates to read, the one who spends all his time playing video games—are these just "boys being boys"? Or is there something else at work? Are they responding and adapting to rules created long before they were born?

The sexual revolution, feminism, civil rights movements, technological innovation, globalization: taken together, these movements have altered, to an unprecedented degree, what it means to be male. "I began to realize that something seismic had shifted the economy and the culture," writes Hanna Rosin in her 2012 best seller, *The End of Men and the Rise of Women*.[10] "Not only for men but for women, and that both sexes were going to have to adjust to an entirely new way of working and living and even falling in love." Recounting the ways that some women have surpassed some men—in schools, in the workforce, and in the home—Rosin argues that the balance of power has profoundly and irrevocably been transformed. And as old notions about masculinity and femininity fall away, there is a palpable angst about what should replace them. This time of instability and change has given rise to a pervasive belief that gains in rights and power for women must mean men are losing out. And this thinking has trickled down to girls and boys as well. According to a 2015 poll by MTV on gender bias, young men have mixed feelings about equality.[11] Twenty-seven percent of boys aged fourteen to twenty-four said gains by women have come at the expense of males, while 46 percent of them said feminism implies negative feelings about men.

It's not hard to understand why boys and young men might see it that way. If we imagine gender equality as solely focused on empowering girls, then what's in it for boys? What would induce them to participate in dismantling a status quo that continues, in many ways, to serve them? As Gloria Steinem once said, "I'm glad we've begun to raise our daughters more like our sons, but it will never work until we raise our sons more like our daughters." Put another way: in order for change to be real and lasting, feminism can't stop at transforming the lives of girls and women; it has to transform the lives of boys and men, too.

My friend Elvira Kurt, a comedian and writer, has a son and a daughter. In one of her stand-up shows, she did a bit on being a feminist mother raising a boy and a girl. With her daughter, she said, she's always trying to fill up the basket of her self-esteem, telling her she's talented, smart, and strong and can do whatever she wants when she grows up. As for her son—who, she pointed out, is at the top of the pecking order as a white male—she thought it would be a good idea to take a few things *out* of his basket, to lower his self-esteem a little, to even things out. She was kidding, but she also revealed an uncomfortable dilemma for anyone who cares about the well-being of young men. How do we uncouple their maleness from misogyny and male entitlement? How do we encourage them to think critically about the messages they receive about masculinity and push back against gender expectations that hurt themselves and others? And what can we learn from feminism and the fight for equality for girls and women to create more liberating, positive, and expansive forms of masculinity for boys and men?

Boys grew out of a desire to make sense of these questions for my own son, not only because I want to raise him to be a good person, but also because I want him to feel freer to express his whole self. This book isn't an argument against masculinity. It's a case for how we might rethink and reimagine the meaning of manhood for all our sakes, men's and women's, boys' and girls', and for those who don't conform to any of those categories.

I begin with a look at the social and biological basis of gender and sex. Chapter 1 explains the idea of the "Man Box"—a metaphor used to describe common attitudes and understandings about what it means to be a man as well as the consequences of those beliefs. Chapter 2 focuses on the science of sex and gender difference and the attendant anxiety about those who don't fit the norms. Then in Chapters 3 through 6, I look at some of the spaces where these beliefs about boys and masculinity play out: within friendships, at school, in sports, and in popular culture. Finally, in Chapter 7, I profile a remarkable sex-education program for boys in Calgary, Alberta, that puts all of this into action, teaching participants to think critically about gender rules, to build healthy friendships and romantic relationships, to be good communicators and positive leaders, and to tend to their emotional and psychological health.

Throughout the process of writing *Boys*, especially after a story broke about the latest boy crisis, in which a young man was either a perpetrator or a victim of violence or in which boys were reported to be in some general state of dysfunction or despair, I'd be asked by a friend or colleague if I felt optimistic about the possibility of better outcomes for boys. I was and remain hopeful, and here's why: A few months after my son's encounter with his friend on the street, his hockey team traveled to another city for a tournament. The team's families took over a floor of a hotel for a weekend. On the first night, a half-dozen boys congregated in our room to hang out and raid our stash of junk food. I was tidying up nearby when my son grabbed his teddy bear, which we had tucked away, and gave him a snuggle. Our son was ten or eleven, an age when a lot of kids have long since given up their stuffed animals and blankets. But Blue Bear had been with our son longer than we had, had comforted him through his transition from his foster family to us, and had taken on a talismanic quality. He was not easily relinquished, and he traveled with our son everywhere. Almost at once the other boys noticed our son holding his bear, and their playing stopped. I froze, fearful that they—a collection of hulking jocks just shy of puberty—would ridicule him. There was a moment of silence, as all of us waited to see how this would play out. My son broke the tension with a little joke. "Guys, meet Blue Bear," he said. Immediately, the other boys relaxed and began comparing notes: One had brought a stuffed dog; another kid had a toy elephant. One boy said that he had wanted to bring a few of his own stuffed animals but worried no one else would have them. Then the boys shifted back to wrestling and swapping Pokémon cards.

As for me, I was embarrassed. Not for my son, but for myself. This roomful of goofy, burping, rowdy boys had just schooled me on what it means to embrace a full range of humanity, where a person, whatever their gender, could be tough and soft, brave and vulnerable, competitive and compassionate. This book is for those boys.

1

THE BOY BOX

The Making of Masculinity

The first time I heard about the Man Box was five years ago in a college classroom on the outskirts of Toronto. Jeff Perera, a public speaker and community organizer who regularly talks to schools, businesses, and sports teams about gender equality, was leading a workshop for students on stereotypes about masculinity. He drew a large square on the blackboard in chalk and labeled it "The Man Box." Inside it, Perera wrote a string of words and phrases describing traditional views of masculinity: *tough, strong, head of the household, stud, stoic, in control, brave, emotionless, heterosexual.* Outside the box were words used to describe men who don't meet these standards: *pussy, fag, batty boy, bitch, mama's boy.*

He then asked the small gathering of college students for suggestions to add to his two lists. Shouts of "Wimp!" "Leader!" "Boss!" "Queer!" bounced around the room. As Perera wrote them down, he explained that the object of the exercise was to show that "the formula for manhood is the denial of everything perceived as soft, or gentle, or emotional, or feminine." In other words, a man might be described as being in every way the opposite of a woman.

Perera, professorial with a shaved head and rectangular-framed glasses, is a born performer, funny and gregarious. In his talk, he drops references both pop cultural (*Breaking Bad*'s Walter White is an example of "toxic manhood") and personal, drawing on his own childhood growing up as a man of color in Canada and the son of immigrant parents from Sri Lanka. To explain how early boys receive these messages, he tells a story about having once conducted an exercise with fifty boys in the fourth grade to see how much they'd begun to internalize the limits of the Man Box. He asked them to write down what they didn't like about being boys, and they returned a list that included "Boys smell bad," "Supposed to like violence," "Supposed to play football," "Having an automatic bad reputation," "Not supposed to cry," and "Not being able to be a mother." He projected an image of the actual list, made all the more heart wrenching by the wobbly printing and typos (*suppost* and *vilence*).

The concept of the Man Box is used by sociologists and equality advocates to describe the behaviors and expectations associated with a conventional, rigid form of manliness, an exaggerated, archetypal machismo that academics describe as "hegemonic masculinity." Admittedly, the metaphor of the Man Box is a little cutesy, but its utility lies in how it clearly separates sex and the biological identity of maleness from gender and the cultural creation of masculinity. (A caveat: there are some who argue that sex is, at least in part, a construction as well, but I'll get into that in the next chapter.)

This is a significant, even radical, distinction to make, since these markers of masculinity continue to be seen not only as normal but also as the rightful traits of those who do and should hold power. It's why we associate a deep voice with authority, while a higher voice sounds weak or shrill; why a suit and tie seem more fitting in a corporate office than a dress does; and why the socially awkward solo inventor, rather than the emotionally attuned collaborator, has become our go-to image of a tech genius.

For all the power these gender biases exert, the idea of "manliness" or "masculinity" as a fixed or natural thing has until recently rarely been questioned. Like whiteness, masculinity has been considered the default—think about how we address a mixed-gender group as "you guys" but never "you gals," much as we use adjectives like *ethnic* and *exotic* to describe every group but WASPs. In the 1990s, whiteness studies and masculinity studies (or men's studies, as it's sometimes called) began to crop up on college campuses. These fields of research seek to debunk the belief that "white" and "masculine" are the norms from which other identities diverge and deviate. Rather, "whiteness" and "maleness" are constructions and deviations of their own, deployed to concentrate power among some people and deny it to others. The myth that people of European descent are distinct from and superior to those with African ancestry, for instance, was the undergirding of slavery and segregation. Yet as the sequencing of the human genome has revealed, there is no meaningful biological difference or distinct dividing line between racial groups. Neither are racial categories stable or "pure." Human history is the story of migration and mixing. As social anthropologist Audrey Smedley once phrased it, "Race as biology is fiction, racism as a social problem is real."[1]

When it comes to gender and sex, the study of masculinity seeks to confront male identity in a similar way. As with race, the definitions of masculinity and manliness are not static either. The attributes that Perera wrote inside the chalk outline of the twenty-first-century Man Box, such as being heterosexual and stoic, are not the same ones that would have described a so-called real man in other centuries. In ancient Greece, for example, a sexual relationship with an older man was a common coming-of-age experience for a future free male citizen. And the poetry and art of the romantic period of the late eighteenth and early nineteenth centuries were rife with effusive male emotion and tenderness among men.

Even now, what's seen as acceptable male behavior isn't monolithic but shaped by factors such as race, class, ethnicity, nationality, and sexuality—blue-collar men, for example, express a different sort of masculinity than men in corporate boardrooms. And merely being male is not enough: boys and men have to be the correct kind of male. Homophobia and hostility toward those who are transgender or androgynous, for instance, are the most pervasive ways to police boys and men who fail to present themselves as sufficiently masculine. Gay men and transgender people are frequently targeted, often violently, for transgressing the rules of male identity. LGBTQ people are more likely than any other group in the United States to be victims of a hate crime. According to the Federal Bureau of Investigation, nearly a fifth of the 5,462 hate crimes reported to the agency in 2014 were a result of the target's perceived or actual sexual orientation.[2]

As Perera noted, these messages about what it means to be a "real man" come early. Sociologist C. J. Pascoe spent a year and a half embedded in a working-class, racially mixed California high school in the early 2000s, studying how boys utilized homophobic slurs to define and regulate male behavior in themselves and each other. In her 2007 book, *Dude, You're a Fag: Masculinity and Sexuality in High School*, she investigates how boys used the term *gay* as both a neutral description of homosexuality as well as a generic put-down equivalent to calling something dumb or uncool. *Fag*, on the other hand, was employed both to mock gay kids and more broadly to call out behavior that didn't fit masculine norms. Pascoe observed that making jokes about "faggots" was central to boy culture. One student told her, "To call someone *gay* or *fag* is like the lowest thing you can call someone. Because that's like saying that you're nothing."[3] Interestingly, girls were not routinely

4

called *dykes* or *lesbians*. Instead, the most common slur directed at them was *slut*. And this usage of *fag* and *slut* as insults reflects the opposing gender-based expectations regarding sex: boys must be aggressively (hetero)sexual, and girls must be chaste.

As a result of this culture, an openly gay boy endured near-constant harassment and eventually dropped out of school. But being straight didn't inoculate other boys from homophobia. "Becoming a fag has as much to do with failing at the masculine tasks of competence, heterosexual prowess, and strength or in any way revealing weakness or femininity as it does with sexual identity," Pascoe writes, noting the ever-present threat of being perceived as a fag. "This fluidity of the fag identity is what makes the specter of the fag such a powerful disciplinary mechanism... [teaching boys to] recognize a fag behavior and strive to avoid it."[4]

Though anxiety about appearing unmanly was universal, Pascoe reported that the definitions and rankings of manliness were also shaped by factors such as race. Black boys at the high school, for example, were among the most popular kids, and they were seen as more athletic and more masculine than other boys. This perception is consistent with prevailing racial stereotypes that associate black men with traditional masculine traits such as strength and athletic skills. That said, many of the black boys at the school also adhered to culturally specific standards of masculinity that diverged from the rules followed by other boys. White boys at the high school tended to think it was "faggy" or unmanly to care about personal grooming and fashion. Black boys, on the other hand, tended to take pride in their appearance. Looking attractive and stylish was, in part, a way to express their personal taste, cultural identity, and connection to other young black men. Yet while many black boys at the school enjoyed a high status among their peers, outside those social circles, stereotypes about blackness and masculinity held serious negative consequences for them. Teachers and administrators frequently perceived black boys at the school as being *too* masculine and presumed them to be violent, sexually precocious, and disruptive. Teachers were also more likely to punish black boys than nonblack boys for misbehavior, such as acting up in class.

Race and racism shape expectations of masculinity for other boys, too. Sociologist Alexander Lu has noted that male status is tied to ethnicity, observing that the common stereotypes of Asian men and boys are emasculating ones: they are seen as studious, obedient, nerdy, and weak—all traits that fall outside the Man Box. In 2013 Lu coauthored a study of Asian American men's personal experiences of masculinity and being male. Many of the respondents reported feelings of stress, Lu writes, "from trying to fulfill an idealized form of masculinity—a man who is tough, physically attractive, unemotional, and a ladies man. However, stereotypes about Asian American men make it very difficult for them to conform to this ideal."[5]

Oliver S. Wang, another sociologist, has also addressed the impact of these stereotypes on Asian American men. In his writing on music, entertainment, and sports, he's pointed out the paucity of images of cool, powerful Asian men in contemporary Western popular culture. The result, he says, is that some Asian boys have gravitated toward black culture and black heroes. Writing about National Basketball Association (NBA) player Jeremy Lin in the *Atlantic* in 2012, Wang observed, "For many of us, growing up Asian American meant having few of 'our own' male role models in the public sphere. As a result, hip hop—besides its sonic and textual pleasures—held a strong appeal because it was also a space in which we could witness brazen displays of masculinity, *especially* in defiance of whiteness." Given the "pathetically narrow" representation of Asian boys and men in popular culture, the emergence of Lin as a basketball powerhouse "offered up something we rarely get to see: an Asian American man, excelling in the most athletically masculine of all American sports, and doing it with passion, emotion and a cocksure swagger."[6]

Muslim boys of South Asian and North African descent have been subjected to similar stereotypes, as diligent students and "model minorities"—a designation I talk about in the chapter on education. But recently, due to fears about Islamist terrorism in Europe, the United States, and Canada, that old stereotype has been swapped out for a new one: lurking extremist threat. Consider the story of Ahmed Mohamed, a fourteen-year-old high school student in Texas who dreamed of becoming an engineer.[7] In September 2015, he showed up for class one day in a NASA T-shirt, excited to show his teacher a digital clock he had built himself out of a plastic pencil case. Instead of praising Ahmed for his initiative, however, his school alerted the police. A teacher had assumed the clock was a bomb. Ahmed was led out of the school in handcuffs and taken to a juvenile detention center. He was fingerprinted, had a mug shot taken, and was interrogated by police. He was subsequently suspended from school for three days. It's difficult to imagine a white, non-Muslim boy being treated like this. What could be more wholesome and typically male, after all, than a desire to tinker with machines? Isn't this why boys are given Lego blocks and chemistry sets? If not for his race and religion, perhaps Ahmed would have been hailed as the next Steve Jobs instead of branded a terrorist in the making.

The performance and expression of masculinity are complex. The same tactics that give boys power in one situation make them vulnerable in another—the ability to silently endure pain and emotional wounds might please a coach or a parent, but that repression in turn thwarts young men's capacity for intimate connection. Because no boy can live up to all the male norms all the time, manliness is a fragile quality. Perera likens masculinity to a house of cards, a slippery identity that must

constantly be reinforced through macho acts: a catcall, a loud apprecia-
tion of sports, a shrugging off of emotions. As women increasingly stand
out in arenas once reserved for men—for instance, as breadwinner or
boss—men are increasingly struggling to evaluate their own worth, he
says. "In your relationship, if you're not the funny one, or the ambitious
one, or the one with the money, what do you bring to the table?" Perera
asks. Without the old definitions, "What does it mean to be a man?"

Over the years since I first heard him speak, Perera and I have kept
in touch. When we met for coffee in the fall of 2017, his question had
taken on greater urgency. Twelve months earlier, Donald Trump had
been elected president, just a few weeks after a tape from the TV show
Access Hollywood was released, in which Trump bragged about grop-
ing women without their consent. His admission appeared to be backed
up by allegations from more than a dozen women that he had harassed
or assaulted them. In the year that followed, a series of powerful men
in politics, media, business, and entertainment were publicly accused
of sexual misconduct, among them Hollywood producer Harvey Wein-
stein, comedian Louis C.K., TV hosts Bill O'Reilly and Matt Lauer,
and Alabama politician Roy Moore.

Meanwhile, Trump's campaign and election had emboldened and
galvanized reactionary far-right groups, who decried immigration,
racial equality and civil rights, feminism, and political correctness.
Michael Kimmel has pointed out that almost all violent extremists,
whether Islamist militants or neo-Nazis, are young men who feel in
some way emasculated. And "proving one's masculinity," he writes,
"plays a central role in recruitment, or entry, into the movement. Entry is a gendered effort to ward off the shame that comes with their
failures—their failures as men."[8] For those of us raising or caring for
boys, this alarming anger, this mounting backlash, these tensions between men and women were a personal emergency as well as a soci-
etal one. At the beginning of what became known as the #MeToo

reckoning, a friend who has a little boy sent me a message on Facebook: "How are you talking to your son about all this?" And one of the first questions out of my mouth when I saw Perera was "What's going on with men these days?"

"What you're seeing," he told me, "are a lot of young men who feel threatened because they have this narrow idea about being a male, particularly a white male." Couple that with growing economic and political insecurity, he said, "and you have in President Donald Trump the embodiment of all their anger and bitterness."

━━━━━

When I began my research on *Boys* in 2015, gender progress seemed to be marching, slowly, forward. A 2014 Pew Research Center survey of American millennials, the generation just ahead of my son and his peers, found that this generation is optimistic and open to change, less attached to political and religious institutions than older adults, more likely to have been raised in a single-parent or blended family, more likely to have children outside of marriage and to wait until they are nearly thirty years old to settle down, more open to interracial and same-sex relationships, and more receptive to immigrants.[9] The Obamas, America's first black first family, still occupied the White House, and Hillary Clinton, widely believed to have a lock on the presidency, was set to be the first woman to break that "hardest, highest glass ceiling." In Canada Justin Trudeau was elected prime minister, seducing the world with his embrace of refugees, his appearances at Pride Day parades, his gender-balanced cabinet, and his feminist sweet talk about reproductive rights. Opposition to this progressive state of affairs by men's rights activists, white nationalists, extreme conservatives, and Internet trolls felt like howls from the fringe, the death cries of those on the wrong side of history.

We know what happened next. Those howls are no longer fringe but rather the voice of a powerful blowback, demanding that old borders and divisions be reentrenched. After spending several years attempting to disprove Obama's citizenship, Trump announced his own candidacy for president with a plan to build a physical wall between Mexico and the United States. Britons voted for Brexit, as nationalist, anti-immigration movements continued to spread across Europe, the United States, and Canada. After a period that held the promise of greater openness, inclusiveness, and empathy, now it seemed that new, starker battle lines had been drawn, not only between political parties but also between races and classes, sexualities and gender identities, men and women.

In 2017 the global nonprofit group Promundo, which works with boys and men to promote gender equality and stop violence against women, published an instructive snapshot of how young men were processing this moment and their place within it. For a study entitled—what else?—"The Man Box," researchers surveyed a racially and socioeconomically representative group of nearly four thousand young men in their teens and twenties in the United States, England, and Mexico to get their thoughts on contemporary manhood. Promundo's researchers referred to the respondents as "being in the Man Box" if they had significantly internalized and strongly agreed with seven "pillars of masculinity": being self-sufficient, acting tough, being physically attractive, sticking to traditional and rigid gender roles, being heterosexual, having sexual prowess, and using aggression to resolve conflicts.

The findings are fascinating—in some areas, the men were progressive, in others quite retrograde. Young men in the United States were most in the Box, with guys in the United Kingdom following not far behind, and Mexican men displaying less traditional and less conservative attitudes across the board. The majority of respondents said they encountered messages and rules about masculinity in society, particularly when it comes to self-sufficiency, toughness, and hypersexuality; however, in many cases they were less likely to respond that they agreed with those messages personally. Young men in all three countries overwhelmingly rejected the idea that men are superior to women. And most respondents believed that men should be involved in domestic labor; only 22 percent of US men, 27 percent of UK men, and 11 percent of Mexican men agreed with the statement "A husband shouldn't have to do household chores." At the same time, a large number of men showed support for the belief that real men should be tough and repress their emotions: 59 percent of US men, 51 percent of UK men, and 48 percent of Mexican men agreed that "guys should act strong even if they feel scared or nervous inside."[10] (Promundo's general findings are consistent with a 2017 study of American attitudes about gender difference by the Pew Research Center, which reported that the majority of millennial men felt they were expected to behave in traditionally masculine ways. Nearly 70 percent said there is pressure on men to be willing to throw a punch if provoked; 61 percent said there is pressure to have many sexual partners, and 57 percent said they felt pressure to join when other men are talking about women in a sexual manner.)[11]

Shortly after the Man Box report was released, I met with Gary Barker, one of the study's authors and the president and chief executive officer (CEO) of Promundo, at his office near Dupont Circle in Washington, DC. Five months earlier and a few miles to the south, an estimated half-million people had taken to the streets for the Women's March, to protest the election of Trump the day after his inauguration. Like millions of others around the world—from Paris to Lima to Nairobi to Antarctica—my wife and I, along with our son, had joined the solidarity march in Toronto. These demonstrations, organized under the banner of women's rights and representing support for economic equality, racial inclusion, social justice, human rights, and environ-mental protection, are considered to be largest single-day protests in US history. Given this recent resurgence in feminist activism, I began by asking Barker where young men saw themselves fitting into all this. "It's a confusing moment when it comes to masculinity," he told me. "We can see from this study and others we've done that young men are largely accepting of social change. In general, they recognize that women should be treated equally. When it comes to LGBTQ rights, there's a lot of acceptance." Well over 80 percent of men in all three countries felt it was totally normal and fine for straight guys to have gay male friends. But then Barker pointed out this finding: when asked, "If a guy has a girlfriend or wife, he deserves to know where she is all the time," 46 percent of US men, 37 percent of UK men, and 26 percent of Mexican men agreed.[12]

He said this suggests that many young men are still scared of wom-en's freedom and how they might be left behind. They have come of age at a time of enormous change, both social and economic and, unset-tled by it, may be espousing more traditional beliefs about gender roles. "These guys are looking at the world and thinking, 'I don't know what work looks like in an Uber economy. And I don't know what a mar-riage looks like now that relationships are more fluid,'" Barker said. "So a version of manhood that we thought was dead, or at least dying, has come back, as guys continue to cling to some of these masculine markers."

Holding these beliefs, or "being in the Man Box," however, has "immediate, sometimes contradictory, and often harmful effects on young men and on those around them," the researchers found. Guys in the Man Box reported being more satisfied with their lives than other respondents—likely because aligning themselves with traditional forms of masculine behavior and attitudes provides them with a sense of be-longing and identity, albeit one that now feels under threat.

At the same time, the guys in the Man Box seem to be in serious trouble. They're more likely to take risks with their health and safety (such as binge drinking and having unprotected sex), more likely to be the perpetrator or victim of violence, and more likely to sexually harass women. They're also more likely to experience depression and think about suicide, and they're less apt to have intimate friendships and seek psychological and emotional help. Tellingly, when they do ask for support, it's from the women in their lives, especially their mothers. (The men say a significant barrier for asking for help is the fear of appearing vulnerable or gay.)

Barker said one of the most troubling findings is how alone the respondents in Britain and America felt. (Guys in Mexico, who had closer ties to their families, didn't feel as isolated.) Also troubling: Barker noted that black respondents in the United States felt most under siege as men, followed by South Asian men in Britain. In a UK focus group, young men from the town of Batley, which has a large South Asian population, reported being treated roughly by police and security guards who suspected them of being criminals or belonging to gangs. The young men said they were targeted for wearing hoodies and for hanging out in groups. In response to this treatment, the young men said they would sometimes act out in anger. As one of them put it, "We turned into what they made us out to be."[13]

Against the current attention being paid to the failing fortunes and bubbling resentment of white working-class men, the experiences of men of color are being overlooked, Barker said. "There are all these stories in the media about how automation and artificial intelligence is going to put men out of work. And the alarm is sounding now because it's affecting white men. But this has been the story of African American men throughout US history." Conversations about the current decline in educational and economic opportunities for white men, and their attendant loss of status, rarely acknowledge those who have been systemically denied access to those opportunities in the first place. At the end of 2017, African American workers had the highest unemployment rate nationally in the United States, at 7.3 percent, followed by Latino (4.8 percent), Asian (3.4 percent), and white workers (3.3 percent).[14] Young black men, meanwhile, continue to be disproportionately arrested and incarcerated. According to the Sentencing Project, a criminal justice reform advocacy group, black men are nearly six times more likely to be jailed than white men. (Hispanic men are 2.3 times as likely.)[15]

Tyvon Hewitt heard firsthand about these experiences from many young men of color. He's a social worker at Washington's Latin American Youth Center, where he leads a program called Manhood 2.0, and for Promundo's study he interviewed young men aged sixteen to twenty-two, most of them black and Latino. Many spoke about their experiences being followed around stores by security guards, being stopped by police, and being perceived as a threat. "You could hear the pain in their voices," Hewitt says. "Because, yes, there's a Man Box, but there are other factors like racism that push young men further and further inside themselves and make them feel like they don't have value in the world." Many spoke about the push-pull of needing to project an image of invincibility while also trying to maintain an emotional openness.

He says depression was the most common theme among the older guys. While the younger men still expressed optimism about their future and about what it means to be a man, guys over the age of eighteen voiced a sense of failure about not living up to masculine expectations. Hewitt calls it a sign of "the provider's complex." If the young men didn't have external signifiers of success, such as a big salary or a fancy car, they didn't feel like real men. "The search for fulfillment was outside themselves. Some of them felt that if they weren't a financial provider then they had nothing to bring to a relationship."

Hewitt, who at twenty-six is not much older than the men he surveyed, says messages about what it means to be a real man "begin the moment the doctor says, 'It's a boy.'" Conforming to the rules of masculinity, he says, is not just something boys and young men do to themselves or monitor within their own social groups—pressure comes from partners and families as well. For instance, a small but significant number of respondents in all three countries said their girlfriends would expect them to use violence to defend their reputation. But for most men, these messages start at home. The majority of young men surveyed in the United States and Mexico said their parents taught them to hide feelings of nervousness and fear, to "tough it out" when they were going through difficulties, and to "man up" when they expressed vulnerability. (In the United Kingdom, 47 percent of respondents reported hearing this message.)

If young men feel anxiety about whether they are masculine enough, it's often in large part due to how much anxiety emanates from the adults around them. Hewitt says that sometimes those messages come with good intentions. Parents might tell their sons to toughen up in order to protect them from being hurt. Or they might want boys to conform for fear of the consequences for them if they don't. But having these beliefs aired and reiterated and reinforced over time, Hewitt says, causes "parts of you to die off," because you feel you can't express who you really are.

———

Though the current configuration and contents of the Man Box are new, anxiety about boys and young men not living up to the standards of manliness is not. "From the very moment masculinity was invented," historian Stephanie Coontz tells me, "it was a source of worry." Coontz is the director of research and public education at the University of

Texas at Austin–based Council on Contemporary Families and the author of several books about marriage, family, and gender. She traces the origin of the current definition of masculinity to the late eighteenth and early nineteenth centuries, when gender identities began to be seen as a dichotomy and women and men were delegated to separate spheres, with women as homemakers and men as economic providers. Certain qualities and dispositions began to be associated with femininity, such as delicacy, sexual purity, nurturance, and sensitivity, and others with masculinity, such as rationality, stoicism, physical courage, and intellect. (Prior to this time, Coontz says, women weren't so much seen as opposite to men but simply as inferior to them.)

At that time, white middle-class young men were a cause of concern. Like our current era, this was a period of massive transformation: urbanization and industrialization, the end of western expansion in the United States, the beginning of the movement for women's suffrage. In periodicals and journals, fretful essays argued that boys had become feminized and weak, they were spending too much time in the company of their mothers and female teachers, and they were losing touch with their natural wild natures. Social reformers, including American Henry William Gibson and Englishman Robert Baden-Powell, stepped in to toughen boys into upright, moral, manly men through sports and outdoor adventures.

Gibson was a leader in the Young Men's Christian Association (YMCA) and author of the 1916 character-building manual *Boyology; or, Boy Analysis*, and Baden-Powell was the founder of the Boy Scouts. Both endeavors were predicated on shoring up what Christopher Greig, a Canadian gender historian at the University of Windsor and author of the book *Ontario Boys: Masculinity and the Idea of Boyhood in Postwar Ontario, 1945–1960*, calls "a colonial imperialist kind of masculinity." These sporting and scouting regimes were intended to build dutiful, honorable men who would serve their nations' interests. The idea, Greig tells me, "was to teach boys enough discipline and self-control so that they could be enlisted as foot soldiers in the economic army, or soldiers in a real army."[16]

Over the next hundred years, anxiety over boys—whether it was that they were too brutish or not brutish enough—has persisted, flaring up during moments of social change and upheaval. The 1950s was a similar period of flux and fear: defined by postwar prosperity and growth, the civil rights movement, the space race, the Cold War, and the Red Scare. Alfred Kinsey's *Sexual Behavior in the Human Male* was published in 1948 and *Sexual Behavior in the Human Female* in 1953, opening up the conversation about sexuality, including homosexuality. Teenagers had more money, more leisure time, and new ways to enjoy both: dancing to rock and roll and hanging out at drive-in movies watching bad boys like Marlon Brando in *The Wild One* and James Dean in *Rebel Without a Cause*. Male deviations from clean-cut mid-century conformity—whether it was juvenile delinquents or effeminate "sissies"—alarmed parents and teachers. Millions of public school children were subjected to hygiene movies—hammy and ham-fisted, these short films tackled everything from cafeteria etiquette to drunk driving and petting at the prom.

The latest concern over a boy crisis began in the 1980s. Fears about crime and disorder in the United States led to the ruinous War on Drugs and the rise of mass incarceration. Big-city newspapers ran inflammatory reports about "wilding" by gangs of boys, a term that came into use in 1989, when five black and Latino teenagers were arrested and falsely convicted for the rape of a white woman jogger in New York City's Central Park. (More than a decade later, all of them would be exonerated.) Donald Trump paid for full-page ads in New York newspapers, calling for them to get the death penalty. In 1996, then first lady Hillary Clinton warned of a kind of young male offender she called a "superpredator," with "no conscience, no empathy."[17] A few years later, on April 20, 1999, two Colorado teenagers named Eric Harris and Dylan Klebold entered Columbine High School, where they were seniors, just before lunch period, armed with bombs and guns. They killed twelve students and a teacher before killing themselves. The massacre was variously ascribed to bullying, mental illness, the proliferation of guns, violent video games, goth subculture, and the music of Marilyn Manson; panic grew about alienated and antisocial white boys like Harris and Klebold, resulting in a growing preoccupation with zero-tolerance bullying policies in schools.

Boys were not only to be feared but also to be frightened *for*, especially when it came to education. Alarm at the boy crisis in school began to sound more than a decade ago, when boys were reported to be falling behind or dropping out. As I discuss in Chapter 4, blame was assigned to an education system that was too feminized and feminist, as well as to an inherent difference between boys and girls in learning style and even in the makeup of their brains.

All these worries about boys have since been magnified. And there are genuine reasons for concern. In the United States, two-thirds of students diagnosed with learning disabilities are boys.[18] And as with attention deficit/hyperactivity disorder (ADHD) and autism spectrum disorder (ASD), diagnoses of mental illness such as depression and suicidal ideation have exploded among boys. Young men, especially young black, Latino, and indigenous men, are among the primary victims of violent deaths—in some cases at the hands of police, such as eighteen-year-old Michael Brown in Ferguson, Missouri, and Tamir Rice, the twelve-year-old boy in Cleveland, Ohio, who was shot in 2014 after he was spotted playing with what turned out to be a toy gun. In both cases, the officers responsible said they thought the boys posed a threat—a charge often used to justify the harassment and criminalization of young men of color. As Columbia University professor Jelani Cobb wrote in the *New Yorker* following Brown's death in 2014, "I was once a linebacker-sized 18-year-old, too. What I knew then, what black people have been required to know, is that there are few things more dangerous than the perception that one *is* a danger."[19] The United States leads the world in locking up children: sixty thousand kids sleep behind bars every night in America;[20] a disproportionate number of them are black and Latino, and as many as 70 percent of juvenile offenders have a mental health disorder.

What do we make of all these struggles and challenges facing boys? How do we account for the ways in which they are acting up, shutting down, or being harshly punished for crimes both real and perceived? The most common response to the boy crisis has been to point to something intrinsic to boys themselves. A hundred years ago it was their wild nature. Today it's too much testosterone or their "boy brain" wiring. But the model of the Man Box points to another possibility: What if the crisis isn't about boys but, rather, masculinity?

2
BORN THAT WAY?

Examining the Science of Gender and Sex

———

When my friend Tori was seven months pregnant with her first child, she posted a picture of herself on Facebook. Sitting on a sunny dock by a lake, she looked lush and serene, a fertility goddess in a tight vintage strapless swimsuit. She wrote in the caption that though she and her husband had decided to wait until the baby was born to learn its sex, her body's dimensions had betrayed her. In South Korea, where she had been living at the time, a grandmotherly woman at a public pool eyed her up and down and confidently informed her she was carrying a boy. A few days later, a younger acquaintance told Tori she was absolutely certain the child was a girl, because Tori's belly was so "pretty and round." On a visit back to Canada, where the dock picture was shot, Tori was told by another friend that because she was carrying out front and high, and not wide and low, the baby was, *most positively*, a boy.

These days, most people aren't satisfied with this sort of folk wisdom and ask to be told the sex during their ultrasound. Tori and her husband's no-spoilers attitude places them in the minority. Studies I've come across indicate that most parents (anywhere from 58 percent cited in an American journal[1] to 69 percent of pregnant women surveyed in a Dutch study[2]) wish to know the sex of their baby before it's born, usually finding out around the twenty-week mark. Whatever the exact number, the practice is so common that the baby's sex is one of the first questions asked of a woman when she begins to show: *What are you having?* comes on the heels of *When are you due?*

To exploit this curiosity, a niche but thriving industry has emerged over the past decade servicing gender-reveal parties, affairs where parents-to-be announce the sex of their future baby. On Etsy, you can buy "guns or glitter?" and "baseball or bows?" invitations, and parenting websites share tips on how to stage the big announcement: the sonogram results are passed along to a party planner or baker, who prepares a piñata filled with pink or blue confetti, bakes a cake with pink or blue icing hidden inside, or fills a crate with pink or blue balloons. Guests takes guesses at what the sex might be, and then, at the designated moment, the piñata is clobbered, the cake is cut, the balloons are released, and *Ta-da! It's a...boy!* Thousands of videos of gender-reveal announcements have been uploaded to Facebook and YouTube and watched millions of times. In one image that went viral in 2016, a member of the US Army Special Forces let the world know his fiancée was carrying a boy by shooting his rifle at a box filled with gunpowder and colored chalk, creating a small explosion and a cloud of blue dust[3]—a display so charged with metaphors about sex and masculinity, guns and ammo that it bordered on parody.

If we want to be precise, "sex" (a biological identity) is what's being revealed, but it's "gender" (a set of social behaviors and expectations) that's being celebrated. Specifically, gender reduced to opposing extremes—reflecting nostalgia for a fantasy past in which girls were delicate princesses and boys were dirty-faced scamps. Some parents may very well be heavily invested in one outcome over the other, but I suspect that in many cases the desire is simply for an outcome that is comfortingly definitive. Blue or pink. Pistol or pearls. Boy or girl.

In the context of this era of change, this quest for control is understandable. Writing in the *New York Times Magazine* in 2015, culture critic Wesley Morris says the second decade of the twenty-first century has been marked by a "great cultural identity migration. Gender roles are merging. Races are being shed. We've been made to see how trans and bi and poly-ambi-omni- we are.... After centuries of women living alongside men, and of the races living adjacent to one another, even if only notionally, our rigidly enforced gender and racial lines are finally breaking down. There's a sense of fluidity and permissiveness and a smashing of binaries. We're all becoming one another. Well, we are. And we're not."[4] In hindsight, though, the celebration of boundary smashing seems premature, and even by the end of his article, Morris observes that this new fluidity has agitated deeply conservative forces that would prefer things stay the same or, even better, revert to an earlier order. To some people, the instability of identity—evident in the rising number of interracial relationships producing multiracial children, in the growing movement for transgender rights and visibility, in population projections indicating that by the 2040s white people in the United States and Canada will be the minority—isn't only disorienting. It signals the beginning of the end-times. The current backlash to change, whether in the form of anti-immigration sentiment or legislation to force people to use a bathroom that conforms to the sex assigned to them at birth, is a way to turn back the clock to more familiar power dynamics and demographics.

And when it comes to sex and gender, we're a mess of contradictions. On the one hand, boys and girls and men and women live lives that are progressively more similar. We go to school together, work together, engage in many of the same social activities, binge-watch the same TV shows, chatter and fight with one another on social media, and have cross-gender platonic friendships. On the other hand, despite all this—or possibly because of it—beliefs about the differences between the sexes are more heightened and embraced of late. Male style and grooming have gotten more distinctively masculine, with men in their twenties and thirties growing bushy beards and mustaches. Meanwhile, there's an outspoken desire for segregation of social spaces: women get away on a girls' weekend, while guys retreat to man caves. Given that modern heterosexual romance is often still predicated on a Venus-and-Mars, opposites-attract difference between the sexes, no wonder the blurring of gender identity has caused such discomfort. It's upending fundamental beliefs about sex, romance, and marriage as well.

So the question "What are you having?" isn't an innocent or small one. Even those who have lived counter to the status quo and have most keenly felt the weight of parental aspiration and disappointment can be seduced by the siren's call of the sonogram. A lesbian acquaintance of mine once attended a prenatal class run by an LGBTQ parenting group. The participants were a mixed and modern bunch, creating families that would have seemed impossible twenty years ago. There were several lesbians pregnant by anonymous sperm donors, a gay male couple using a surrogate mother, and a trans man who had temporarily suspended taking testosterone in order to carry the child of his cisgender (or nontransgender) male partner. Of this group, only my acquaintance and her partner had turned down the offer to learn their baby's sex at the twenty-week mark. "Everyone said they did it so they'd know 'what to expect,'" she tells me. "As if any of us turned out to be what our parents expected."

Of course, the reason everybody is susceptible is because the uncertainties of pregnancy, childbirth, and parenting are myriad and terrifying. Sonograms and gender-reveal parties are just the current manifestation of a long-standing preoccupation. In her 2010 book, *Origins: How the Nine Months Before Birth Shape the Rest of Our Lives*, Annie Murphy Paul cites a three-thousand-year-old Egyptian scroll that instructs pregnant women to pee on wheat and barley seeds and wait for them to sprout—if the wheat does, it's a boy; if it's the barley, then a girl. "There's something about the opaque orb of the pregnant belly that invites such speculation," Paul writes. "It's a silent oracle, a blank crystal ball. The sex of the fetus within becomes the hook on which we hang our multiplying questions about what the future child will be like."[5]

Historically and globally, the natural odds slightly favor giving birth to a boy: there are about 105 boys born for every 100 girls—it's been theorized that this imbalance is to compensate for men's higher mortality rate. Human bias, however, has almost always favored boys. In previous eras, boys were preferred for their power to confer status, to carry on a name, and to inherit a trade or business. Girls who were deemed burdensome were killed at birth, abandoned, or relegated to servitude. Even now, there remains a sense of success attached to having a boy—families with firstborn daughters are statistically more likely to go on to have more children, suggesting that parents might keep trying until they have a male child, the true genetic prize.[6]

Since the use of ultrasounds and other prenatal screening devices became widespread in the 1980s, parents who want a son can selectively abort female fetuses. Worldwide, the United Nations Population Fund estimates that tens of millions of pregnancies have been terminated for this reason over the past generation. There are more than 117 million "missing" girls and women across Asia, eastern Europe, and the Caucasus region, distorting standard sex ratios. In some areas, there are 130 male births per 100 female ones. In Canada researchers examined birth and sex data between 1990 and 2011 and found that Indian-born women with two children subsequently gave birth to 138 boys for every 100 girls. (They focused on families from India, since they have among the highest birthrates of immigrants in Canada.)[7] Based on this birthrate disparity, researchers estimated there is currently a deficit of 4,400 Indian Canadian girls.

There is only one situation where parents have consistently opted for girls: adoption. Studies in the United States show that prospective adoptive parents tend to specify a desire for a female child, whether they are adopting domestically or internationally. (There is also a similarly marked desire among white adopting parents for white children.)[8] There are theories about why boys are less likely to be adopted. Parents may prefer girls because they seem more vulnerable, or parents may believe boys more liable to bring with them disadvantages or defects from their family of origin. Potential adoptive parents may also be more familiar with the notion of girls moving from one family to another through marriage. In this case, a boy brought into a new family through adoption might be seen as a pretender to the throne. Or else, it's been ventured, since biological parents prefer males, perhaps if they place a son for adoption, it is because he is troubled in some way.

My wife and I had heard about this preference for girls from our social worker while we were filling out the dozens of forms required for our home study, the package of information collected as part of our adoption application. Sex—male, female, or either?—was among the many preferences we were asked to consider. There were also race and age and whether we would accept a sibling group or a kid who was the product of incest or rape. The questions were relentless: Would we accept a child with a club foot or a cleft palate or whose biological parents were addicts or mentally ill? Would we adopt a child who was blind, or had cerebral palsy, or was both blind and had cerebral palsy? Who was missing limbs? Who had cancer? Who was aggressive, withdrawn, on the autism spectrum? One who had been molested or beaten?

The purpose of the exercise was to weed out people with unrealistic expectations about the sort of children they might adopt. Since the early 1970s, the availability of birth control and abortion has changed the demographics of domestic adoption. Today, public adoption systems tend to house children who've been relinquished by parents unable to look after them or those who have been removed from unsafe homes. Many of the children are traumatized or come with histories of parental alcohol and drug abuse. Very little magical thinking is permitted with adoption: there is a surplus of children needing homes but few who conform to the idealized children that adopting parents may have had in mind when they planned to create a family.

Compared to every other question we were asked, the one about sex was easy: we ticked "either." If one of us had given birth, we wouldn't have chosen to know the sex beforehand, and we treated adoption the same way. We weren't leaving the decision about which child we'd get to fate, exactly; we were accepting that we had little control over it. Within a couple of months, we attended a conference where child welfare agencies meet to present their hard-to-place cases, children who could not find a home in their district. "Hard to place" is most often applied to children with disabilities, groups of siblings, older kids, and children of color. To make these children more appealing, the conference takes on the aspect of a trade show. Social workers talk up the kids to prospective parents. In a separate room, videos of the children run on an endless loop, with a narrator summing up their situations ("Jacob is a quiet seven-year-old who really wants a forever family. It would be best for him if he were a youngest or only child. He loves kittens and playing with his trucks") over footage of them romping at playgrounds and riding bikes. The ethics of this sort of marketing are questionable, but the approach is effective. Child welfare agencies that aggressively advertise their kids like this do so because they are more likely to place them in permanent homes.

At the conference we watched a short video of our son—not on the big screen but on a small monitor at a booth where we met his social worker. Our boy was beautiful, round-faced with lively eyes, warm brown skin, dressed in a fuzzy green onesie, and laughing with delight as he rolled over on a blanket. *Please consider us*, we said, handing over the contact information for our social worker. Next to that booth, we noticed a line that snaked a dozen or so couples long through the convention center. Of all the agencies present that day, it was the only one with a white female infant available for adoption.

I thought about the answer that parents-to-be sometimes offer when asked about whether they want a boy or a girl or when, as with my friend Tori, others try to predict. They say, "All that matters is that it has ten fingers and ten toes." I wonder if that's true for anyone at all. Because sex matters long before a baby is born.

———

Let's go back to what makes a boy or a girl in the first place. The creation of human beings requires both a female sex cell (an egg, or ovum) and a male one (a sperm). Every other kind of cell in our body contains twenty-three pairs of chromosomes, long stringy collections of genes. Sex cells contain just one chromosome from each pair. At the moment of fertilization, those twenty-three chromosomes from our mother's egg unite with twenty-three from our father's sperm to form the ultimate forty-six. Those chromosomal pairs will copy themselves many times over and pass on genetic data to each new cell, determining characteristics like eye color or a predisposition to hypertension. Sex is decided by the X and Y chromosomes. The egg can contain only an X to create females, but the sperm can have either X or Y. A double X makes a girl; an X and a Y make a boy.

Chromosomes are just the beginning, however. Each of us, in our earliest weeks, starts out as female, with rudimentary sexual organs that are "bipotential," meaning they can go either way. Left alone, we'd each continue to become female, growing fallopian tubes, uteruses, ovaries, and clitorises. But for some fetuses, around six weeks the sex-determining region Y gene located on the Y chromosome inhibits the development of female sex organs and kicks off the growth of the testicles, scrotum, and penis. In a couple of weeks, the nascent testicles begin producing androgens, a group of hormones that include testosterone and help to refine the development of male genitalia. And so, in the dark, warm protection of the womb, boyhood begins.

Outside the womb, another kind of boyhood begins, as expectations for who that child will be are already being forged. Thirty years ago, sociologist Barbara Katz Rothman wrote about the consequences of learning a baby's sex before birth. She asked a group of mothers to describe the movement of their fetuses during the last trimester. Women who knew they were having a girl characterized the activity in gentle terms, like "lively, but not excessively energetic." Those who had been told they were having a boy, by comparison, described it as "punches" and "earthquakes." Those who didn't know the sex of their baby didn't fall into a pattern in their descriptions. Similar gender-based sentiments have been revealed in birth announcements. A 2005 study from Montreal's McGill University surveyed nearly twenty-five hundred newspaper announcements and found that parents were more likely to express pride at the birth of a boy and happiness at the birth of girl. Researchers theorized that parents unconsciously think about their new daughters in terms of emotional attachment and their new sons in terms of status.[9]

From infancy on, this gender messaging only builds. Diapers and pull-ups are sold in male and female (blue and pink) versions, as is almost everything else in baby and toddler land: socks, hats, soothers, bed linens, tooth brushes, shoes, and backpacks. Good luck finding anything plain or unisex: boys' T-shirts come emblazoned with rugged markers, like a dinosaur, a football, or an army Jeep; girls' jeans and tops are dolled up with sparkles and unicorns. And let's be clear: a baby doesn't choose a sweatshirt that reads *Daddy's Little Princess* in pink cursive or *Mommy's Little Troublemaker* in blue block letters. It's parents who want to announce their infant's gender and the qualities they feel align with it, and it's toy and clothing companies that strive to profit from emphasizing gender difference. Writing in the *New York Times Magazine* in 2006, journalist Peggy Orenstein recounts her feminist-mom frustration in observing "the relentless resegregation of childhood" while shopping with her princess-obsessed young daughter. "A year ago, when we shopped for 'big girl' bedding at Pottery Barn Kids," she writes, "we found the 'girls' side awash in flowers, hearts and hula dancers; not a soccer player or sailboat in sight. Across the no-fly zone, the 'boys' territory was all about sports, trains, planes and automobiles. Meanwhile, Baby GAP's boys' onesies were emblazoned with 'Big Man on Campus' and the girls' with 'Social Butterfly'; guess whose matching shoes were decorated on the soles with hearts and whose sported a 'No. 1' logo?"[10]

So relentless is this segregation that it was newsworthy in 2015 when Target announced it was phasing out gender-based signage in its kids' departments, meaning there would no longer be "Boys' Bedding" and "Girls' Games" but instead "Bedding" and "Games."[11] Target wasn't the first large store to embrace gender-neutral marketing. Two years earlier, a Toys "R" Us superstore in Sweden stopped grouping toys by gender altogether. The company also distributed a catalog throughout northern Europe that featured pictures of boys playing with hairdressing kits and girls firing rounds from automatic toy guns.[12]

On this side of the Atlantic, though, some parents and conservative media outlets reacted to Target's plan to change its signs as though the apocalypse had arrived. But as much as the critics wanted to drum up alarm over the perversion of the natural sexual order of Mattel products, there's little proof of a universal, inflexible, in-built boundary between things boys and girls like to play with. While there are some gender differences in style of play (due to varying rates of the development of certain skills, like language and self-regulation), kids share plenty of common interests in activities and items that aren't strongly associated with a certain gender, such as coloring and puzzles, board games and hide-and-seek, swimming and climbing on monkey bars.

In fact, much of what boys and girls are drawn to is the result of socialization and savvy marketing, not intrinsic preference. Take the prevalence of pink for girls. It wasn't always thought of as a princess shade—a century or so ago, it was a masculine color. Prior to the early twentieth century, pink was seen to represent vitality, strength, and power, and it was routinely worn by young men. Blue, meanwhile, was seen as more suitable for girls; it was delicate and dainty, and it was the color of the Virgin Mary's robes, symbolizing purity. Similarly, fads in toys and kids' clothing are usually less a reflection of natural inclination than of current attitudes and anxieties about gender roles. Sociologist Elizabeth Sweet has studied the history of children's toys in the twentieth century, and she found that between the 1920s and 1960s, a period of relatively strict gender norms, girls' and boys' toys were produced and marketed according to stereotypes. Girls' items emphasized domesticity and motherhood. A 1925 ad in a Sears catalog for a pint-size toy broom read "Mothers! Here is a real practical toy for little girls. Every little girl likes to play house, to sweep, and to do mother's work for her." Boys' toys, by contrast, focused on mechanical tasks. That same Sears catalog pitched an Erector Set like this: "Every boy likes to tinker around and try to build things. With an Erector Set he can satisfy this inclination and gain mental development without apparent effort."[13]

These gender-coded toy advertisements began to disappear in the early 1970s, however. By then, more women were working outside the home, fertility rates had dropped, and the feminist movement was calling gender stereotypes in advertising into question. (This was the era of Virginia Slims ads targeting liberated women by assuring them, "You've come a long way, baby.") In the Sears catalog ads from 1975, fewer than 2 percent of toys were explicitly marketed to either boys or girls. In fact, many ads of that era depicted boys playing with kitchen sets and girls hammering away at a toy tool bench. Sweet notes that this changed again in the late 1980s, as gendered advertising crept back in, to the point that, by the early 2000s, the gendered advertising of toys was even more extreme than it had been in the 1920s and '30s— hence the hearts-and-flowers versus sports-and-trucks division that Orenstein observed.

Sweet attributes this reversal to several factors. One is economics. By segmenting the children's toy and children's clothing markets into boy things and girl things, companies can sell more versions of the same item. She says nostalgia also comes into play, as parents and grandparents like to give children toys they remember from their own childhoods.

But mainly, she argues, this marketing reflects an uneasiness with gender fluidity and exploits deeply felt convictions about traditional male and female roles. We like to believe a preference for dolls or toy guns is natural. Nearly every parent of sons I know has said, at some point, "We didn't do anything to influence his interests. It was natural. He just loves trucks!" (or footballs, or Star Wars Lego, or some other boy-defined item). However, given the prevalence of these pink-and-blue divisions, how early they start, and the degree to which they're reinforced in books and movies, in advertising, and in implicit and explicit adult expectations, it's impossible to separate the biological from the social. We can't truly know what toy or T-shirt a child might naturally choose for themselves—they're rarely given the space in our culture to do so. And these divisions become self-reinforcing, Sweet observes. "As toys have become more and more gender segregated, the social costs of boundary crossing and the peer pressure to stay within the lines are huge, for kids and parents alike," she wrote in a 2012 *New York Times* op-ed.[14] This is especially true for boys. "Parents tend to stick with gender-typed toys for boys," she noted, "either because they understand that the social costs for boys who transgress into the 'pink' zone are especially high in a homophobic culture or because of their own desire for gender conformity."

Fueling this is the popularization of brain science to explain how biological sex differences shape our personalities and behavior. The science of sex difference has tended to double down on gender stereotypes, by arguing that we can't help our preference for dolls or trucks— we were born that way. The invention of brain imaging technology and the mapping of the human genome have given a professional veneer to broad and sometimes dubious generalizations. A storm of magazine articles, books and TED Talks have focused on our brain-based, hormone-derived differences, popularized by experts like University of California psychiatrist Louann Brizendine, author of *The Female Brain*, who has written that women are born with a talent for verbal agility and "a nearly psychic capacity to read faces and tone of voice for emotions and state of mind," and University of Cambridge psychologist Simon Baron-Cohen, author of *The Essential Difference: The Truth About the Male and Female Brain*, who has theorized that "the female brain is predominantly hard-wired for empathy, and that the male brain is predominantly hard-wired for understanding and building systems."[15]

Male and female brains do appear to differ in a few ways. Men's brains tend to be larger, for one. And there's research indicating that boys' and girls' brains may mature and develop at different rates in select areas, such as memory and language and sensory processing. Rates of diagnosis suggest that boys are more prone to conditions like attention deficit disorder and autism spectrum disorder. Overall, though, boys' and girls' brains start out very much the same, which suggests biology is only part of the story; culture, experience, and environment help shape brains over time. (I'll get into this more in Chapter 4 when talking about schools—where this thinking about brain-sex difference has been influential.)

The debate about sex-based brain difference—whether men and women are hard-wired differently or whether sex differences are the result of culture and environment—is highly polarized. The work of experts in the hard-wired camp has come under fire for amplifying small discrepancies and for overlooking the considerable overlap and similarity between the structure of male and female brains. And when studies on sex-based brain difference are translated from the lab to popular media, the result is often overhyped claims about intrinsic gendered capacities, such as boys being inherently aggressive and mechanically inclined, while girls are naturally nurturing and sensitive. Australian psychologist and author Cordelia Fine refers to this phenomenon as "neurosexism." In her 2010 book, *Delusions of Gender*, Fine critiques the science of brain difference with tart, pitiless precision. "There remains in some quarters, a Victorian-style attachment to notions of innate, immutable, inevitable qualities" belonging to boys and girls, she writes. Reviewing the research, Fine concludes that measurable inherent differences between the sexes are minimal—or, as she puts it, "The male brain is like nothing in the world so much as a female brain."[16] Instead, she argues that our behaviors and aptitudes are a result of a complex interplay between our genes and our environments, a constant back-and-forth between our inherent potential (what we are born with) and cultural reinforcement (what we experience and are taught out in the world).

Like Fine, American neuroscientist and author Lise Eliot has written about the allure and harm of using brain science in understanding and categorizing children. "Unlike a generation ago, when parents actually worried about stereotyping their children, the new focus on nature seems to be encouraging parents to indulge sex differences even more avidly," she writes in her 2009 book, *Pink Brain, Blue Brain*. "The more we parents hear about hard-wiring and biological programming, the less we bother tempering our pink or blue fantasies, and start attributing every skill or deficit to innate sex differences."[17] After assessing the current research on everything from how boys and girls play to how they fare in school, Eliot concludes that boys' and girls' brains are, in most ways, remarkably alike. And while noting that there are differences between boys and girls when it comes to rates of development, some physical abilities, and play styles, she argues there's danger in overstating these discrepancies. We begin to see only what we expect to see, and those expectations "crystallize into children's self-perceptions and self-fulfilling prophecies." If a girl opts even once for a Barbie, later she is less likely to be given Lego to play with. If a boy runs around rather than sitting quietly with a book, the response is—often approvingly—"He's just a typical little boy," and he won't be as readily encouraged to develop a love of reading. This isn't to say that biology is meaningless. But assuming that the psychology and behavior of children are, to use Fine's term, *inevitable* dooms boys and girls right from the start.

———

Where thinking on gender, sex, and biology becomes even more complex and urgent is in the experiences of children who don't fit rigid definitions of male or female. The past decade has seen a growing understanding and visibility of children who are transgender (don't identify with the sex they were assigned at birth), gender nonconforming or nonbinary (don't conform to the social norms of gender identity or who reject being labeled a boy or a girl), and intersex (born with a reproductive system or sexual anatomy that doesn't appear to fit, or is inconsistent with, the typical definitions of female or male). They might be kids whom Jake Pyne, a Toronto academic and advocate for trans youth, describes as gender independent—kids who are "a bit more fabulous than the others."[18] Or they might be transgender kids, like a child announced to be a girl at birth but who later tells his parents that he's a boy. Or kids like prominent teenage trans activist, author, and reality TV star Jazz Jennings, who describes herself as having "a girl brain but a boy body."

Girl brain, boy body. The experiences of trans people reveal that sex can be both inherent and changeable and an identity that doesn't always comply with typical physiological markers, such as chromosomes and genitalia. (That is, having a penis does not necessarily mean you are a boy.) And the number of children who identify this way is growing. A 2017 study from the Williams Institute at the University of California–Los Angeles (UCLA) School of Law estimated 0.7 percent of kids aged thirteen to seventeen (or 150,000 youth) identify as transgender in the United States. This group, thirteen to seventeen, also has the highest estimated percentage of individuals who identify as transgender. Figures from Britain's National Health Service's Gender Identity Development Service indicated a huge uptick in referrals for children, increasing about 50 percent per year since 2010–2011.[19]

What this means is that young people today are coming out as trans much younger than in previous generations and in higher numbers. Clinics, counseling services, summer camps, and support networks have been founded in dozens of major centers around the world, specifically to care for transgender and gender nonconforming children and their families. The visibility and increased awareness are helping kids get treatment and care. Without support from families, schools, and the medical community, as well as legislation and policies that ensure their rights, transgender children can experience discrimination and isolation that can lead to emotional distress. One study of transgender youth in Boston found that they had a two- to threefold increased risk of depression, anxiety disorder, suicidal ideation, suicide attempt, and self-harm compared to cisgender young people.[20]

In many cases, transgender children are at the front line of a gender war zone, as school boards and local authorities grapple with policies and legislation regarding who can use which bathroom or participate on which team. Gavin Grimm, a seventeen-year-old high school student from Virginia, was the lead plaintiff in a case that went all the way to the US Supreme Court in 2017.[21] Grimm had transitioned to male when he was fifteen years old. At first his school administrators were supportive and allowed him to use the boys' bathroom. But when some parents and students got wind of the situation, the school board barred him from using the boys' washroom and instead required him to use a separate single-user restroom. The American Civil Liberties Union, who represented Gavin, argued that this was a case of sex discrimination. (The US Supreme Court ultimately decided not to hear the case.)

There are thousands of Gavins—children whose gender identity history is called into question when they attempt to use washroom facilities at their school or try to join single-gender clubs or teams. Around the same time Gavin Grimm's case was moving through the courts, Mack Beggs, a seventeen-year-old high school wrestler, won his weight class against girls at the Texas state wrestling championships.[22] The victory was protested by some of his competitors and their families, because Mack is a trans boy who had been taking testosterone as part of his transition, and that was seen as giving him an unfair advantage over the girls. Mack would have preferred to wrestle boys but was prevented from doing so under state law.

These fights over bathrooms and sports teams expose deep-seated panic over what it means to be male and female. Yet there is nothing new or unfamiliar about a range of sex and gender identities. Transgender people, intersex people, and those who were seen as being of a "third gender" or having aspects of both male and female identities have existed throughout human history and around the world, in India, Japan, among indigenous people in the Americas, and elsewhere. Our genes, hormones, and anatomy do not determine, in every case, whether we are male or female or something else, though many of us rarely consider the meaning or source of our gender identity. In an interview, Dr. Joey Bonifacio, a pediatrician at Toronto's Hospital for Sick Children (SickKids) who works in the hospital's Transgender Youth Clinic, points out to me that transgender children are required to account for and explain their identity, while cisgender children (and adults) aren't expected to do the same. "Before you ask a transgender kid why they know or believe they are a girl or a boy," he says, "you should ask yourself, 'Why do you believe you're a woman?'" It's an exercise everyone should try: Why do you believe you're male or female? What does it mean to feel like you are one sex or the other?

Gender awareness—understanding that there are both boys and girls and knowing which one you are—emerges as early as eighteen months. This can be difficult for children who are transgender or those who consider themselves something in between. It's often at this point that they begin to tell their parents that they are the other sex. Other typical signs that emerge in the toddler and preschool stage are certain bathroom behaviors (girls want to stand to pee, for instance, or boys only want to sit), preference for opposite sex bathing suits and underwear, and a desire to play with toys that are typically associated with the opposite gender. "Consistent, persistent, insistent" are markers used by doctors to determine whether a child is transgender, meaning this isn't short-term or occasional behavior.

Pamela Valentine, a writer, educator, and mother living in the Chicago suburbs, began to notice behavior like this when her son Jake, who was born in 2007, was a toddler. Told that Jake was a girl when he was born, Valentine imagined a warm mother-daughter relationship with her first child. "I'm a feminist," she tells me over the phone, "and even though I didn't fit the feminine standard in every way, I still imagined passing down this culture of womanhood to my child." Jake had other plans. By two he'd announced to his mother and father that he was a boy. At three Jake asked his mom why she wouldn't love him if he was a boy. "I love you no matter what you are," Valentine recalls responding. At four Jake switched to a boy's wardrobe; a year later he shaved his head. And just shy of his seventh birthday, Jake transitioned socially, identifying fully with a male identity.

"His courage takes my breath away," Valentine wrote on her blog, *Affirmed Mom*, about parenting a transgender child. "When you have a gender non-conforming child, you're forced to confront a lot of your preconceived notions about what makes a boy 'a boy' and a girl 'a girl.' You have to take all of the assumptions and ideas and expectations you had and let them go."

But how easily these expectations can be relinquished can also depend on the natal sex of the child (what they were called at birth) and the sex and gender they embrace. Jake's transition occurred earlier than is typical for trans boys, which is usually around eleven or twelve years of age, while many trans girls are referred for care around age four. For a girl to act in male ways is socially acceptable to a point, whereas a boy acting like a girl is more anxiety provoking. There is license for the tomboy to play sports and wear jeans but suspicion about the boy who wears skirts and plays with dolls. This double standard reflects the different values given to male and female traits. Dr. Daniel Shumer, an American pediatric endocrinologist who works with transgender children and adolescents, tells me natal boys are referred to gender-identity clinics at a younger age than natal girls, as parents grow concerned about their son's inability or unwillingness to adhere to typical boy behavior or clothing. "Masculine girls can be that cool girl who plays football with the boys. But the only words I can think of that are used to describe feminine boys have a negative connotation."

Valentine concurs. At first she and her husband thought Jake was a tomboy. "I was proud that I had what I thought was a strong spunky girl, or a future butch lesbian." It didn't bother her and her husband at all that their child only wore pants and hated princessy things—both of which conferred a certain kind of girl-power status. Then Valentine shared a story with me during our conversation about how this might have played out differently had Jake been a natal male and transitioned to female.

Valentine's husband is open-minded, and he was fully supportive of Jake's transition. But when the couple's younger child, Rudy (a boy who identifies as male), was two, he went to a little girl's birthday party. Rudy wanted to join the girls in dress-up, to try on a tutu and put pink coloring in his hair. Valentine said her husband later confided that he felt some discomfort with Rudy acting like a girl. "When Jake was two, he was wearing boy pull-ups and boy everything. But for Rudy to dress in girl things, that was a problem," Valentine says. Because we value masculinity more, we see girls acting as male as a step up. But to be seen as male and favor female activities and clothing? That's a loss of status and power.

When I reported about transgender children for a parenting magazine a few years back, a mother I spoke to shared a similar story. Melissa Schaettgen recalled her child Warner telling her at age two that "God made a mistake."[23] A mistake because Warner, like her twin brother, Emery, had been identified as male at birth, but while Emery embraced stereotypical boy stuff like trains and trucks, Warner preferred dolls and dresses, fairies, and the color pink. Melissa and her husband are Catholic and live in a conservative rural community in Canada. They didn't know what to make of a child who felt she was born into the wrong body. "We had no previous experience with LGBTQ issues," Melissa says. "No exposure—nothing."

They wanted Warner to be happy, and so at home she was allowed to dress like a girl, provided she put on boys' clothes when she was in public. For the next few years, the family lived a double life: one in which Warner was a boy, the other in which she was a girl. Melissa and her husband feared their then son would be bullied and that they would be seen as bad parents. "We tried to make Warner something she wasn't. A boy."

Warner began to get upset every time she had to return to her boy identity. The summer before she entered first grade, she had been allowed to let her hair grow shaggy, and the prospect of a back-to-school haircut led to a meltdown. "She said, 'I'd rather *die* than be a boy,'" Melissa says. She hoped it was a phase, but Warner's persistence and increasing unhappiness at living as a boy were something that couldn't be ignored. Soon after, Warner transitioned socially to identifying as female in public as well as at home.

Until recently, the standard treatment for children like Warner and Jake was what's called conversion or reparative therapy that aimed to treat gender nonconforming kids by encouraging feminine boys to be more masculine and masculine girls to be more feminine. The practice has been discredited, and some cities, states, and provinces have legally banned it. Today the standard protocol in North America and northern Europe is to provide social support for kids to live as the gender that feels right to them until they are in their teens, when they can explore medical interventions such as hormone treatments or surgery.

But what about children who don't identify with a specific gender or who are raised without gender labels? In 2011 a Toronto couple named Kathy Witterick and David Stocker went public with their decision not to tell anyone whether their newborn third child, Storm, was a boy or a girl. Aside from themselves, the midwives who delivered Storm, and Storm's two older siblings, Jazz (then five) and Kio (then two), no one knew Storm's sex. The couple didn't want any assumptions to be made about the baby's sex until Storm could decide what felt right. When people cooed over the infant and asked whether it was a boy or girl, Witterick and Stocker declined to answer.

In an email to friends and family, Witterick and Stocker explained their decision as "a tribute to freedom and choice in place of limitation, a standup to what the world could become in Storm's lifetime (a more progressive place?)."[24] After an article about the family appeared in the *Toronto Star*, the story was picked up around the world, and the couple was roundly attacked. Witterick and Stocker were accused of conducting an abusive social experiment on their child, received hate mail, and were harassed. On the street, people screamed "Boy!" at Storm.

When the *Toronto Star* caught up with the family five years later, though, they didn't seem like such outliers. The visibility of transgender people had already grown. Mainstream media has covered stories about trans children, as well as those who don't conform to either a male or a female identity and who use gender-neutral pronouns such as *they* and *them* instead of *he* or *she*. A handful of jurisdictions have begun to issue gender-free identification; Canadians and Australians have this option on their passports, and California was the first US state to introduce birth certificates that didn't specify male or female. In 2016 the Witterick Stocker family reported that Storm identifies as female. Jazz, who was identified as male at birth, is a transgender girl who uses the pronouns *she* and *her*. Kio uses the pronoun *they* and identifies as nonbinary.

Joey Bonifacio says that it can be more challenging for children who identify as gender nonconforming to find care and support. "Our broader culture divides us into this binary of male and female," he says, "and the main way we've been treating transgender children is to help them fit their affirmed identity as male or female. But we're witnessing more and more children who don't fit into those categories, and we need to start talking about how we help them." Daniel Shumer has observed a similar evolution. "There has been a rapid shift driven by young people who are rejecting the binary gender idea," he tells me. "I don't think that even five or six years ago we would have been seeing people describing themselves as 'genderqueer,' or 'agender.'"

This is a "mass identity migration," as Wesley Morris so aptly described it. And the evolution continues. Pamela Valentine says that since Jake transitioned, he's grown more comfortable in his own skin. When he was younger, he hated everything girlie. Valentine suspects that when his gender identity was still in question, he needed to assert his masculinity to prove to the world who he was. In a way, it was a trans boy's version of the Man Box. Jake wanted to live up to male expectations.

But now he's loosened the rules. He's met adult trans men whose self-presentation runs the gamut from he-man to feminine, and he's learned, Valentine says, that he "can choose whatever flavor of manhood and masculinity he wants." Right now, he likes to have his fingernails painted—because who says boys can't wear nail polish?

3

NO HOMO

Boys and the Need for Love and Friendship

━━

From the start, my son was a social creature. His foster family lived several hours away from us, in the same city as our longtime friends, a couple with a six-year-old boy we consider to be a nephew. We stayed with them every weekend during the summer that we met our son, who had just turned one, as we gradually transferred his attachment from his foster family to us. Initially, over the six-week transition period, we'd take him for a short walk in his stroller, then out for an entire day, feeding him, changing his diaper, putting him down for naps, and learning the vocabulary of his cries and smiles, before we brought him home with us for good. Our friends were usually with us, their six-year-old an instant hit with our kid, who would reach for him and later, when he began to walk, chase after him on his wobbly legs. Sometimes he would fling himself at our nephew, hugging and kissing him. The other boy's dad is a photographer, and he shot dozens of pictures of the two of them. One of my favorites is a close-up of the two boys lying on a bed. My nephew is on his back, my son is sprawled on top of him, and their faces are turned to the camera. They are tender, unguarded, in love.

Our son's circle grew from there: the baby of another friend, a pair of toddlers from the neighborhood drop-in, a kid a few years older from up the street. Only children sometimes acquire, by necessity, a certain self-sufficiency to entertain themselves, becoming avid readers and dreamy inventors. My son's aloneness had the opposite effect: it turned him into a schmoozer, a gadfly forever angling for a playdate, a quality that persists into his early adolescence. He returns from the first day of summer camp, or a visit to a skate park or a city pool, reporting he's made another new friend, and his network of contacts through social media and online video games is endless. He seems to exemplify the notion that boys are social but superficial, a belief prevalent enough to have inspired a parody news story on The Onion website: "12-Year-Old Couldn't Begin to Guess Name of Friend Whose House He Visits to Play Xbox."[1]

Yet for my son, a smaller subset of close friendships has emerged, boys he pines for when they are apart. His domestic aspirations aren't, at the moment, remotely romantic. Adulthood, as he imagines it, isn't about building a life with a family; it's a perpetual hangout with friends, sharing an apartment someplace cool and magical, like Los Angeles or New York, and supporting himself as a professional athlete or game designer.

But while my gregarious and funny son made friends readily when he was younger, he found keeping them harder. A constellation of learning disabilities—including ADHD and a motor-speech disorder called apraxia of speech—meant he was much slower to speak than his peers, and he has lagged a year or two behind in his social skills. He was too much at times, too loud, physical, silly, persistent, emotional, eager. He was sometimes left behind by peers who matured more quickly than he did. That's typical of kids with disabilities like this, as well as other conditions such as autism spectrum disorder. Making friends requires complex verbal skills, social perceptivity, and self-control. Children with disabilities can come across as awkward or aggressive to other kids. Some boys who visited our house a dozen times never reciprocated with an invitation to their place. There were birthday parties and sleepovers to which our son wasn't invited.

Each rejection crushed me—more so, I think, than it did him. I was unpopular in elementary school, not so much bullied as always on the periphery, and I still recall that feeling of loneliness. I didn't want that for my child. But as he got older, he developed a couple of closer connections, usually with boys who are a little complicated themselves—too anxious, too nerdy, or too rowdy—and each won my devotion and gratitude. This was something I hadn't known to expect about having a child: the significance of their friends. As early as preschool, friendships are crucial to children's development and well-being. They create a sense of belonging and safety and help diminish stress. They teach children how to communicate, cooperate, and respond to the emotions of others. There's research showing that friendships play a role in children's mental health. For instance, a 2010 longitudinal study followed 230 elementary school students in Maine over three years and found that having just one friend helped prevent anxious, withdrawn children from developing full-blown depression. While children who are shy and have a sad affect tend to become even more withdrawn and sad as they enter adolescence, the students who had one friendship at any time during the study suffered less, and they even reported that their sadness declined. Researchers believe that friendship conferred psychological resilience.[2] So, while some parents fantasize about their kid's future, their graduation, and their wedding day, my dreams are more immediate: they're about the kids who will have my son's back, who will be his voice of reason, support, and encouragement, who will make him laugh and feel loved.

Male friendship, in fact, has been idealized throughout Western history, foundational to society, culture, and art. This romanticizing of men's friendships can be charted as far back as ancient Greece.

Aristotle called the friend "a second self," and the biblical David said his friend Jonathan's love for him "was wonderful, passing the love of women." From Renaissance Europe, there's French philosopher Michel de Montaigne's essay "Of Friendship," in which he describes his connection with a deceased friend as "souls mingling and blending with each other so completely that they efface the seam that joined them."

Before women were considered equal to men and before marriage evolved into a romantic and companionate union, these male bonds stood above all. Some of this was sexual, what we'd now understand as gay, but homosexuality as a discrete emotional, social, and political identity is a modern concept. This has led to lively debates about whether we might retroactively reconsider the nature of some of these friendships, as well as the sexual inclination of historical figures like Abraham Lincoln. As a young man, the future president had a habit of sharing beds with his close male friends—not an unusual practice in the nineteenth-century American Midwest, when housing was limited and nights were cold. (For what it's worth, one of those friends did reportedly tell a biographer that Lincoln's "thighs were as perfect as a human being could be.")[3] Whatever the connection between Lincoln and his friend, overt displays of affection and confessions of love between male friends were, until recently, common and unremarkable.

And on it went through the eighteenth and nineteenth centuries, at a time when women and men rarely socialized together outside supervised gatherings or family groups. This led both genders to turn to same-sex companions for emotional sustenance. Historians and sociologists point to "romantic friendships" among women, evidenced by fervent letters and mushy diary entries in which women rhapsodize about their enduring (mostly platonic) love for other women. Men's experiences at the time were similar: all-male societies, such as professional guilds and workplaces, religious orders, universities and colleges, service clubs, sports teams, and the military, fostered adoring friendships, particularly among younger and unmarried men.

Then the culture shifted. In the late nineteenth and early twentieth centuries, women began moving beyond their domestic duties, some playing integral roles in social justice causes such as the abolitionist, suffrage, and labor movements. Places of employment, schools, and political movements were no longer all-male environments. The sexes were increasingly integrated in public life. As the social spheres of women and men began to overlap, love-based marriage and the nuclear family displaced male friendships and male societies at the center of culture and society.

At the same time, homosexuality became more visible as an identity. Like gender fluidity, same-sex desire and sex have existed throughout history and across nearly all cultures. But sex was understood to be something you did, not something you were. In the West, it wasn't until the mid-1800s that the categories of heterosexual and homosexual were created. By the late 1800s in Europe, doctors and scientists—including Richard von Krafft-Ebing, Henry Havelock Ellis and Magnus Hirschfeld, as well as Sigmund Freud—were beginning to study and catalog the range of human sexual behavior. The sensational 1895 English trial of playwright Oscar Wilde for indecency—more specifically, for having sex with other men—brought to light tales of London's vibrant gay underground. While scientists like Hirschfeld pled for tolerance, society saw homosexuality as a perversion and a threat to Victorian values. This fear about same-sex desire soon made platonic male friendships seem suspicious as well. Taken together, women's advancement, the idealization of the nuclear family, and the visibility of homosexuality helped forge a new definition of manhood that still exists within the Man Box today: the male as the opposite of the female, as the provider and head of the household, and as heterosexual.

In her landmark 1985 book, *Between Men: English Literature and Male Homosocial Desire*, cultural theorist Eve Kosofsky Sedgwick observed that as gay identity became more prominent and visible, there emerged a distinction between "homosocial" relationships and "homosexual" ones. The former are emotional and related to male group loyalty (think bros and buddies), the latter to sexual desire (think gay love and sex). For women, relationships exist on a spectrum: women and girls are able to connect with and love each other in a variety of ways, without one possibility excluding others. It's understood that women have a capacity to care for one another—as mothers, sisters, daughters, friends, lovers—without any of those relationships upending the definition of femaleness (perhaps with the exception of women who identify as masculine or butch). But that same capacity isn't believed to translate to men and boys. As men loving men began to be seen as suspicious and unnatural, a sharp line was drawn between homosocial and homosexual relationships; in fact, homosocial bonding often involves homophobic slurs and put-downs, as a way to deflect any suggestion that the bonding includes sexual desire. And under these new rules of masculinity, intimate same-sex connections became antithetical to being "a real man."

———

In 2017 former US surgeon general Vivek Murthy identified the biggest threat to public health: not heart disease, diabetes, or cancer—but loneliness. Isolation and weak social connections, he wrote in the *Harvard Business Review*, "are associated with a reduction in lifespan similar to that caused by smoking 15 cigarettes a day and even greater than that associated with obesity. Loneliness is also associated with a greater risk of cardiovascular disease, dementia, depression, and anxiety."[4] Murthy was drawing on a large body of research, culled from more than two hundred studies involving more than 3 million subjects worldwide, that found that we are in the midst of a loneliness epidemic. The culprits include the fluidity of modern life (we move and change jobs more); the weakening of community institutions, such as service organizations and faith groups; and the gig economy, which has allowed for greater flexibility but fewer face-to-face interactions. Our reliance on social media has also had an impact. Facebook, Instagram, and Twitter offer potentially massive social networks, but often the connections and interactions we find online don't prove to be as reliable or supportive as those in real-life friendships.

Men, in particular, are affected by the loneliness epidemic and by attendant feelings of depression and despair. Over their life spans, they tend to lose connections with male friends, depriving them of the protective effect of social bonds—which have been shown to increase happiness, help people cope with trauma, and extend longevity. Men typically base their friendships around activities such as sports or work rather than intimate talk, resulting in those connections being more casual and harder to sustain. The rules of masculinity render men reluctant to show vulnerability or ask for support, so they are less likely to reach out to other men when they're struggling or to make an overture to a new acquaintance to deepen the friendship.

There's also the seeming fear of being perceived as gay or feminine. If straight men and boys wish to connect and be vulnerable with one another, there is a price. Call it a masculinity tax: platonic male intimacy requires a rejection of homosexuality and a hostility toward anything that seems unmanly. Think of the saying "bros before hoes," which is male bonding predicated on putting down women, or the slang expression that emerged in the late 1990s "no homo." That term was used like an incantation to affirm a guy's heterosexuality after he said something that might be seen as too feminine. For example, "I love you, man." Chased immediately with "no homo."

More recently, another expression emerged that, despite being endearing, reflects a certain discomfort with male affection. "Bromance"—the rugged *bro* combined with the flowery *romance*—was coined to tag male friendships of a dewy variety. In 2016, during a meeting and state dinner in Washington, DC, the mutually admiring Justin Trudeau and Barack Obama were said to be sharing a bromance. The term celebrates same-sex fondness but with a smirk—as if two men caring for one another is so remarkable that it must be explained and justified.

Male friendships haven't disappeared, of course. Indeed, the fact that many men struggle to make and sustain intimate connections with each other in real life seems to have deepened their affection for images of male bonding. When I put out a call on Facebook asking for examples of male friendships in pop culture, both real and fictional, comments flooded in from my male acquaintances. From movies, there are the kids in *Stand by Me*, Andy and Red in *The Shawshank Redemption*, Harold and Kumar, Frodo and Sam. From TV, Bert and Ernie, Felix and Oscar, Captain Kirk and Mr. Spock. From comics, Archie and Jughead as well as Batman and Robin. From children's literature, Frog and Toad, Harry Potter and Ron Weasley. In sports, soccer's Neymar and Lionel Messi, the National Hockey League (NHL)'s Mike Richards and Jeff Carter, the NBA's Kyle Lowry and DeMar DeRozan.

Given my son's never-ending quest for new buddies, it's not surprising that he loves the *Fast & Furious* action-movie franchise. Kicked off in 2001, these aren't great films by any critical measure, but they're thunderous, speedy, and appealingly implausible. They're set in a postracial-divide fantasyland, featuring a multiethnic and attractive gang of car racers and thieves. The heart of this hip alternative family is the friendship between Brian O'Conner, played by Paul Walker, and Dominic Toretto, played by Vin Diesel. In 2013, during production on the seventh film, Walker was killed in a car accident. His real-life death was subsequently woven into the series' mythology: his character,

Brian, through the magic of CGI and stunt doubles, dies in the series' seventh installment, released in 2015. A tribute song by Wiz Khalifa and Charlie Puth, "See You Again," plays at the end of the movie. Throughout the summer of 2015, this ode to male friendship and requiem for the bond between Brian and Dom was an inescapable radio earworm. Like most guys in his circle, my son loved it; when it came on the car radio, he and his friends would sing along reverently. "See You Again" has been likened to "My Heart Will Go On," the epically and wonderfully sappy Céline Dion ballad from *Titanic*. And with this deeply sentimental soundtrack, Walker/Brian's death and Diesel/Dom's grief took on the sheen of a hero's tale of old.

—————

For nearly thirty years, first as a high school counselor and now as a professor of psychology at New York University, Niobe Way has studied the emotional lives and friendships of boys. She estimates that she's interviewed and talked with somewhere around fifteen hundred pubescent and teenage boys, and they've told her in language both vehement and tender how important their friends are to them. Here's how a fifteen-year-old named Justin characterized his relationship with another boy: "[My best friend and I] love each other.... I guess in life, sometimes two people can really, really, understand each other and really have a trust, respect and love for each other. It just happens, it's human nature."[5]

Way's 2011 book, *Deep Secrets: Boys' Friendships and the Crisis of Connection*, is filled with professions of intimacy and love just like Justin's. She tells the stories of hundreds of boys living in cities in the northeastern United States—primarily black, Latino, and Asian, many of them poor and working class—as they traverse adolescence, tracking the ebb and flow of their friendships. Some of the boys were interviewed multiple times over the course of several years. They articulate the importance of friendships for their happiness and mental health.

Though plenty of books and articles have come out in the past decade worrying about the state of young men and the "boy crisis," few have examined the psychological and social well-being of this demographic. And from these boys comes a consistent call for emotional support and love. Take fourteen-year-old Kai, who said, "You need a friend or else you'd be depressed, you won't be happy, you would try to kill yourself." Or Benjamin, who when asked what he likes about his best friend, said, "Most everything. His kindness. Everything. I know he cares for people, [like me], I know."[6]

Counter to the entrenched idea that boys are less communicative and less capable of vulnerability and intimacy than girls, Way's findings reveal that boys are equally so. "Boys have this enormous capacity for emotions, but somehow people ignore it," she tells me in a phone interview. A mother of a son and daughter, she says her interest in boys' emotional development dates back to when she was a teenager watching her younger brother struggle after losing a friend. Her brother had been very close to another boy, and one day the two of them had an abrupt falling-out. Way remembers her brother trying to make up with the other boy, knocking on his door and repeatedly being told the other boy was busy or didn't want to spend time with him. Way says the end of the friendship broke her brother's heart, and to this day the loss remains a bruising memory.

Of the boys Way has interviewed, she observes, "Their closest friendships share the plot of *Love Story* more than the plot of *Lord of the Flies*. Boys valued their male friendships greatly and saw them as essential components to their health, not because their friends were worthy opponents in the competition for manhood but because they were able to share their thoughts and feelings—their deepest secrets—with these friends."[7]

Way also found that in early adolescence, at ages fourteen and fifteen, boys specifically seek out friendships with other boys rather than friendships with girls. (That changes in older adolescence when serious dating begins and straight boys pursue emotional intimacy with girls.) Younger teenage boys cherish and protect their male friendships, not because of similar, gendered interests in sports or video games but because of their shared emotional terrain. Way suggests that the preference for male friendships at this age "may be rooted in boys' desire to connect to other boys right at the time their voices are cracking and their bodies feel awkward. They may feel too vulnerable to be vulnerable with those they do not perceive to be experiencing the same changes."[8]

Way also notes, however, that despite the importance of these childhood friendships, boys begin to lose their close male friends during later adolescence. Relationships fade and grow less intense. At this age, boys become distrustful of one another and less comfortable expressing their feelings. Way says that as straight boys enter manhood, they are more self-conscious about same-sex intimacy and instead turn their attention to romantic relationships. It's not a coincidence, she says, that boys' late adolescence is also marked by an increased risk for depression and feelings of isolation; their now more superficial friendships don't provide them with same degree of emotional sustenance as when they were younger. Way believes the "crisis of connection" that young men are experiencing is in no small part the result of being told that real men can't be close to one another.

———

Judging from media accounts, you'd imagine that all boys are hapless oafs, out of touch with their emotions. While girls are perceived earlier on to be socially adept, emotionally literate, and in possession of "soft skills" like empathy, research on boys' socialization focuses on their aggression, emotional numbness, and inscrutability. Stanford University psychologist Judy Y. Chu found something very different during her two years spent observing the emotional and social development of a cohort of six boys from prekindergarten through the first grade at an independent grammar school in New England. Chu sat in on their classes, stood lookout in the schoolyard and lunchroom, and spoke regularly with the boys, their parents, and their teachers.

In her early visits to the school when the children were four, she noticed that the boys were really interested in playing guns. There were no toy guns at the school, but the boys built them out of blocks or used their fingers. This activity bothered the teachers, who banned the game, fearing it reflected violent impulses and aggression. Initially, Chu thought the same but then noticed that playing guns had a different meaning for the boys than it did for the adults. First of all, the boys weren't angry or hostile. They were delighted to chase and be chased, to play stick-up, and to pretend to shoot or be shot.

On closer observation, Chu understood that playing guns was primarily a "quick, effective and distinctly 'masculine' way for the boys to engage and bond with each other."[9] By the age of four, they'd already absorbed the idea that a gun is a "boy thing," like dress-up is a "girl thing"—recall the pistols-or-pearls-themed gender-reveal parties—and so opted for gunplay as a way to align themselves with other boys. They didn't choose to play guns exclusively, though; they also played with less gendered objects such as building blocks and puzzles, and they drew and read. But it was the gunplay that teachers and parents noticed and objected to. That objection wasn't unreasonable. In 2015, according to a report in the *Washington Post*, American toddlers found guns and accidentally shot people at a rate of about once a week.[10] We *should* be mindful of the messages kids absorb about firearms and the ways in which we have become desensitized to shootings.

Chu's point, though, was that parents and teachers were wrong about what they assumed the boys' gunplay implied. Boys weren't drawn to the game because of some inherent bloodlust. Rather, it gave them an opportunity to play with other boys. As they got older, their interest in guns waned and was replaced by Pokémon cards and sports. Though the toys and activities changed, the desire to bond and identify with other boys remained.

The six boys Chu observed had individual temperaments and preferences, and while they shared a number of common interests, they made deliberate choices about when to act masculine (be tough or bossy, make fun of girlie things, and so on), depending on their wishes and needs at any given moment. Boys like Mike and Min-Haeng, who liked status and power, were most likely to adhere to boy norms like competitiveness, while others, such as Dan, a happy-go-lucky kid who played with girls as easily as he did with the boys, and Tony, a withdrawn kid dealing with the upheaval of his mom's recent remarriage, seemed less interested in or less capable of fitting in with the boys' clique. All the boys tended to moderate their behavior when adults were present, intuiting that they were seen as more troublesome and mischievous than girls. A typical example is a moment when Mike admired a rifle-shaped object that Min-Haeng had put together from blocks: "What a long gun!" he said. Min-Haeng's mother overheard and insisted it was not a gun. Both boys went silent. When Min-Haeng's mother left and the boys didn't think any adults were around, Min-Haeng boasted to Mike that the thing he built was *absolutely* a gun.

Chu wrote up her findings in a 2014 book titled *When Boys Become Boys: Development, Relationships, and Masculinity*—the title capturing her central conclusion, that the characteristics and qualities typically associated with boys are not universal or innate but rather are deliberate and calculated responses to social conditioning and cultural expectations. "The boys' adaption to norms of masculine behavior was neither automatic nor inevitable," she writes.[11] Boys chose how much like "boys" they would be, some because that's what suited their tastes and inclinations best, some because of a wish to conform and belong to the group.

This idea—that boys aren't born "boys" but choose to become "boys" (or, as Chu puts it, boys are "active participants in their gender socialization")—is significant. And it squares with other research indicating that from as early as infancy, boys are subtly, even unconsciously, coached to ignore or stifle their emotions and are perceived by adults as being aggressive or hostile. Neuroscientist Lise Eliot, whose work I look at in the previous chapter, has highlighted studies showing that adults perceive boy babies as being more angry than girl babies and girl babies as being more social than boy ones. (In fact, in that study, observers were told the wrong sex of the baby—that those angry boys were girls and vice versa.)[12] Other small studies have observed that parents use larger and more complex vocabularies to talk about feelings with girls than they do with boys. This feeds into the common myth that boys are naturally competitive and emotionally oblivious. As a result, as boys get older, they aren't encouraged to develop skills like empathy and communication that help create and sustain intimate friendships.

But what if, like Chu and Way, we are interested in how boys rebel against the expectation that they be stoic and tough? How might we build on that resistance?

━━━

In the spring of 2016, I visit an elementary school in a small city just north of Toronto. Like many of the suburbs that ring the city, the community consists of sleepy cul-de-sacs lined with townhomes and freshly built bungalows, and six-lane thoroughfares strung with strip malls, synagogues, mosques and churches, big-box stores, and hockey arenas.

Though the area was previously home to Italian and Jewish communities, over the past two decades waves of immigration have increased the city's diversity: its population is now a mix of Caribbean, Chinese, Korean, Iranian, Russian, South Asian, and Filipino Canadians. The five hundred or so students at the school provide a fair reflection of the city's demographics. Alongside the regular mainstream program, the school houses an elite arts academy for students in fifth through eighth grades, which draws kids from across the district, skewing its student body a little bit whiter and wealthier than the surrounding middle-class and immigrant-rich neighborhood.

The bell to announce the end of the school day has just rung. I'm there to sit in on a session of Next Gen Men, an after-school program for boys in seventh and eighth grades that's run by a trio of friends in their twenties. They dreamed up the program a year earlier and funded it with a small seed grant for initiatives devoted to men's and boys' mental health. Over ten weekly sessions, Next Gen Men uses sports, team-building exercises, and group check-ins to help boys become more emotionally literate, empathetic, and self-aware.

Jermal Alleyne runs the after-school programs. While the boys burn off their end-of-day energy playing basketball, he and I chat at the side of the gym. In trainers and glasses, Alleyne is jockish and thoughtful, a former chess-club kid as well as a competitive athlete. Before launching Next Gen Men, he earned a degree in public health and worked as a case manager for a youth organization. While we talk, the boys circle him, passing him a ball, asking him to join in the game. In developing Next Gen Men, Alleyne and Jake Stika, who have been best friends since college, along with another friend, Jason Tan de Bibiana, imagined the kind of program they wished they'd had when they were in middle school, one that delved into issues that boys find hard to discuss, including peer pressure, sadness, crushes, friendships, and jealousy.

"It had to be fun," he tells me. "It couldn't feel like homework. And it had to be safe. Safe for them to talk about their feelings and safe for them to air their opinions without being shot down or made fun of."

After basketball, he gathers the ten boys into a circle and opens the session with a check-in. The boys aren't generally forthcoming—they mention a birthday party one of boys had, video games they like. Then one boy mentions spending the weekend with his dad, and a couple of the other boys perk up. "That's great," they tell him. "Cool." (I later find out the boy's parents are divorced, and he doesn't see his dad that often, so the visit is a big deal, and the other boys know it.) Meanwhile, a new kid to the school, a tall boy with an eastern European accent, can't sit still. He repeatedly gets up, wanders toward the far end of the gym, and chases the younger brother and sister of a skinny boy in glasses who is also in the group. Alleyne keeps patiently shepherding him back to the circle, until everyone has had their turn at sharing.

Then Alleyne divides them into groups of three and four to do a short exercise about gender stereotypes. He tells them to make two lists of words, one describing women and girls, the other describing men and boys. The boy who's just seen his dad senses a trap. "Are you asking for stereotypes? Or real descriptions, like, based in reality?" Alleyne tells them just to write down what comes to mind. When the group reconvenes, the list for women includes the following: *smart, loving, joyful, mother, weak, emotional, beautiful, hot* [this gets snickers], *arty, nice, happy, sensitive.* For men: *athletic, strong, tough, army, gangs, money, tuxedo, guns, brave, fearless, creative.* Alleyne takes them through an examination of why they ascribed certain qualities to one gender or the other. When he asks them if they know any males who are, for instance, sensitive, a chatty, curly-haired kid shoots up his hand. "Me! I'm *really* sensitive."

The gender analysis doesn't last long. The tall kid keeps wandering around the gym. The little brother and sister of the skinny kid demand a snack. The sensitive boy tells a rambling story about evolution and male hunters and female gatherers. When after several minutes he's interrupted by another boy, a slouchy kid who has barely spoken since the exercise began, the sensitive boy wails, "Why does everyone always tell me to shut up all the time?" The session seems to be falling to pieces, but then the kid with the divorced parents steps in to referee, asking them politely to stop bugging each other, so everyone can get a snack. Alleyne wraps up the discussion and closes the session by asking each boy to say something nice about another one. The compliments are sweetly earnest: "You tried hard today." "You've improved a lot in basketball." "I think you're the best *League of Legends* player I know." "You're always a good friend."

In addition to these boys' groups, Next Gen Men has held gatherings called Wolf Pack for adult men to talk about issues such as body image, romantic relationships, and mental health. They hope meetings like this will promote a healthy version of masculinity and help men build friendships with one another. Alleyne says that in the "culture of being a man," there's little room for authentic conversations and connections, because there's such a fear of looking weak or being judged. He's spoken with adult men as well as boys who they think they're "inherently bad." And he says he hears from a lot of men who want to support women and girls and address the ways in which they may have behaved badly and caused harm, but they worry they'll say or do the wrong thing. "They're not bad," he tells me. "They're trying to figure things out. I try to meet them, wherever they're at, with empathy."

Several boys in the group are obviously popular. One wears immaculate Vans skater shoes, and the kids tease him, admiringly, about his fashion sense. He's close to three other boys, who together form an almost impenetrable clique. Lying on the floor filling out their male/female word lists, they lean into each other's shoulders and knees. Other guys, like the slouchy one, the sensitive one, and the tall kid, are obviously outsiders to this group, and they seem to lack the confidence of the popular boys. (Later, the slouchy kid tells me his best friend moved away a couple years ago, and he hasn't made a real friend since.) Alleyne says he sees boys like these try to connect with other boys and fail. At one point, the tall boy, who seems harmless, sneaks up behind the stylish kid, the smallest in the group, and picks him up. It's an awkward overture. The short kid laughs it off, but he's clearly uncomfortable.

What's tough for boys, Alleyne explains, is that when they attempt a connection and it doesn't work, they may never try again. It's too hard for them to be vulnerable, to extend themselves and be rejected. He says that even with him, if a boy ventures to confide something personal and he misses the moment, because he's distracted or busy, it can take weeks before that boy shares something personal again. "By the time boys get to ten or eleven, it's already ingrained in them that men figure out things on their own," he says. "The message is that needing help means you're a failure as a man. So, if you work up to the courage to reach out, and it doesn't get picked up on, some boys, if they haven't seen healthy models of masculinity, will just shut down."

This is what Chu identifies in her research on boys as a negative feedback loop. In their desire for male approval, boys learn to become guarded and withholding, which then prevents them from bonding with each other. The skills that are required to become a real man are detrimental to becoming a real human. Or, as Niobe Way explains it, "Boys' problems at their very root are not related to their biology or their psychology but to a culture that refuses to see boys (and men, girls and women) as more than a set of gender, and in the case of boys of color, racial stereotypes. Given the nature of these stereotypes, the very social and emotional skills that are necessary for boys to thrive are not fostered."[13]

This sounds bleak, but given that boys have the potential for empathy, connection, kindness, and affection, then it's merely a matter of figuring out how to encourage those qualities. Way says that deep, intimate friendships are one of the ways that boys can resist the conventions of masculinity. To illustrate how, she tells me about a talk she gave a couple years ago to a group of boys at a middle school in New York City. She shared quotes from *Deep Secrets* and asked them to interpret. What did they think about boys' friendships? About an hour into the conversation, a boy came forward and told a story about wanting to be friends with another boy and being rejected. The school was small enough that everyone knew the identity of the other boy. Way was surprised to hear one of them speaking candidly and publicly about having his feelings hurt.

She was even more surprised when another student asked her, "Professor, who did you write this book for?" Here's how she describes the moment: "It totally took me off guard. And I said, 'I wrote it for parents and teachers.' Well, he looked at me, so irritated, and said, 'Why didn't you write it for us? Because we're the ones who need to hear this because then we'd feel less alone.' He hit it on the head. Boys don't think their feelings are normal; they don't get told it's normal for a boy to feel scared, vulnerable, sad, jealous, hurt."

Then a different boy chimed in, saying, "Professor, can you tell us how to make a good friend?" Way turned the question back on the kids. "You tell me," she said. And 150 boys spent the rest of the day talking about strategies for making and keeping good friends. "And that," Way tells me, "is the resistance." It may be that we don't need to tell boys anything at all, she adds. "We might just need to start listening to them better."

4

THE BOY CRISIS

Who's Really *Failing at School?*

———

Nadia L. Lopez gives the impression of a woman who hates the idea of waste—whether it's wasted time, wasted money, or, especially, wasted talent. She's the founder and principal of Mott Hall Bridges Academy, a public middle school located in eastern Brooklyn's Brownsville neighborhood, one of the poorest communities in New York City. When I meet with her in late fall 2016, she is elegant in a shift dress and cardigan in the school's trademark purple and black ("royal colors," she tells me—she and her students wear the colors every day) and seated at a vast table in the center of the school's administrative office, with stacks of papers, a laptop, and a smartphone all within close reach. As we talk, Lopez will be interrupted several times to take a call from a parent, to respond to a teacher's question, to decide whether to accept a speaking engagement, and, most important, to talk with a boy of about eleven, his small hands balled into frustrated fists at his sides, who looks like he's been having a rough morning.

Lopez's students, whom she calls "scholars," live in a neighborhood commonly defined by its struggles and its crime statistics. Brownsville lies only a few miles east of Brooklyn's gentrified Park Slope, with its brownstone homes valued in the millions, but might as well be in another country. According to a 2017 survey by the nonprofit child advocacy organization Citizens' Committee for Children of New York, 40 percent of people in Brownsville live below the US federal poverty level—in 2016 that was $20,160 per year for a family of three—and more than half the neighborhood's nineteen thousand children are growing up in poor households.[1] Brownsville's predominantly black and Latino residents reported that they feel left behind by city and state legislators and power brokers. Their neighborhood is short on basic resources: banks, grocery stores, after-school and summer programs for children and teenagers, parks, libraries, and public transportation. And this is what political and economic neglect means for the prospects of Brownsville's children: fewer than 16 percent of those in grades 3 through 8 are proficient in math and English-language arts, and just over a third of students in high school will graduate. During our conversation, Lopez repeats a familiar line of hers—that she "opened a school in order to close a prison."

Lopez and her school became famous in January 2015 when a sweet-faced eighth-grader named Vidal Chastanet, who aspired to become a chef and an actor, appeared on the popular *Humans of New York* blog, which features photos and short profiles of locals. The site's creator, Brandon Stanton, had bumped into Vidal on a Brooklyn street and asked him who had inspired him the most in his life. Vidal answered, "Ms. Lopez." "When we get in trouble, she doesn't suspend us," he went on to say. "She calls us to her office and explains to us how society was built down around us. And she tells us that each time somebody fails out of school, a new jail cell gets built. And one time she made every student stand up, one at a time, and she told each one of us that we matter."

Within days, the post was shared more than 150,000 times, and it soon received more than 1 million likes on Facebook. Stanton set up a fund-raising page, which quickly racked up $1.4 million in pledges.[2]

(The money has been earmarked for summer programs, a college scholarship fund, and field trips to postsecondary schools.) Lopez and Vidal met President Obama in the White House and appeared together on *Ellen*.

Like those hundreds of thousands of others who saw his *Humans of New York* post, I found Vidal's thoughts about Lopez's inspiration touching. But his comment about her policy on discipline struck me. It seemed like an unusual thing for a boy his age to notice and remark on. What did it say about a thirteen-year-old black boy's expectations and experiences that he found it noteworthy that his middle school principal was reluctant to suspend children?

Knowingly or not, Vidal had hit upon a troubling fact about how boys—especially boys of color—are treated within educational systems in the United States, Canada, and Britain. Teachers and administrators discipline boys more often and more severely than girls, and they discipline boys from certain racial groups (black, Latino, and indigenous in the United States; black and indigenous in Canada; and black and Caribbean in the United Kingdom) to an even greater degree than other children. Experiencing exclusionary punishments at school, like suspensions and expulsions, is associated with higher incidences of contact with law enforcement—meaning kids who are singled out for punishment by school officials are also more likely to be singled out by police. Though black children make up less than 14 percent of all American kids under eighteen, black boys represent 43 percent of the male population in juvenile detention centers (black girls make up 34 percent of incarcerated girls).[3]

When discussions turn to boys and schooling, an overly generalized idea of a boy emerges. He's restless and rambunctious and hooked on video games; he'd rather shoot hoops than read a book; he's more likely to be found in the principal's office than on the honor roll. As the mother of a son who pretty much exemplifies this type of boy, however,

I don't think this "typical boy" is typical at all. Boys like my son are simply more visible than the boys who get along well in school, earn decent grades, and generally stay out of trouble. But over the past two decades, a scare narrative about the "boy crisis" in education contends that modern boys as a group are in deep trouble: they are being left behind, while girls surge ahead. Citing statistics about male versus female elementary-school literacy levels and postsecondary enrollment, proponents of the boy crisis maintain that girls' success has come at the cost of boys'. It has many parents worried about their sons' prospects. To be sure, plenty of boys are struggling in school for all sorts of reasons, whether structural and social inequalities, learning disabilities, or family challenges. The case for the boy crisis, however, depends upon a few shaky premises: that all boys are fundamentally the same and share similar capacities and interests, that all boys have equal opportunities and are treated equally in their classrooms, and that boys and girls have distinct and different neurological systems. A closer look at the history of education and how we perceive boys and assess their character and capabilities suggests the focus of this alarm is misplaced. There is, in fact, a boy crisis, but we're not reaching the boys who most need help.

One initiative at the academy is a boys' group called I Matter that hosts mentoring sessions and workshops in areas such as communication and relationship skills, sexual health, and social justice. Not long after the school was founded, Lopez established a girls' group but then turned her attention to boys, recruiting male acquaintances and community leaders in various fields to serve as role models and mentors for her male students. "I care about every one of my scholars," she explains, "but I find that when I deal with the boys, I feel such a sense of urgency."

"Boys can learn to, quote, 'manage their behavior' if they're punished enough," Lopez says, "but that doesn't deal with the underlying issues of what might be causing them to be anxious or act out in the first place." After our conversation, Lopez's assistant, Donsha Jones, gives me a quick tour of the school. On my way out, I bump into Lopez, who is walking down the school's main corridor, her hand resting on the shoulder of the little boy who had come to her office earlier that morning with a head full of steam. He's been crying, his eyes are puffy, and his shoulders slumped, and he looks incredibly young. It's a look I recognize from my son's middle school years—one minute he would be full of preteen bravado, and the next he'd be tearfully reaching for a hug. Lopez is talking quietly to her scholar, encouraging him to tell her what's going on. She catches my eye and smiles at me above his head. "It's hard being a boy sometimes," she says.

—————

Up until about 150 years ago, the only children who enjoyed a formal, comprehensive education were upper-class white males. If poor children, or children of color, or girls were schooled at all, they were sent into trade apprenticeships or were taught just enough to make them obedient workers or wives. The establishment of local coed public schools began in Canada and the United States in the early nineteenth century, and over time elementary schools began to take their current shape—students were separated in grades based on age, teachers were trained at professional institutions, and the curriculum was standardized. By the early decades of the twentieth century, high school attendance was mandatory.

Universal public education has been a revolutionary force in creating the opportunity for class mobility. But it's also been a force of social control. Led by social reformers, one mission of those early nineteenth-century public schools was to teach morality, citizenship, and civic virtue to lower-class children, who were seen as wayward and undisciplined. Enslaved children were forbidden from being educated, and several statutes criminalized anyone who taught literacy or numeracy to enslaved people. During the Jim Crow era, throughout much of the United States, public schools were segregated by race—specifically black and white, but in some states indigenous children and Mexican American children were also banned from whites-only schools. Segregated black public schools were vastly underfunded compared to white schools and often housed in dilapidated buildings. (Some regions in Canada had de facto segregation as well, with white school administrators discouraging Asian and black children from attending white schools.) Though the US Supreme Court struck down laws segregating schools in the 1954 *Brown v. Board of Education* ruling, desegregation efforts lasted well into the 1970s.

Indigenous children in Canada, meanwhile, were the victims of the country's policy of "aggressive assimilation," or, as it was more coarsely phrased, "to kill the Indian in the child." Beginning in the mid-nineteenth century, indigenous children were forcibly removed from their homes and sent to federally funded church-run residential schools. (Parents were threatened with prison if they refused to relinquish their kids.) While there, children were assigned a new European name, as well as a number, and were denied contact with their families back home (siblings at the same school would often be kept apart as well). Children were punished, often with whippings and beatings, if they were caught talking in their language or practicing their culture. Illnesses, such as tuberculosis, swept through the poorly maintained dormitories. Many children were sexually abused by teachers, priests, and nuns. In all, about 150,000 indigenous children were sent to residential schools, and thousands are estimated to have died while in attendance.[4] Those who returned home did so with a deep disconnect, in many cases unable to communicate in the same language used by their parents. Countless survivors of these schools, which operated into the

1980s, experienced the lasting effects of trauma, including mental illness and addiction.

Laws and policies regarding education may have changed, but racial inequality and segregation persist. Children living on reserves receive 30 percent less funding for their education than Canadian children overall. Many remote communities don't have local high schools, which means kids are forced to move away from their families and board with strangers to receive an education, a situation that unnervingly replicates aspects of the residential school system.

This same disparity in support, resources, and opportunity exists in other school districts that educate marginalized students. Mott Hall Bridges Academy, for instance, located in liberal, diverse New York City, is part of one of the most segregated public school systems in the United States. Most black and Latino kids in New York attend schools where less than 10 percent of students are white. And white children make up just 15 percent of those in public schools; half of them are concentrated in 11 percent of the city's schools, most of them known to be high performing and racially and economically homogenous.[5]

Whiter, wealthier public schools have better resources—everything from new computers, modern science labs, and musical instruments to the advocacy of a well-connected parent body able to fund-raise and volunteer. In New York City, as elsewhere in the United States, schools with large numbers of black and Latino kids are less likely to have experienced teachers, advanced courses, up-to-date instructional materials, and modern, well-kept facilities.

Mott Hall Bridges Academy was established in 2010 in part to address this disparity. The school takes up the third floor of a blocky, low-slung building. On my visit, the floors are freshly mopped and the walls recently painted. Tidy bulletin boards display notices of clubs and events, as well as student projects and artwork. In the classrooms, high windows let in light. Academy students share the basement cafeteria and a full-size gym with students from another school, also located in the building, but Lopez has turned a large classroom on her floor into a minigym to give her scholars a space to move around when they need it. Another classroom filled with comfy chairs and couches serves as a chill-out area and meeting room. With very little, Lopez has done a great deal to create an environment that feels calm, safe, and encouraging. "If you can show that children in this community can thrive with the minimal amount of resources and support," she tells me, "just imagine what would happen if they had the kinds of resources that kids in wealthier neighborhoods have."

———

Lopez is clearly a gifted teacher and principal, though I'd argue that her success is due not solely to her extensive pedagogical skills but also to her personal investment in her students and their ability to see themselves in her. She's black, the daughter of immigrant parents, and she grew up not far from Brownsville. Academically gifted and encouraged by her parents, she sees that same potential in her scholars.

The relationship between teachers and administrators and their students can have a huge impact on a child's—particularly a boy's—life trajectory. Studies have shown that black children who encounter black teachers are more likely to be recommended for gifted and advanced placement programs. Long-term tracking of one hundred thousand black students in North Carolina's public schools found that having at least one black teacher in elementary school significantly increases the chances that low-income black students will graduate high school and consider attending college. For poor black boys, having just one black teacher was transformative—it decreased their risk of dropping out by nearly 40 percent.[6] And for both low-income black boys and girls, exposure to at least one black teacher in grades 3 to 5 increased the likelihood that they would aspire to attend a four-year college.

One of the unintended fallouts of school desegregation in the United States was the plummeting number of black teachers and school administrators. After *Brown v. Board of Education* in 1954, black schools were shut down, and black children were integrated into formerly all-white schools. Black educators were fired en masse, and their numbers never bounced back. Just 2 percent of US public school teachers today are black men[7]—meaning few black boys in America will be taught by someone who resembles them and shares, to some degree, their life experience.

What are the consequences when public school systems in Canada and the United States are increasingly diverse, yet most teachers are white? Those educators may be well intentioned, but they may hold unconscious biases and have lower expectations for their male students and students of color. Implicit bias in education is a rising area of research for social scientists. The idea is that all of us, no matter how open-minded we imagine ourselves to be, harbor unconscious prejudices related to race, gender, sexual orientation, age, and so on. The good news: studies have shown that once you're aware of your reflexive prejudices, you can learn to lessen them. Bias is often due to a lack of familiarity with a specified group or the result of persistent stereotypes about that group. The bad? Unchecked, these biases—dismissing a kid as having no prospects rather than seeing him as having promise— can be destructive to the lives and aspirations of those they are leveled against.

Several small-scale studies have looked at implicit bias toward particular groups of children by adults, including teachers and police officers. In one study, a group of college students was told a hypothetical story about a child with challenging behavior and then shown a randomly selected picture of said child.[8] Those who were given a picture of a black child rated him or her as being significantly less innocent and far more blameworthy for the challenging behavior than those who were given a picture of a white or Latino child. Participants also assumed that the black children in the photos were, on average, 4.5 years older than they really were.

The belief in the innocence of children is fundamental to our culture and is at the basis of laws that protect children: it's the reason there are age requirements for working, getting married, driving, drinking alcohol, and enlisting in the army, and it's why children aren't named in the press during legal proceedings. But this belief in the fundamental innocence of children is not extended equally. Think of the case of Tamir Rice, the boy shot by a police officer in Cleveland. The person who spotted Rice playing in the park with a toy pellet gun and called 911 told dispatchers the child was a "juvenile," and the gun was "probably fake." Yet one of the officers who arrived on the scene shot the boy within seconds of getting out of his patrol car. Defending the man who killed Rice, the president of the Cleveland Police Patrolmen's Association said, "Tamir Rice is in the wrong. He's menacing. He's five foot seven, 191 pounds. He wasn't that little kid you're seeing in pictures. He's a 12-year-old in an adult body."[9]

Adultification is the term used to describe this perception of children to be older, more culpable, and more responsible for their actions than their chronological and developmental age would suggest. Black children, both boys and girls, appear to be commonly "adultified"— and research suggests the degree to which authority figures assume them to be older and more mature than they actually are is a factor in how harshly those adults punish them. What's more, this assignment of blame based on race and sex begins when children are very young. In one example, a group of researchers at Yale University's Child Study Center recruited preschool educators at a large conference to study how implicit bias might affect their perceptions of their students and their disciplinary choices.[10] In one task, the preschool teachers were seated facing a laptop computer screen and told they would be shown a video of four preschool-aged children—a white boy, a white girl, a black boy, and a black girl—and would be tested on their ability to detect potential challenging behavior before it became problematic. In fact, none of the children in the video behaved badly or inappropriately. The prompt was a ruse to prime the preschool teachers to look for trouble. And while they watched the video, the direction and duration of their eye gaze and attention were monitored to track which child they watched the most.

The result: participants spent more time gazing at boys and at black boys most of all. When the preschool teachers were explicitly asked which of the children required most of their attention, 42 percent said the black boy, followed by 34 percent for the white boy.[11] These findings suggest that preschool teachers may have different expectations of their students' behavior based on race and sex. And this bias may explain why schools disproportionately suspend and expel boys, especially black ones: boys in US preschools are 3 times more likely than girls to be suspended one or more times, and black preschoolers are 3.6 times as likely as white ones to receive one or more suspensions.

Of course, all children misbehave at times, and some more so than others. But the biases held by teachers and school administrators may sway how they interpret and address children's behavior. When a teacher sees a boy fidgeting at his desk, or poking a classmate, or ripping up a math sheet in frustration, does that teacher wonder whether the boy is struggling at home, or is hungry, or is feeling overwhelmed, or does the teacher assume he's just a troublemaker? If it's the latter, over time a child who is regularly seen as a problem will inevitably become one and will likely view school not as a place of learning and care but as a place where they're unwelcome.

Racial and class bias in how students are disciplined, coupled with children's alienation from their school environment, accounts for what's called the "school-to-prison pipeline"—the statistical likelihood that children who are suspended and expelled (many of whom are growing up in poverty, have histories of abuse or neglect, or have learning disabilities) will later end up in trouble with the law. Having seen this trajectory in Britain, when he was the director-general of the national prison system, Martin Narey once remarked that "the young people excluded from school each year might as well be given a date by which to join the prison service later down the line." Data from the United Kingdom and Canada on exclusion rates from school reveal a similar racial disparity to that in the United States: in Britain black Caribbean and mixed white-and-black Caribbean children are excluded at rates three times greater than that of white children.[12] According to statistics from the Toronto District School Board, 48 percent of the children who were expelled between 2012 and 2016 were black, compared to 10 percent who were white.[13]

Zero-tolerance school policies that came into force in the 1980s and '90s were an extension of the "tough on crime" philosophy of the era, which saw the rise of policies like the US War on Drugs and mandatory minimum sentencing requirements, alongside an explosion in incarceration rates. Zero tolerance was also an example of the then-popular "broken windows" theory of crime—the idea that tolerating minor acts of vandalism, graffiti, and the like would lead to greater crimes and violence. If you crack down on the small transgressions, the theory goes, you can prevent bigger troubles. But as police in cities like New York began to routinely stop people to question, search, and fine them for tiny infractions, incidences of police misconduct and abuse skyrocketed. Today, the thinking among some sociologists and criminologists is that broken-windows policing may have done much more harm than good. It turns out that these policies played only a small role in the dramatic plummet in violent crime throughout the United States and Canada over the past thirty years—a widespread and persistent downward trend credited to demographic changes (an aging population commits fewer crimes), immigration (high rates of immigration are associated with less criminal activity), and a decline in crack cocaine use.[14]

Despite this, many institutions that are part of the growing charter school movement are built on broken-windows principles—or what's called "no excuses" discipline. Publicly funded but privately run either as nonprofit or for-profit businesses, these schools largely serve poor, urban, low-performing, black and Latino school districts like Brownsville in Brooklyn. (In post-Katrina New Orleans, charter schools almost entirely replaced the public schools that had been damaged or destroyed in poor black districts.) In the most extreme cases, students are subjected to strict and absurd rules, such as having to walk single file in hallways, keep shirts tucked in at all times, and raise their hands in a prescribed manner. Charter schools are praised for instilling discipline in what are considered "high-risk" kids, but they've also been criticized for their high rates of suspensions and expulsions. For example, in Washington, DC, during the 2011–2012 school year, charter schools accounted for forty of the fifty schools in the city with the most suspensions and expulsions that year, yet they enrolled only 41 percent of the student population (and most were clustered in low-income minority neighborhoods).[15]

What's even worse is that suspension and expulsion aren't effective forms of discipline—kicking a kid out of school just moves him and his problems elsewhere and eventually, statistically, to prison. Diversion and restorative justice programs, which focus on getting to the whys of violence and misbehavior through counseling and mediation, are proven to be far better at reducing recidivism among children who are frequently in trouble.

Some charter schools have been successful in raising literacy and graduation rates,[16] and there are parents in low-income neighborhoods who feel charter schools offer their children a more structured, safe, and enriched environment. But the no-excuses school culture of conformity demands a degree of compliance that can crush the soul and spirit. There is no space for the artsy oddball kid, the shy kid, or the tender kid who feels things deeply. And this strict-discipline approach is distinctly at odds with the current push in education toward experiential and self-directed learning and the expansion of boutique programs like gifted classes, language immersion, and schools devoted to elite athletics, robotics and coding, or visual and performing arts.

At Mott Hall Bridges Academy in Brooklyn, Nadia Lopez and I spoke about how the supportive and encouraging messages from parents and teachers in neighborhoods like Brownsville can sometimes lean more heavily on qualities such as hard work, grit, and discipline than on self-expression and curiosity. Those former qualities are valuable, and that emphasis may make a certain sense in Brownsville, where, she tells me, boys must navigate violence daily, from the gangs that want to harm or recruit them to the police who suspect them of being up to no good. Simple survival requires determination and vigilance. But having to toggle between a tough-guy attitude on the streets and total deference in school leaves little room for error and little opportunity to be a carefree and curious kid. One of the challenges for teachers at the academy is getting boys to lower their guard while at the same time raising their ambitions to more than survival in five-year increments. Lopez wants children at her school to feel free to experiment and to learn it's okay to make mistakes: "A lot of my children don't feel safe to ask questions or put forward a new idea because they don't want to be seen as foolish or defiant." Lopez would like her scholars to have a sense of entitlement and to believe that they are deserving of big, bright futures. When she takes older students to tour colleges, her choice of institutions is deliberately lofty: Harvard, Yale, Columbia, and Howard.

———

My own son has had a challenging school career. By the time he was eight, he'd been suspended twice. He's affectionate, funny, guileless, and charming, but he's also impulsive and reactive. He exhibits what's called "dysmaturity"—he behaves younger than his chronological age. When he was in fourth grade, we were advised to enroll him in an anger-management program, which included a training course for parents. While the kids were sent off with cheerful, earnest social workers to role-play and learn emotional-regulation techniques, the parents sat round a large table discussing how to de-escalate triggering experiences: transitions to bedtime, trips to the grocery store, homework. After a couple of sessions, it was clear that every child—all of them boys—had some sort of disability (autism spectrum, ADHD, anxiety disorder) and that all the parents had tried desperately to secure them proper support at school. We were there because we'd failed to do so, and our unpredictable, volatile sons had been labeled as "bullies," "troublemakers," or "unmanageable."

We were warned of our son's potential for trouble when he was very young. His doctor advised a MedicAlert bracelet noting his disabilities, so police would be aware of them in case he ever had a run-in with the law. He was five or six at the time. The calls from principals and the suspensions soon followed. Our son got frustrated. He erupted. He got taunted. He fought back. If his class was told to line up, he raced to the front, elbowing other kids out of the way. If he was scolded, he bolted out of the classroom and out of the school, to hide in the farthest reaches of the schoolyard.

In an era of zero tolerance, the line between bad kid and good kid, aggressor and victim, is now thickly drawn. Bullying is a grave problem, multiplied considerably by social media. Some children have experienced such prolonged torment at the hands of their peers that they've harmed themselves or committed suicide. Yet the label of "bully" is often too readily applied to common incidents of childhood conflict, without an understanding of the underlying dynamics or without realizing that the conflict might be mutual. My son, for instance, has been on the receiving end of violence as well: an older boy once punched him in the face and gave him a bloody nose; another time, a schoolmate held him down and spat on him. It shows how thoroughly we have vilified acts of aggression between children that I have often felt an odd relief when my child was the one being picked on. At least then, someone else's kid was to blame.

Bullies, of course, may be victims themselves—of the school system, of structural inequality, of their parents. A kid might act out in scary ways because he needs emotional support or because of a disability. His aggression may reflect the violence he negotiates in his neighborhood, and acting tough by throwing the first punch could be a smart survival technique. It's true that in a small number of cases, a childhood bully will grow up to be an abuser or sociopath. But measures such as mediation, counseling, and diversion programs are effective in helping the truly troubled kids. And plenty of people who were unkind as children grow up to be decent adults. Ask adult siblings how they treated each other as children, and you'll hear tales of torture: a little brother locked in a closet, a big sister with a bite mark on her back. (That would be *my* big sister, by the way.) Empathy, cooperation, restraint, respect for boundaries, and sharing don't come naturally to most of us. These qualities need to be taught.

Heavily punitive solutions for bullying and conflict don't reflect this reality, though. "Applying the bullying label carefully and sparingly is crucial because of the stigma it carries for kids," writes Emily Bazelon in her book *Sticks and Stones: Defeating the Culture of Bullying and Rediscovering the Power of Character and Empathy*, "because accusations can often be harder to sort out than they first appear."[17] That stigma is significant, because once a child is labeled as bad or as a bully, it's nearly impossible for them to be seen any other way. Instead of fixing a conflict, exclusionary punishment offloads the problem—a suspended kid doesn't learn emotional-regulation skills and conflict resolution, and kids who are most in need of help end up shoved further to the margins. Consider the statistics above: boys, boys of color, poor boys, and boys with disabilities are the ones most often suspended and expelled; they're also the children who will most likely drop out of school as a result. In my province of Ontario, the mania for zero tolerance hit its peak in the early 2000s, when the Safe Schools Act was passed by the Conservative government of Premier Mike Harris. In force from 2001 to 2008, the law required principals to suspend and expel students for any kind of aggressive behavior—with no exceptions. It had an instant and devastating impact. In the 2002–2003 school year, the number of students suspended in Ontario spiked to 157,436, up by almost 50,000 from two years earlier. Nearly 1 in 5 of the children who were suspended had previously been identified as having a learning disability or special needs.[18]

Boys are identified in this way more often than girls. Over the past two decades, diagnoses of attention deficit/hyperactivity disorder and autism spectrum disorder have mushroomed. According to the US Centers for Disease Control and Prevention, 10.4 percent of American children have ever been diagnosed with ADHD, and 14.2 percent of boys have received a diagnosis, compared to 6.4 percent of girls.[19] ASD, meanwhile, is about 4.5 times more common among boys. It's not yet entirely understood why the rates have increased, whether these conditions are simply better recognized today or whether they are, in fact, more prevalent.[20] Little is known about what causes these conditions, although a 2015 large-scale five-nation study found an association between parental age at conception and risk for ASD. Older parents—women over age forty, men over age fifty—and teenage mothers were more likely to have children later diagnosed with ASD.[21]

It's also unclear why boys are more likely to be afflicted. It might reflect a difference in brain chemistry. It may be that boys' and girls' symptoms present differently, resulting in girls being underdiagnosed. It might reflect gender bias in referrals for assessments. Some of the markers of ASD (lack of social skills, emotional aloofness, obsessiveness) and ADHD (impulsivity, inattention, inability to sit still) might be perceived as more disruptive or more menacing when they come from a boy, making teachers and parents apt to recommend or seek testing and treatment.

It bears pointing out that these symptoms look an awful lot like what are considered defining qualities of boyness, raising questions about whether boys are being *over*diagnosed. Are we too quick to label the archetypical nerd (brainy, awkward, obsessive gamer, and comics geek) as being "on the spectrum"? And isn't ADHD just a clinical term for being energetic, kinetic, rebellious—in other words, an old-fashioned boy? "We are pathologizing boyhood," Edward (Ned) Hallowell, a psychiatrist and the coauthor of *Driven to Distraction* and *Delivered from Distraction*, told *Esquire* magazine in 2014. "There's been a general girlification of elementary school," he goes on to say, "where any kind of disruptive behavior is sinful. What I call the 'moral diagnosis' gets made: *You're bad. Now go get a doctor and get on medication so you'll be good.* And that's a real perversion of what ought to happen. Most boys are naturally more restless than most girls, and I would say that's good. But schools want these little goody-goodies who sit still and do what they're told—these robots—and that's just not who boys are."[22]

Framing any behavior as "the way boys are" raises a red flag. I agree with Hallowell that disabilities like ADHD and ASD, which affect behavior and socialization, are often framed in terms of morality rather than ability. But his characterizations of what's natural girl behavior (being a goody-goody or a robot) and natural boy behavior (being restless) are reductive. Undoubtedly, some children are misdiagnosed or prescribed medication too hastily. But having a child of my own with ADHD and having spoken to dozens of parents of boys with complicated learning disabilities and mental illnesses, I believe the true and pressing crisis is not the mislabeling of a typical kid who is aloof or high-spirited. It's that children who have been legitimately diagnosed are being underserved or pushed out of school. As diagnoses of ASD, anxiety, and ADHD have climbed, more and more education systems are emphasizing the integration of kids with disabilities into mainstream classrooms. The thinking is that inclusion decreases stigma and isolation and helps nondisabled kids learn to be more tolerant. Yet in practice, integration often happens without proper resources or teacher training and with zero education for classmates about disabilities.

What's more, standard discipline doesn't work for kids with autism, ADHD, and other conditions in which executive function—the mental processes that govern the ability to plan, focus, regulate emotions, remember instructions, and move from task to task—is affected. Behavior that might seem intentional is often reflexive or impulsive. A kid with poor communication skills might kick at his teacher when he's exhausted, because he doesn't know how to say "I'm tired." A child who is unable to interpret facial expressions won't get the meaning of the stern *Be quiet, please* look on a teacher's face and will just continue chattering away. With obsessive-compulsive and tic disorders, children may repeatedly touch things or fling their arms around or shout out: they have no more control over these actions than they do over blinking or sneezing. That doesn't mean they can't learn self-regulation and positive social skills, but that takes more investment than many schools are willing or able to provide.

So in the absence of training and support, schools suspend kids with disabilities or, in some cases, have them arrested. If the disabled child is also male as well as black or indigenous, his chance of being suspended multiplies. In the United States in the 2011–2012 school year, administrators suspended, at least once, more than one in every four black, indigenous, multiracial, and Pacific Islander boys who were identified as having a disability.[23] (Only 3 percent of all Asian boys and 6 percent of all white boys received an out-of-school suspension that year.)

In the spring of 2016, while reporting a story about education for children with special needs,[24] I traveled to a suburb outside Toronto to meet a twelve-year-old boy I'll call Connor (his family asked not to be identified). Connor has been diagnosed with a web of disabilities, including autism spectrum disorder, attention deficit disorder, tic disorder, and anxiety. He's also extraordinarily smart. After he welcomes me into his house by playing the *Star Wars* theme on the piano and we break the ice with chitchat about first-person-shooter video games, Connor tells me that for the most part he finds school "evil."

He has attended nine schools over the previous eight years. His sensitivities and behaviors make it hard for him to sit still, focus on his work, interpret social cues, regulate his emotions and behavior, remain calm, stay quiet, and write legibly. The typical elementary classroom feels like an impossible, hostile place to him. He has cursed, insulted his teachers, had explosive tantrums, and run down the hallway pulling posters from the walls. He's also been yelled at, restrained, and sent home.

After Connor retreats upstairs to play video games, his mother sketches in his school history: he has spent all the years since preschool bouncing among public and private schools, special education classrooms, tutors, and gifted programs. Connor is tall for his age, verbally precocious, but emotionally young. He has been seen as unmanageable and, at times, dangerous. His mother explains that on a few occasions, parents have lobbied to have him removed from a class or from school altogether. She likens this to being "chased by villagers with pitchforks." She isn't joking. Her son has been treated as though he is a monster.

She didn't downplay his challenges—she acknowledged his combativeness, the ways he can get locked into a battle of wills, his "impressive" vocabulary of swear words. At the same time, he had rarely been taught by someone who understands kids with complicated disabilities or has the expertise to teach them. Hence, the punishments. "But how do suspensions help a child with disabilities learn social and emotional skills?" she asked me. When we meet, Connor has just started a new program in a new school that seems promising, but they'd been through this too often to feel anything but wary.

My son hasn't struggled to the degree that Connor has, but I suspect he also thinks school is evil, at least some of the time. A few teachers have been kind and empathetic. Up until the fourth grade, he attended a school that was specifically created for indigenous children. It taught language and culture (mainly Ojibway and Cree) and celebrated indigenous traditions and histories. But it lacked the special education support he needed, so he had to move to another school. He has been labeled a "problem," has been punished and excluded from social activities and field trips, and has sensed that teachers disliked him—a feeling that was compounded by our concern that, in some cases, racial bias was at play in how he was treated. One teacher wrote him an end-of-year letter saying our son had "disappointed" him.

Eventually, he was placed in a small class with extra support, modifications in his lessons, and counseling for his behavior. His grades improved, and he became happier. But even when he's doing well, I can't

shake the knowledge of his vulnerability. On top of all the usual parental worries about speeding cars and child snatchers, there's also the
consciousness of the realities of racism and how he's perceived by the
world as an indigenous teenager. No matter how much we love him
and how diligently we protect him, there is always the knowledge that
adults and authority figures are tougher on boys like him.

———

So, is the boy crisis real? If you've followed conversations and news stories about sex, school, and success over the past decade or two, and
most parents I know have, you're probably convinced it is. Since the
1990s, there's been a recurring cycle of media-driven panics about boys
losing their social, cultural, and political edge in schooling and job opportunities. Now, once again, magazine features, TV news documen-
taries, newspaper stories, and, increasingly, online men's rights activist
groups are raising the alarm about the failing state of boys. The problem, these experts and commentators say, is a mounting hostility toward boys in our culture and in our schools. Young men are at risk
of falling so far behind, they'll never catch up. "It's a bad time to be a
boy in America," warned Christina Hoff Sommers, a leading conservative chronicler of the boy crisis, in the *Atlantic* in 2000.[25] And again
in *Time* in 2013, she wrote, "As school begins in the coming weeks,
parents of boys should ask themselves a question: Is my son really welcome?"[26] Psychologist Michael Gurian, author of *The Wonder of Boys*
(1996), as well as physician Leonard Sax, author of *Why Gender Matters* (2005), and others have argued that sex differences are innate and
fixed. By their reasoning, boys aren't hard-wired for the modern education system with its emphasis on emotional intelligence and literacy,
which instead favors the soft-skilled female brain. And so girls, being

more adept and favored by their female teachers, are now ascendant. They talk sooner, read sooner, and have better self-control.

Despite inconsistent data on boys' academic achievement, these fears have gained traction. Anecdotal evidence is everywhere: as I've laid out above, ADHD and autism among boys is rising; everyone seems to know someone with a teenage son stuck in the parental basement, unable to launch into adulthood. In the wake of the 2016 US presidential election, the plight of white working-class boys and men has become a media obsession. With blue-collar jobs lost to automation and globalization, many of these young men are unemployed, adrift, and angry—and hoping to Make America Great Again.

And it's true: there *are* so many bright young women, thriving and busy with ambition. At my son's eighth grade graduation, his cohort of a hundred or so classmates gathered to receive their diplomas in an auditorium decorated with a series of portraits of the school's founding principals. It was amusing to watch girl after girl, all of them young women of color, called up on stage to receive the school's top academic and leadership awards, under this gallery of solemn white men.

Before we pronounce the death of the patriarchy, however, let's look seriously at the evidence. Struggling boys do exist—I've spent most of this chapter detailing their circumstances. But that doesn't mean the entire sex is experiencing a crisis. In fact, research shows there is a greater difference in school achievement and graduation rates *among* boys than between boys and girls.

When the data on school achievement is broken down by ethnicity and economic status as well as sex, what stands out are race and class inequalities. Research emerging in the past couple years has found that the female-male educational advantage at school—in other words, the boy crisis—is larger and has increased more among black students and poor children than among white and more economically advantaged children. Boys seem to be more sensitive to disadvantage than girls; even within the same families living in poor neighborhoods and enrolled at the lower-quality public schools, they fare much worse than their sisters. They are more likely than girls to skip school, exhibit behavior problems, perform poorly on standardized tests, and drop out of high school.[27]

Some theories have been floated to account for this. Physiologically, boys seem to suffer more from stress than girls, and since boys are discouraged from expressing their emotions or asking for support, they may not seek out help when they need it. Low-income families are also often led by single mothers, and boys may struggle with the absence of a same-gender role model. (Black boys in communities where there are high numbers of black father figures and mentors, such as uncles, coaches, and teachers, had much better outcomes.) Racism is another contributing factor: black boys who grow up in more racially tolerant communities, where white people exhibit lower levels of racial bias, earn more money as adults and are less likely to be incarcerated.[28]

Racism and poverty, it appears, are far more responsible for boys' struggles than are sex differences in the brain—or the "girlification" of school, as Ned Hallowell put it. The most marked contrasts in test scores, grades, graduation rates, and postsecondary school enrollment are not divided along gender lines but along race and class ones. Boys' test scores, for instance, are inconsistent, with their results occupying much of the top end and bottom end of the spectrum, while girls' scores are more concentrated in the middle. Meanwhile, white suburban and middle-class boys are, as a group, doing just fine. On average, this group isn't dropping out of school or abandoning postsecondary education.[29]

Nor have education systems changed course so radically in the past two or three decades as to suddenly set themselves against boys. Even though young women now match or slightly outnumber young men in some undergraduate programs and in law and medical schools, technology and engineering programs are still dominated by men. If boys as an entire sex appear to be doing worse, it's largely because the surge in girls' achievements and advancements has been dramatic in comparison. That shouldn't be surprising. This is what it looks like when playing fields are leveled: boys no longer dominate every class and win every award.

As for boy brains versus girl brains? As I note in Chapter 2, there are biological and physical differences. But what this means in terms of capability and intelligence—if it means anything at all—is nowhere close to being understood. Remember, it was only about a century ago that women were thought to be too ignorant to vote and doctors warned that too much intellectual stimulation would draw blood from women's wombs up to their brains, ruining their fertility. Today it's well accepted (one hopes) that these attitudes about the inferior female brain were ridiculous and sexist. As neuroscientist Lise Eliot has pointed out, much of the research on sex differences in the brain has been done on adults. Given the brain's plasticity and the growing understanding of the complex interplay between our genes and our environment, there is no consistent evidence that these differences are necessarily innate and static. We are creations of both nature and culture; very little of what makes us male or female is down to one of those factors alone.

The argument that boys are now in crisis because of their brains requires a rather convenient forgetting of history. Until the 1980s and '90s, it was boys who made up the majority of class valedictorians and student leaders, boys who went on to fill the spots at prestigious universities. If the male brain isn't wired for schooling, how do we account for these previous achievements? If the male mind lacks a capacity for language, reading, and wordplay, then how do we explain the presence of so many men in the Western literary canon? If boys struggle to sit still and concentrate, why are so many CEOs, university presidents, and politicians men?

It's far sexier and more headline grabbing to cast problems in education as a battle of the sexes. If girls are up, then boys have to be down, right? But framing the problems of education as primarily about gender overlooks the entrenched social inequalities that really are a grinding problem for so many boys.

It is useful, too, to consider what has led to girls' current success. For one, we've altered our expectations. We encourage girls to take advanced courses, play sports, join clubs, run for class president. Girls, in turn, work hard in school. They spend more time studying than boys do, and they are more likely to say that it's important to them to get good grades and that it's important to please their teachers.

While girls changed, boys didn't. As girls occupy more spaces that were traditionally the domain of boys—as student leaders, top scholars, champion athletes—boys seem to have developed an identity crisis. If boys and girls are defined as opposites, then what happens when girls are good in school? Does that mean boys aren't or shouldn't be? Does being good at school make you appear feminine? Perhaps the boy crisis isn't about brain difference or an anti-male culture at schools. Perhaps ideas about school and masculinity are what's causing boys to fail.

———

The experiences of boys in Toronto's Portuguese community might hold some answers to these questions. There are about 170,000 people of Portuguese descent in Toronto, the now elderly immigrants who arrived in a vast wave in the 1950s and their children and grandchildren, many still concentrated in blue-collar but rapidly gentrifying Little Portugal on the city's west side. Other immigrant groups, such as those from Italy and India, have found social mobility through migration, but the Portuguese community's trajectory has been different. While economically secure—Portuguese men are prominent in the city's construction industry, and the home-ownership rate is high—there hasn't been much class mobility. Levels of academic achievement are low. According to a Toronto District School Board report, Portuguese Canadian kids have the highest dropout rate in the city, at 34 percent. Portuguese Canadian boys are also less likely to graduate than their female cohort.[30]

These numbers have puzzled sociologists and educators. One theory is that low literacy levels among working-class people in Portugal has been carried over to second- and third-generation children. Another is that Portuguese Canadian students face discrimination of lowered expectations. Since their fathers are visible working in construction and their mothers as domestic laborers and cleaners, teachers don't encourage them to consider college.

David Pereira, a PhD candidate at the University of Toronto who is of Portuguese descent, has another theory. Boys don't believe it's manly to do well in school. For his master's thesis, he spoke to a dozen Portuguese men in their late teens and twenties about masculinity. They told him that within their families and community, manliness was defined in traditional and conservative ways. Being a man meant being self-sufficient, a provider, and a home owner, and all of that was closely tied to physical work. "Whether, as participants mentioned, it is being a handyman so as to not need to pay others to fix something, or being financially secure and stable enough to purchase what one needs or wants without asking for assistance," Pereira writes, "masculinity is understood as getting the job done without needing to ask others for help." (Pereira's theory is supported by research from the United States indicating that poor and working-class boys in communities where men work physical blue-collar jobs associate doing well in school with being "gay" or "feminine.")[31]

This shapes boys in a number of ways. Among students in Toronto, kids of Portuguese ancestry worked the longest hours at part-time jobs and the fewest hours on homework. Many gave their families part of their earnings. The belief in self-reliance means Portuguese boys are reluctant to ask teachers for help. Boys who dropped out of school could find work through their family networks in the trades, reducing the incentive to stay in school.

Yet even as many of the young men subscribed to these beliefs, they recognized how such beliefs could be used against them. Nearly half the young men Pereira spoke to said that what they least liked about being Portuguese were negative stereotypes about being uneducated, aggressive, lazy, and manual laborers. One young man named Bruno said his male friends would never ask a teacher for help with schoolwork. "They would rather do it on their own, [and] if they can't do it on their own, then find something else to do, because clearly school isn't something that you're going to excel in," Bruno said. "So find something that you are going to do well in." When Pereira asked Bruno what teachers thought of him and his friends, he answered, "Dumb kids."[32]

Another dynamic Pereira identified was a tension between educated sons and their less educated, working-class fathers. Fathers had mixed feelings about their sons' advancement: they wanted them to do well and have better economic opportunities, but they also felt threatened and belittled by what they perceived as a "sense of superiority." This left the boys caught between dueling expectations about what it means to be male and Portuguese and what was needed for them to do well in school. The tools that gave them success in one realm failed them in another. Pereira believes there is bias against Portuguese students, but he doesn't think boys are entirely passive in their experience of schooling, either. He suggests they may be "de-selecting" themselves from academic success both because schools don't recognize their potential to do well and because academic success challenges their community's idea of what it means to be a man.

Research showed a similar dynamic with indigenous students in the United States, who have the lowest educational attainment rate of any group in the country. Just 46 percent graduate from high school, compared to a national average of 89 percent.[33] When asked why they dropped out, these students said they felt that teachers and students were hostile toward them. They also said they were bored. The curriculum wasn't relevant to them and their communities. In fact, only 8 percent of indigenous students drop out because of academic failure. Similar to Portuguese boys in Toronto, indigenous students in the United States felt they had to choose between success at school and their cultural identity.

This is why conversations that generalize about the "boy crisis" aren't helpful. From the first day of kindergarten, boys must negotiate a tangle of expectations—about gender, about class, about race, about social status—that vary based on their personal histories and identities: one boy has a jail cell waiting for him, while another is a dumb kid who will drop out to become a laborer.

Even positive stereotypes about the types of boys who do well in school can be confining and damaging. One study of teacher bias in California found that educators describe East Asian and South Asian boys as more cooperative, self-controlled, eager to please, perfectionistic, academically successful, and having fewer overall behavior problems when compared to their peers.[34] The belief is bolstered by stereotypes of Asian parents as exacting tiger moms and dads. The "model minority" trope may seem to work in favor of Asian boys— they are perceived to be on a track for success, typically in high-status fields like engineering and medicine. But the reverse side of this myth is that it's used to pit Asian children against those from other racialized groups, particularly black kids. If Asian children are doing so well, the argument goes, then educational systems couldn't possibly be racially discriminatory.

But this thinking overlooks factors that have led to the academic achievement of Asian children. For kids whose families are recent migrants, there's the fact that immigration policy favors highly skilled and educated adults, whose children will inherit certain socioeconomic advantages. The other is that racist attitudes are expressed differently toward different groups, and racism toward Asians, according to some historical surveys in the United States, has diminished more over time than racism directed at black people.

The other problem with the model minority image is that Asian children are perceived to be less assertive, less expressive, and less socially skilled than their peers. This sets up Asian kids to be stereotyped and bullied for being studious, and for boys particularly to be viewed as nerds. This perception also means that educators may overlook or misinterpret Asian children's struggles in school. For instance, teachers who believe that it's normal for Asian kids to be perfectionists may not recognize the signs of mental health disorders such as anxiety.

In some cases, the view that Asians are excellent students has tipped over into a sense of resentment that they are doing *too well*. There is a growing backlash that fears Asian students are overrepresented at elite postsecondary programs. In 2010 the Canadian newsmagazine *Maclean's* ran a story about race-based enrollment quotas at universities with the headline "Too Asian?" Sociologist Carolyn Chen, who teaches at the University of California at Berkeley, has written that Asian students have told her "they feel ashamed of their identity—that they feel viewed as a faceless bunch of geeks and virtuosos. When they succeed, their peers chalk it up to 'being Asian.' "[35]

Too Asian, too black, too tough, too hyper, too dumb, too emotionless, too dangerous, too nerdy. Whatever the stereotype and expectation, it inhibits boys' growth and development. But once we're conscious about how boys shape their male identities in school, solutions aren't difficult to find. Take the study from North Carolina. If having a black teacher radically reduces the dropout rate for poor black boys, it suggests boys will do better if they have teachers who are culturally connected to them and can serve as role models. That's the thinking behind the Manhood Development Program created in 2012 by the Oakland Unified School District in California. Taught by black men, the series of elective courses—in black history, politics, and culture—is geared to African American boys in grades 3 through 12. Similarly, Portuguese teachers and social workers in Toronto have formed a group to tutor and mentor Portuguese students, with the hope that seeing adults from their community who've graduated and gone to postsecondary school will counteract myths about identity and academic success.

———

In 2016 I witness another model of this at work at Robert W. Coleman Elementary School in West Baltimore.[36] Seated cross-legged on a yoga mat at the back of the school gym next to two giggling boys, I am being led in meditation by a fourth grader. "Inhale deep, and exhale," he repeats. There are about fifty children in the gym, and under the guidance of a small group of instructors, they take turns leading the others through a series of yoga postures and short meditation exercises. The room is sticky with heat, and most of us teeter as we attempt tree pose—balancing on one leg, with the other one bent and its foot pressed against the thigh of the standing leg. One of the giggling boys beside me whispers and points to me: "Keep your eyes on one spot, miss," and shows off his moves. Occasionally, the instructors, mostly young men in their late teens and early twenties, circulate through the group to gently hush the talkers or demonstrate a tricky posture.

West Baltimore is a neighborhood a lot like Brownsville. More than 80 percent of students qualify for free or reduced-cost lunches.

Many don't have stable housing; a number have family members who are currently or have been incarcerated. Several students exhibit signs of emotional distress. In 2015, following the death of twenty-five-year-old Freddie Gray in police custody, the neighborhood was the center of mass protests against police brutality, followed by eruptions of violence with arson and looting. A state of emergency was declared, and the National Guard was sent in to patrol the nearby streets.

Nearly ten years ago, a nonprofit organization called Holistic Life Foundation started an after-school meditation and yoga program to help students cope with stress and anxiety and to reduce suspensions and expulsions. Since then, the foundation has set up a permanent office in Robert Coleman, leading short meditations over the PA during the day and running an extensive afternoon program, with enrichment classes, homework support, and yoga.

Andres Gonzalez, who started the foundation with brothers Atman and Ali Smith, gave me a tour of the school before yoga class. As we walked the halls, children ran up to him with arms open for a hug. Everyone involved with the foundation is a hugger. When I'm introduced to staff and instructors and reach out for a handshake, I inevitably wind up being pulled in for an embrace.

As part of the program, students who act out in class are sent to the Mindful Moment Room, a quiet space filled with pillows and yoga mats. There, foundation staff members encourage them to talk about what led to their removal from class and then do breathing exercises to help them calm down. Suspensions have been dramatically reduced.

Wanting to be mentors to young black and Latino men, Gonzalez and the Smiths started running free recreational programs at the local YMCA fifteen years ago. Eventually, the three, who are longtime yoga practitioners and meditators, began to show the boys breathing techniques and simple yoga postures. At the time, Gonzalez says, the boys thought yoga was "only a thing white women in expensive stretchy pants did," but after trying it they realized it would help them with focus and improve their performance in sports. Soon the boys were more interested in doing yoga than in playing football or basketball.

Jamar Peete was one of those early students. He was ten when he met the Smiths and Gonzalez. He played baseball and lacrosse and was first drawn to yoga because it made him a better competitor. "Yoga was my secret weapon for dealing with pressure," he says. Then he began practicing yoga for its own sake. Now he works for the foundation as a teacher and mentor.

It's a testament to the program that after graduating college, Peete returned to take a job at the foundation. A number of former students are instructors now—a positive cycle of mentorship. Gonzalez says it's important for boys in the program to see men practicing yoga and providing them with emotional support. Boys generally aren't taught to channel their feelings in healthy ways. "They aren't supposed to cry, or look foolish, or be vulnerable," he says, so they shut down at a young age. Yoga and meditation quell the chaos and create a sense of safety that's largely absent in their lives, he says. It lets them open up. I can see it, in the abundant positive encouragement and the sensitive approach taken with the kids. Peete tells me, "A lot of kids start this program, and they're angry all the time. I remember asking one kid, 'Why are you always so mad?' And he said, 'I don't know what else to feel.'"

As we're talking, a little boy who looks about six or seven years old storms into the Mindful Moment Room in his socks. He took off his shoes for yoga, and another boy took them home with him. The child is furious, and his eyes brim with tears. How will he get home without shoes? How will he explain it to his mom? Why did that other kid steal from him? A man on staff patiently listens to the little boy until he's finished. Then he takes a few deep breaths with him and helps him brainstorm an action plan. Within minutes, a call is made to his mother and the mother of the other boy to explain the situation and ensure the shoes will be returned the next day. A spare pair of shoes is found in a lost-and-found cupboard for the boy to wear home that night. He gets a glass of water and a snack. When his mom arrives a half hour later to pick him up, he's calmed down and smiling. After one final hug from the staff, he heads home with her in his borrowed shoes.

5

MAN UP

How Sports Build Boys

One of the things our son's foster mother told me about him, during our first conversation over the phone, was that he liked sports. She and her husband were soccer fans, and whenever there was a match on TV, he'd follow the ball with his eyes—rare, she told me, in a child so young. It was projection on her part, I think, but I knew little about infants and toddlers at the time, and nothing at all about what sense my future son's brain could make of a soccer ball on a television screen, so I took her at her word. It was projection on my part too: this detail about my son made him real to me. Suddenly, there was an image of him in my head as a budding jock that fleshed out the scant details we knew from his file. The idea was comforting. Given all the unknowns, all the ways in which my son's life experience and history would be seen as different—as an Oji-Cree and Ojibway adoptee with white lesbian parents—his interest in sports felt pleasingly normal. And if I'm being honest, there was a small part of me that surged with a kind of pride at a talent that might make him special.

At our first in-person meeting with our son, at an office of the child welfare agency in the city where he lived, we brought a small basketball, so we could play with him. He rolled it back and forth to us with enthusiasm until his attention turned to exploring and he crawled off to climb on the furniture. Ever since, my son has remained in constant motion. He doesn't simply enter a room; he runs, slides, or tumbles into it. He's not a prodigy, but he's been gifted with coordination and balance and quickly picks up the basics of most games he tries—skateboarding, skiing, baseball, swimming, basketball, and rock climbing.

Hockey is his mainstay sport, one he's played since preschool. It wasn't entirely of his choosing. My wife played as a kid, when few girls did, encouraged by her adoring father, and she continues to play as an adult and volunteers to manage our son's team. To her, the game is wedded to tradition and family. Hockey's detractors find its stoicism, low scores, and lack of colorful personalities dull. Comedian and author John Hodgman once called it "a game of intensely watching things almost happen."[1] But that's part, if not much, of the appeal for fans. It's such a grinding, gritty, and unglamorous game that its grace and thrills become all the more evident by contrast. So unless our child showed absolutely no aptitude or interest, it was inevitable that he'd play. Skating lessons began at age two, and when he turned five, he started to play a rudimentary version of hockey. Like most beginners, he skittered across the ice in a slippery *bourrée*, falling frequently with a splat.

Basketball and football, when reduced to their fundamentals, can be played with minimal equipment in a park or on a playground and can provide gratification quickly. Hockey requires months, even years, of skating practice just to become adequate. It's tough to learn, equipment is cumbersome and costly, and rinks and ice time are limited. In his 2008 best seller, *Outliers: The Story of Success*, Malcolm Gladwell uses minor hockey to illustrate both the rule of ten thousand hours of practice—that's the amount of time he says is required to perfect a skill—and the ways in which the emphasis on early selection for more competitive streams preempts opportunities for younger, less-developed boys to ever enter the elite levels of the sport.

My own evolution as a hockey mom has taken years as well, and I remain reluctant.[2] During the seasons when my son played in a competitive league where the players—and the parents—were more aggressive, I often distracted myself during games by working out calculations in my head, tallying up the hours and dollars we'd spent on his lessons and fees and equipment, and calculating the odds my son's head would be slammed into the boards or smashed onto the ice. At one game, when he was about ten years old, he went headfirst at full speed into the metal frame of the net. He crumpled to the ice and lay there, limp and still, for a full minute that felt like a century. He was lucky. He was shaken but not concussed.

That's hockey. It's a rough, dangerous sport and an aggressively masculine one. Not as nakedly violent as boxing or as overtly driven by a desire for domination as football. But it's still a sport that teaches boys as young as age twelve to bodycheck. And it involves an enforcer (or a goon), a mediocre player who revs up fans by taking to the ice, tossing off his gloves, and slugging it out with an opposing player. In Canada, in the past decade, sports-related brain injuries have shot up among kids, with a 45 percent rise in emergency room visits by children aged ten to seventeen and a 78 percent increase by children nine and under. Sixty-two percent of the children were boys.[3] The sports most likely to cause these injuries are hockey, cycling, and football/ rugby; the number of hospital visits for brain injuries from hockey was almost double that from cycling, football/rugby, and skiing/snowboarding. Meanwhile, the US Centers for Disease Control and Prevention has called sports concussions "an epidemic" among young people. An estimated 329,290 children under the age of nineteen were treated in US emergency rooms in 2012 for sports- and recreation-related injuries that included a diagnosis of traumatic brain injury. And from 2001 to 2012, the rate of emergency room visits for sports-related head injuries more than doubled among children under age nineteen.[4] These sorts of traumas can have long-term consequences, including depression, anxiety, and suicidal ideation, as well as violent behavior.

In 2013 the now-defunct website Sports on Earth profiled a mother in Georgia named Monet Bartell, who was deliberating about whether to allow her seven-year-old son, Parker, to continue with football. The daughter, niece, and sister of several National Football League players, Bartell had long dreamed her son would play; he weighed sixty-five pounds by the age four, and his nickname was "Tank." Yet just as Parker joined his first league, she began getting reports that her relatives who had played in the NFL were now struggling with signs of chronic traumatic encephalopathy, such as dementia (CTE can be confirmed only by autopsy). Bartell lived and breathed football. She was conflicted. "Deep down, there's a side of me that would love [Parker] to go to the NFL and keep up the tradition," she said. "Do I *want* him on a football field? Absolutely. Do I know the repercussions? Absolutely. Do I think he *should* play? As a mom, absolutely not."[5]

I understood Bartell's dilemma. Even though my son currently plays in a noncontact hockey league, where the risk of serious injury is remote, several of the boys he's played with have been concussed—one serious enough to have developed severe headaches and mood swings. His recovery required weeks of rest. Hockey gives my son joy, physical confidence, a sense of belonging, and practical lessons in resilience and hard work. But are the risks worth it?

Concussions aside, there are other serious hazards in how sports are used to define maleness and masculinity and in how that definition is cast in opposition to femaleness and, by extension, homosexuality. Sports are at the center of the Man Box and its rules for masculine behavior. You hear it from the coach who tells a flailing player to "man up" and to "stop playing like a girl," or in the trash talk that inevitably deploys slurs like "fag," "punk," and "bitch."

Sports empower boys but can sometimes give them too much power, such as when a championship team gets the lion's share of a school's funds while other programs wither, or when a star player's academic or sexual transgressions are overlooked as long as he delivers on the field. Sports foster loyalty but also encourage conformity, as when a kid unquestioningly takes direction from a coach who puts his safety at risk. It says a great deal about how much we believe sports to be an essential part of boyhood and manhood that it can override the instincts of even the most protective and thoughtful parents. Parker Bartell eventually quit football. His mother was relieved but said, "It's like a drug or alcohol addiction. Leaving the sport is like trying to quit cold turkey. It's very difficult to lose it." Not only is football a defining feature of manhood, but it's also central to American culture.

The association of maleness—and boyness—with sports is assumed to be natural. A lack of interest in sports is considered a suspicious sign of male failure. Boys' identities are invested in sports—70 percent of US boys in grades 3 to 5 and 63 percent in grades 6 to 8 say sports are "a big part of who they are" (compared to 35 and 40 percent of girls in the same grades). But what's most telling is that 42 percent of boys who don't even play sports also say sports are "a big part" of their identity.[6]

In his book *Guyland*, sociologist Michael Kimmel observes that an interest in sports is one of the defining features of maleness. Sports remain a male domain, a place where men can find a collective identity; sports are also one of the few venues in which over-the-top male emotion, such as tears of joy or defeat, can be expressed. "Guys live for sports, and live through sports," he writes. "It serves so many purposes—validating our manhood; bridging generational, racial, and class divides; cementing the bonds among men; and more clearly demarcating the boundaries between Guyland and Herland."[7]

When you begin to look, you see the messages about this demarcation everywhere, not only in organized and professional sports but also in casual play in public parks and schoolyards. A few days a week, my local YMCA hosts after-school pickup basketball for teenagers. My son and the rest of the young boys who turn up take half the court for games of two-on-two or H-O-R-S-E. Though it's open to everyone, only once have I seen girls show up. Even then, they played together, in a separate game, coached by a staff member. It's the same on the public basketball courts in our neighborhood. On spring and summer nights, they're full of boys and young men—rarely is a girl or young woman in sight.

Casual sports experiences like these aren't merely about having fun; they teach boys how to negotiate, how to compete, how to engage with strangers. They also teach boys how to claim public space—parks, schoolyards, gyms—as their own. When girls aren't present in these public spaces with boys, not only do girls lose out, but boys begin to believe that girls have less right to them. When girls and boys don't play and compete together, boys don't learn to see girls as teammates and as competitors. And gradually boys learn to take possession of other spaces too. This dynamic has come to be seen as natural: it's believed that sports are male dominated because they are inherently male activities, having evolved out of boys' and men's innate talent, aggression, and drive for competition. The actual history is more complicated.

———

Modern team sports, the ones we recognize now as soccer, baseball, football, rugby, basketball, and hockey, began to take their current forms in the 1800s. One of the main instigators for the popularization of sport was, strangely enough, a novel about religious values. Thomas Hughes's influential 1857 novel, *Tom Brown's School Days*, was set at an upper-class all-boys British boarding school, and its central theme is the transformation of rowdy boys into respectable Christian men. Pious message aside, it was Hughes's characterization of sports that caught on: descriptions of bare-knuckle boxing, rugby and running, and his emphasis on the virtues of physical strength, teamwork, and coopera- tion. What readers took away was a vision of young manhood that was fearless and rugged, forged on the playing field alongside one's loyal teammates.[8]

The formalization of sports as a morally healthy pastime for boys was helped along by Victorian squeamishness about sex. Boys' sexual desires were seen as disruptive and dangerous. Sports, especially when twinned with values like honor and duty, were thought to provide an outlet for sexual urges, as a way to exhaust or sublimate them, espe- cially at boarding schools, which were rife with same-sex crushes and affections. Of course, with all the male bonding in the locker room and grappling out on the field, this didn't exactly work, and the tension be- tween male intimacy and homophobia has bedeviled sports ever since.

Initially, sports were primarily activities for socially superior boys (that is, white, Christian, and upper class). By the late nineteenth cen- tury, rugby, rowing, and cricket had become the marker of a well- cultivated young man. So much so that at the time, a notice on the wall at the ultraposh British boys school Eton College read: "Any lower boy in this house who does not play football once a day and twice on half holiday will be fined half a crown and kicked."[9] At the same time, in North America, Europe, and elsewhere, soccer, hockey, lacrosse, track and field, and boxing were being formalized with rules, clubs, and teams.

For working-class boys, boys in British colonies, and black and in- digenous boys in Canada and the United States, sports had a different goal. The Victorian belief in amateurism—that is, not receiving payment for playing sports—shut out all but those who were wealthy enough to play organized or club sports for free and receive training and coaching at school or college. (The class discrimination baked into the idea of amateurism continues in sports even now, amid the growing calls for college athletes—who make considerable sums of money for their schools and whose talents help fatten endowments—to be paid for their work.) Working-class and black and brown boys and young men were admitted into organized sports initially as a way to socialize them and to impress upon them the power structures of the day. Sports were coached and officiated by white adult men through charitable organizations. The YMCA, for instance, was founded in London in 1844 by an evangelical Christian named George Williams, who wanted to minister to the young, poor, rural men pouring into cities during the Industrial Revolution, looking for jobs. Within a decade, the organization had spread throughout Europe and into the United States, Canada, and Australia, espousing what came to be called "muscular Christianity," a form of faith that valued sports, teamwork, sacrifice, and duty and was skeptical of anything that seemed effeminate or overly intellectual. (James Naismith, the Canadian Presbyterian chaplain and educator who invented basketball in 1891, was a champion of the values of muscular Christianity.)

In addition to instilling young men with religious values, sports—rugby, in particular—were also a way for boys and men to rebel against women's growing independence. Historians and sociologists have pointed out that the coarse, thuggish traditions of rugby developed at the exact same time women were agitating for the vote. As British suffragettes were literally waging a war by chaining themselves to fences, starving themselves, blowing up churches, and setting fires to mailboxes, British men retreated to the bunker of sport. Rugby was a male-only pursuit, and, fortified by fringe activities such as mooning women and singing crude drinking songs, it allowed men to assert their masculinity.

Two other sports juggernauts emerged during the late nineteenth and early twentieth centuries. In France an aristocrat and scholar named Pierre de Coubertin became fixated on the belief that young French men were physical weaklings and inferior to their European peers. In search of new models for athletic education to whip his young countrymen into shape, he seized upon a copy of *Tom Brown's School Days*. After visiting several British boarding schools, Coubertin returned home to France and initiated his grand ambition, a revival of the ancient Olympic Games. Coubertin deliberately barred women from the first Games in 1896 and for most of his life continued to oppose their participation. Like many men of his era, he believed sports were a male birthright and argued that women were biologically incapable of athletic excellence. He also thought the sight of women competing was immoral and would inspire lustful thoughts: "If some women want to play football or box, let them, provided that the event takes place without spectators, because the spectators who flock to such competitions are not there to watch a sport."[10]

In America the military battles and colonizing efforts of the early nineteenth century had come to a close, leaving few arenas for young white men looking to prove their virility and power. Then came along American football, a spin-off of rugby, and with its military formations and focus on gaining and stealing territory, it was the perfect stand-in for army skirmishes and frontier adventures. The first game ever played was in 1869 between Rutgers and Princeton Universities. Early games were deadly, with almost no passing and plenty of fighting, the very definition of blood sports. In pileups players punched, bit, and throttled. Between 1900 and 1905, at least forty-five players died from injuries, including broken necks and backs.

By 1905 there was a movement to outlaw the sport, and several university and college administrators were ready to scrap it, but President

Theodore Roosevelt stepped in to preserve football as a ruggedly American male pursuit. Manliness was an obsession of his: a scrawny, asthmatic, nearsighted kid nicknamed "Four Eyes," Roosevelt reinvented himself in adulthood as a hunting, horse-riding he-man through a program of boxing and wrestling.[11]

New rules opened up the game, spread out players on the field, and emphasized passing. Ivy League schools dominated the sport, but much of the innovation came from the tiny Carlisle Indian Industrial School in Pennsylvania. Like the Canadian residential schools of this era, Carlisle was created in 1879 to "civilize" Native American children; they were made to cut their hair, dress in European-style clothes, and speak only in English. One way in which the students assimilated was through football, and they excelled at it. Ironically, it was these so-called uncivilized students who gifted football with dazzle and skill, refining the game's brutality through their inventions of the forward pass and the overhand spiral. Carlisle's quarterbacks were the first to fake handoffs and rear back to throw passes.[12]

The underfunded and underfed Carlisle students routinely defeated the hulks at Harvard and the University of Pennsylvania. To the students of Carlisle, their triumphs on the football field were a way to assert their humanity and aptitude in contests against the sons and grandsons of those who had stolen their lands. And in 1912, there was remarkable retread of history in a game played between Carlisle and the US Military Academy. Just twenty-two years earlier, the US Seventh Cavalry had slaughtered more than 150 Lakota adults and children at Wounded Knee Creek in South Dakota. (Many students at Carlisle were Lakota.) Talking to his team in the week before the face-off against the academy, the team's legendary coach, Pop Warner, said, "I shouldn't have to prepare you for this game. Just go to your rooms and read your history books."[13] Carlisle beat Army 27–6.

Without Carlisle's refinements, football may have perished. Yet the school's influence has mostly been forgotten. To add insult, pro football, like other pro sports, is riddled with offensive Native mascots and logos of braves and redskins. These cartoon images of generic warriors, unconnected to a tribe or nation, simultaneously erase the contributions of indigenous athletes and mock indigenous people. In a 2013 statement on the continued refusal by the NFL's Washington Redskins to change its name, the National Congress of American Indians wrote, "Widely consumed images of Native American stereotypes in commercial and educational environments slander, defame, and vilify Native peoples, Native cultures, and tribal nations, and continue a legacy of racist and prejudiced attitudes. In particular, the 'savage' and 'clownish' caricatures used by sports teams with 'Indian' mascots contribute to the 'savage' image of Native peoples and the myth that Native peoples are an ethnic group 'frozen in history.' "[14]

━━━━━

This history of violence, sexism, homophobia, racism, and elitism is part of how sports has constructed ideas of masculinity. And throughout the past 150 years, sports were used by anxious adults to toughen up young men, to display patriotism, to uphold racist attitudes, to settle grudges, to depress sexual urges, and to shore up local economies. Mainly, though, sports have been used to express a very specific kind of masculinity, one that is stoic, physically fearless, and driven to dominate.

"Toxic jock" is a label coined by Kathleen E. Miller, a sociologist at the University of Buffalo who studies the way student athletes, both male and female, develop their identity and sense of self through high school and college sports.[15] There is a healthy model of personality related to sports, Miller has found: the "athlete identity," which empha-sizes the mastery of skills and personal excellence. Young people, both boys and girls, who participate and think about sports this way get bet-ter grades, exhibit lower drug and alcohol use, and are in good physical and emotional health.

Then there's the subset of student athletes that Miller refers to as "toxic jocks." Members of this group are not as interested in teamwork and sportsmanship but rather interested in outperforming others and being stars. Toxic jocks have "an ego-oriented approach to sports par-ticipation," Miller writes, and tend to play high-status or high-profile contact sports such as football, hockey, and wrestling. Not surprisingly, this group is predominantly male and strongly embraces traditional ideas of masculinity. Think of any good-looking ringleader quarter-back bully from any teen movie who ever shoved a nerd into a locker: that's a toxic jock. They drink to excess, get in trouble at school, get into fights, engage in unprotected sex. Adolescents don't need any more encouragement when it comes to danger and risk. Most young people don't reach their full capacity for emotional regulation and impulse con-trol until they're in their early twenties. In the meantime, kids are prone to pleasure seeking, driven by their friends' approval, and highly tolerant of risk. With cultural messages that see reckless behavior as manly and cool, boys are hit with a double dose of encouragement to do stupid things that put themselves and others in danger.

While embodying the worst qualities of sports culture, the toxic jock is revered and valued within popular culture. Energy drink com-panies,[16] for instance, routinely exploit these toxic tendencies in their marketing schemes, targeting a consumer base obsessed with gonzo sports and video games. They've been hugely successful in their efforts: 31 percent of kids, mostly boys between the ages of twelve and seven-teen, guzzle these drinks on a regular basis. The drinks, which contain high levels of caffeine, are pitched at young men through sponsorship of extreme sports like motocross, skateboarding, mixed martial arts, and video games. A 2015 study found a cascade effect connecting beliefs about manliness and the efficacy of energy drinks to the high consumption of those beverages: the more a young man bought into masculine ideals, the more susceptible he was to macho marketing associating masculinity with energy drinks, and the more he drank them.[17] In essence, the industry plays on young men's gender anxiety about sports and performance. Some companies sell "gaming fuel" to heighten focus and endurance, aiming them at tween and teen video gamers. Gamma Labs, the makers of G Fuel, has sponsored a popular clan of professional *Call of Duty* players, housing them together and live-streaming their activities, which include the conspicuous consumption of G Fuel products.

The danger is that in aiming their message at the vulnerable young male ego, these companies may exacerbate the dangerous behavior to which young men are already prone. The high levels of caffeine in energy drinks have been found to produce harmful effects, causing anxiety, dehydration, insomnia, and cardiovascular problems. Several fatalities in the United States have been linked to the use of energy drinks and shots, and in 2014 a fourteen-year-old boy in Norway was hospitalized with kidney failure after consuming more than a gallon of energy drinks during a sixteen-hour *Call of Duty* session.[18]

Sports can help boys direct impulsive and aggressive behaviors in positive ways. At the same time, they can also encourage boys to override their own instincts for self-preservation, and put team, coach, and fan expectations first. The toxic jocks are the extreme. But their risk-taking, tough-guy attitude infuses sports culture, whether they're playing through pain and injuries or chugging energy drinks. Sports are likened to the military for good reason: both can use the validation boys are taught to crave—as warriors, as heroes, as manly men—to put them in harm's way. We may assume that this rough, cutthroat culture is what boys want, but it's often the adults in their lives who put them in danger.

━━━

For three years, my son played in the Greater Toronto Hockey League. The mythic GTHL is the largest hockey development organization in the world, with forty thousand kids playing on more than five hundred teams. Just as the De Toekomst youth academy in the Netherlands and La Masia in Spain forge boys with quick feet into soccer greats like Lionel Messi, and as Oak Hill Academy high school in Virginia fashions gangly teenagers into basketball wizards like Carmelo Anthony, the GTHL shapes rink rats into NHL MVPs like P. K. Subban and John Tavares. Families of ten-year-olds with stickhandling brilliance or a gift for goaltending will relocate to Toronto from as far as eastern Europe to meet the GTHL's residency requirements and give their offspring a chance to be coached by former pros. Each December the league hosts a game for top prospects, showing off the forty best fifteen- and sixteen-year-olds. Many will land a spot in the minor leagues en route to the NHL.

My son was never more than a middle-of-the-pack player on a middle-of-the-pack team in the lowest of the league's three levels. It was as no stakes as you can get, a slightly more competitive experience than playing recreationally, with no expectation beyond learning skills and having fun. Still, even that was intense. Despite hockey's blue-collar ambience, it's an expensive and elite sport. Annual league fees are in the hundreds, if not thousands, of dollars. Equipment is pricey: skates cost as much $300 and sticks $200. At the more elite levels, it's not unheard of for families to spend $50,000 for specialized year-round training for boys as young as twelve and thirteen.

Only a tiny fraction of boys will have the talent to make a career out of it, but the long-shot odds don't deter ambitious parents. Contemporary middle- and upper-middle-class mothers and fathers have made their own competitive sport out of overscheduling, overprogramming, and hovering over their children's lives. The outlay of money and time in children's sports fuels an already frenzied parenting culture. And having put so much into their child's extracurricular life, parents claim an outsized ownership of it. It's common to hear a hockey dad or mom use the plural first person when referring to their child's team, as in "We had a great game today" or "We really need to keep our feet moving in front of the net."

An engagement with our children and their accomplishments is an expression of our love and attachment. But that engagement can, and does, turn ugly. Among the more routine incidents of parental misconduct in minor hockey are screaming (at kids, coaches, other parents, refs) and physical fights. One parent I know witnessed a father barge into a dressing room to tell his nine-year-old son, who was in tears following a rough game, to "stop being a pussy." That parent also says that it's commonplace to hear parents scream during games, "Take him out!" Another mother told me that the father of one of her then ten-year-old son's teammates spent games pacing alongside the rink, calling kids "little shits" when they screwed up. A gay dad has a story of his elite-level son being routinely targeted by opposing teams when he was twelve and thirteen, with taunts of "fag" and "homo." He heard that the boys were encouraged to do so by their parents and coaches. Everyone I know has a story like this. I suspect anyone who has a son in any sport has a story like this.

I don't share my wife's delight in hockey, but I recognize what it gives my son. I like that *he* loves it. I like that it's a hard thing he's had to really try at. I like that he's learned thousands of times over how to get up after he falls and that he's learned how to win and how to lose. I like the physical courage it gives him and how he expresses himself on the ice, with a flash and a spark. But I struggle with the ever-present threat of violence. Even without bodychecking and fights, it's a high-contact game, anger flares constantly, and banishment to the penalty box becomes a show of bravado. Violence—whether it's actual hitting or name-calling, whether it comes from players, coaches, parents, or fans—isn't an unfortunate by-product of a sport like hockey. It's an essential part of the game.

The increasing awareness of concussions, however, is slowly changing contact sports like hockey and football. Enrollment in US youth football is on a steep decline, largely due to concerns about brain injuries. (Schools in a number of states, including Maine, Missouri, and New Jersey, have terminated their tackle football programs due to a shortage of interested players.) In response, the national governing body USA Football has changed the rules and format of the kids' game to cut out a lot of the violence. In the new version, the field has been shrunk, and fewer players are on it at any given time. With less room to run and collide and fewer bodies to hit, the sport has become safer and more focused on skill than brute force.[19]

Kids are also abandoning youth hockey in favor of lower-contact sports such as basketball and soccer. Some hockey leagues now delay the introduction of bodychecking until boys are thirteen or fourteen, as a way to reduce injuries and successive hits to the head. A few years ago, I attended a game of the Toronto Non-Contact Hockey League. It was played at Ryerson University's state-of-the-art athletic center, which is housed inside the gutted shell of the city's former hockey cathedral, Maple Leaf Gardens, home to the Toronto Maple Leafs for nearly seven decades.

Facing each other that night, on the expertly tended ice, were the Redhawks and the Wolverines. The boys were fifteen and sixteen years old, well into their adolescent growth spurts and huge. Even without bodychecking, they played tough, fast hockey, digging for the puck and shooting it hard. But what struck me was that the boys played with an unusual lightness. The league was small, with only four teams in that age group, so most of the players had, at one time, been on the same team as their opponents. It was serious but not dour, competitive but not win at all costs. The boys were having a blast. The game looked like what can happen when kids are allowed to define a sport for themselves, without cultural baggage and parental expectation.

Cutting down on the violence didn't affect just the boys. It affected the response of their families. To anyone who has spent time around loud hockey parents, the spectators peppered throughout the stands that night would have seemed conspicuously quiet. A couple behind me murmured praise for the Wolverines' passing in hushed tones. Farther back, a man urged, "To the point! Back to the point!" and then quickly fell silent. When the Redhawks scored, there was staccato applause and a lone whoop before the crowd was once again silent. There was a decorum often missing at other youth games but, more important, a sense among the parents that this wasn't about them.

Many of the parents who brought their sons to the league did so as a kind of protest. Their kids had been hurt or dressed down too often by their coach. One father told me that in his son's previous league, he found the ambitions of some other parents, "all convinced their kid was headed straight for the NHL," exhausting. "I just didn't fit in with those people."

Another dad, who coached his son's team, described that rinkside hysteria as "rabid-parent syndrome." As his son got older, and the games became more serious, he found that he was so tense and anxious that he had to brace himself before the puck dropped. He hated the animosity among the other coaches and the way that the boys, by the age of nine, had already started trash-talking their opponents. The final straw was when his son was eleven and targeted during a game by a group of boys on the opposing team who repeatedly pushed and shoved him on the ice. After one hit, the boy went down with a crash. The dad felt a surge of rage. He found himself on the verge of screaming at the kid who'd hit his son, to intimidate and humiliate him. Then he stopped himself. He was a grown man about to berate a kid. He didn't want to be that guy, he told me, and he didn't want his son to see him being that guy. After that game, he moved his son to the noncontact league.

At its peak, the league had 175 players, and it ran for seven seasons, shutting down in the spring of 2016. Other, bigger, leagues began to ban bodychecking, so the need for a noncontact league petered out. But I think about that game every time I watch my son play. Now in high school, he's since moved to a less-competitive, less-aggressive league himself and plays with an ease and a happiness I haven't seen since he was very young.

———

In the fall of 2016, just a month before the US election, the *Washington Post* received a copy of a decade-old videotape from the TV show *Access Hollywood* with footage of then-presidential candidate Donald Trump talking about his come-on technique with women. "I'm automatically attracted to beautiful [women]. I just start kissing them. It's like a magnet. Just kiss. I don't even wait," he said. "And when you're a star, they let you do it. You can do anything. Grab them by the pussy. You can do anything." If what he said was true, then Trump was admitting that he had committed sexual assault—an offense of which several women had already accused him. But when the story broke, Trump explained it was simply "locker-room banter,"[20] implying that bragging about touching and kissing women without permission was a regular subject of discussion when men were alone together. Almost as troubling was his wife, Melania, dismissing it as "boy talk"—as though this was to be expected from men. Boys will be boys, and famous boys get to grab women by the genitalia and kiss them without consent.

The response from those far more familiar with locker rooms than Trump—namely, professional and amateur athletes—was swift. Many were offended. Oakland A's pitcher Sean Doolittle tweeted, "As an athlete, I've been in locker rooms my entire adult life and uh, that's not locker room talk." Former NBA player Dahntay Jones said, "Claiming Trump's comments are 'locker room banter' is to suggest they are somehow acceptable. They aren't." On the podcast *Edge of Sports*, DeAndre Levy, then a linebacker for the Detroit Lions, said, "When you dismiss it as 'locker-room talk,' the next step is dismissing the actual act [of sexual assault]. I think it's something that needs to be addressed, something that we don't really think about because it's all normalized. It's an idea that a lot of athletes have: entitlement—as Trump said—that you can do whatever you want when you're famous."[21] Just a few months earlier, Levy had written an essay for the *Players' Tribune* about athletes and sexual and domestic violence.[22] His commitment to the issue included helping to raise money, more than $30,000 in all, as part of an effort to test eleven thousand rape kits found in 2009, abandoned in a warehouse by Detroit-area law enforcement agencies, some dating to the 1980s. (As of December 2017, ten thousand kits had been tested, 1,947 cases investigated, and 817 serial rapists identified.)[23]

Meanwhile, at a high school in Oregon, a group of student athletes shot a picture of themselves wearing T-shirts with the slogan "Wild Feminist." The caption under it read, "Sexual Assault Is Not Locker Room Banter." The image went viral. This wasn't the first time high school athletes had addressed sexual violence in such a public way. In 2014 Jerome Baker was a high school senior and a star football linebacker in Cleveland, Ohio, being courted by several colleges.[24]

Disturbed by the recent high-profile sexual assault by two fellow high school football players in nearby Steubenville, Baker came up with the idea of a public pledge signed by fellow high school players to end violence against girls and women. He contacted boys he knew, the best players, the role models and leaders, on teams throughout northeastern Ohio. Within a year, a hundred high school athletes had taken the pledge, which reads, in part, "I promise to never commit or condone acts of physical or sexual violence toward women or girls.... If I hear someone making negative remarks about women/girls or gender-based jokes, I will speak out against it."

Baker, like the young men in Oregon, like the pro athletes who spoke out against Trump, understood the influence and clout they have as sports stars. As DeAndre Levy put it in the *Players' Tribune*, "We have the prominence in our communities to effect real change. When we talk, people listen." Athletes had been primed to take on political issues, as sports culture has become increasingly activism-oriented over the past several years—most markedly after the shooting of Trayvon Martin in Florida in 2012 and the founding of the Black Lives Matter movement. Shortly after Martin's death, members of the Miami Heat released a photo of themselves wearing hoodies pulled over their heads with the hashtags #WeAreTrayvonMartin, #Hoodies, #Stereotyped, and #WeWantJustice.

Since then, a number of professional athletes have spoken out against racism and police violence—a galvanizing and personal issue for the many young black players in the NBA and NFL.[25] In 2014 several NBA players wore "I Can't Breathe" T-shirts during pregame warm-ups, referencing the final words spoken by Eric Garner after he was put in a choke hold by New York City police officers. Two years later, San Francisco 49ers quarterback Colin Kaepernick began to take a knee during the US national anthem as a protest against violence and racial inequality. While some in management and the media criticized

Kaepernick's actions for politicizing sports, to others they favorably recalled the history of activist athletes like Muhammad Ali, and Tommie Smith and John Carlos, who gave Black Power salutes on the podium at the 1968 Olympics.

This current model of activism by pro athletes has in turn inspired young fans and athletes to speak out. Following Kaepernick's example, football players at middle schools and high schools in Colorado, Nebraska, Texas, California, and New Jersey began to take a knee during the pregame anthem. "When Kaepernick kneeled, he gave us an outlet. He gave us something to do," a student in Colorado told the *New York Times*.[26]

Yet even as professional and student athletes have been speaking out against racial violence, other issues, such as sexual and domestic violence by players themselves, have been trickier to address. Despite protests from athletes, Trump latched on to the phrase *locker-room talk* for a reason: sports culture is deeply sexist. The NFL has been criminally lax in its handling of players accused of sexual misconduct or abusing their partners. In college football, there have been a number of high-profile cases of sexual abuse and rapes, from Baylor University and Notre Dame to Florida State and the University of South Dakota. An ambient culture of sexualizing women is a feature of the sport, beginning with the attractive female "hostesses" who greet and guide the most sought-after potential recruits when they tour campuses. A 2017 lawsuit against Texas's Baylor University alleged that thirty-one of the school's football players committed at least fifty-two acts of sexual assault, including five gang rapes, between 2011 and 2014. The suit also alleged that the recruitment of underage prospects included taking them to strip clubs and arranging for women to have sex with them as an enticement.[27]

In the mythology of American football, players are hailed as conquering heroes entitled to spoils—money, sex, and fame. One illustration of this was heard in the defense a father gave for his teenage son in 2016, after the boy was accused of raping a fifteen-year-old girl. The boy played football for De La Salle High School in Concord, California, one of the top programs in the United States. The girl had gone to confront the boy about sexually explicit texts he had sent her. When they met up to talk, she alleges, he assaulted her. The boy's father told the media it was consensual: "He's tall, dark and handsome, he plays for De La Salle, there's a lot of girls that want to be with my son. When young, fast girls see something they like, they go after it."[28] Those comments sound like an echo of the father of Brock Turner, the Stanford University swimmer convicted of sexually assaulting an unconscious woman at a fraternity party in January 2015.[29] Turner's dad wrote in a letter that his son's life "will never be the one that he dreamed about and worked so hard to achieve. That is a steep price to pay for 20 minutes of action out of his 20 plus years of life."

Again and again in the quest for young men's athletic success, young women are turned into an enticement, a reward, or collateral damage. Bad behavior, even violence and assault, is excused or concealed, if the future of a gifted player is at stake—because so much rests on that future. Scandals can cost a school its sponsors and its fans. College sports are enormous businesses, with the best athletics programs and teams earning millions in profits for their schools. Even high school sports have significant impact on local economies. Since its mills began to close, Steubenville, Ohio, a former booming steel town, has seen its population plummet, its downtown businesses get boarded up, and its citizens beset with drug addictions. The high school's state championship–winning Big Red football team is a rare bright spot and revenue generator, bringing in upward of ten thousand fans from the region to its games. The sixteen- and seventeen-year-old players are big men on campus. They're also pillars of their town, who are expected to be shielded from trouble. An inquiry into the 2012 sexual assault by the team's two star players found that the boys' coach had been aware of their conduct and hadn't reported it to police. Three more school officials were indicted for obstructing justice in covering up other sexual abuse cases.[30]

Randy Jackson, however, is not that kind of coach. The week after Trump's "locker-room" comments came to light, the then head coach of the football program at Grapevine High School, in the Dallas–Fort Worth suburb of Grapevine, Texas, gathered his junior varsity and varsity players into the locker room. Under Jackson, character-development lessons were a regular part of the players' curriculum—"taking advantage of this captive audience of boys," as he puts it—to talk about teamwork, respect, integrity, and what it means to be a good man. Jackson often uses current events for discussion, like when former NFL running back Ray Rice was caught on a security camera in 2014 punching his then girlfriend inside a hotel elevator. When Jackson heard about Trump's allusion to "locker-room banter"—comments Jackson calls "deplorable"—he saw it as another teachable moment. Degrading women is never acceptable, he told the boys. What Trump bragged about—touching and kissing women without consent—was assault, plain and simple. Even if a man says something vulgar in a male-only space like a locker room for the purpose of impressing other men, it shouldn't be taken lightly or dismissed as a joke. "You can't compartmentalize your character," Jackson told them.[31]

The day after Trump was elected president, I spoke with Jackson on the phone. He's spent twenty-six years coaching football, the previous three at Grapevine, located in a largely upper-middle-class neighborhood, where, Jackson says, "People can afford to spend six dollars on a cup of coffee." In other words, his players tend to be more sheltered than street smart. "We have to be intentional about making our kids tough," he explains. Football is a tough sport, after all, one that demands mental and physical grit and one that attracts aggressive, type-A alpha boys and aggressive, type-A alpha coaches. But coaches also need to teach boys how to switch off their aggression when they're not on the field. "Because we focus so much on competing and battling for dominance, if you're not careful, you find that you're always rewarding and praising the kid who dominates, the kid who takes what he wants when he wants it," he says. "You have to be intentional in showing boys that being a real man outside of a game means caring for other people, treating women and girls with respect, and standing up for kids who are bullied."

Traditional values are often cast at odds with progressive thinking. Jackson is, in many ways, a traditional man. He quotes biblical scripture, describes himself and his fellow coaches as youth ministers, and calls me "ma'am." But he finds no dissonance in expecting his players to expand their ideas of manly behavior to include being attentive and nurturing within their relationships and families. He and his assistant coaches regularly invite players to their homes for dinner. Partly, this is to create a family atmosphere on the team. Partly, it's to model what it means to be a decent husband and father. The message to the boys is deliberate: real men cherish their spouses, wash dishes, and change diapers.

A month after Jackson and I spoke, the twenty-six-thousand-member Texas High School Coaches Association announced the launch of a statewide program to educate young athletes about sexual assault and consent. It's one of the few places where issues like this are discussed in the state. In the 2015–2016 school year, a quarter of Texas public school districts provided no sex education whatsoever, and nearly 60 percent of districts taught abstinence-only curricula. Most of the abstinence-based sex-ed programs were filled with gender stereotypes, portraying boys as naturally hypersexualized and girls as helpless maidens in need of rescue.[32] Absent other forms of sex ed, interventions by coaches like Jackson are crucial. If serious, lasting transformations of sports culture and negative male behaviors are to happen, the process must start with the kids who are still in the stage of cementing their identities and values. At the end of our conversation, Jackson says, "Parents tell us all the time that we're the only people their sons will listen to."

I hear something similar from Dave Zirin, a sportswriter and commentator in Washington, DC, who covers the politics and culture of the sports world. He's an editor at the *Nation* magazine and host of the *Edge of Sports* podcast. He's also a father and coach himself. "The culture of youth sports is hugely dependent on the kind of coaching kids get," he says. "Boys and sports, left to their own devices, list toward bad conclusions, like a meteor headed into the earth." Too often, he says, even the language used to talk about sports—you crush, you decimate, you destroy your opponent—suggests the endeavor isn't worth it unless you come out on top.

Zirin grew up in New York City and played basketball in school. He remembers an almost constant soundtrack of sexist and homophobic slurs from his teammates. To be on a team with a girl was shameful, he says. To be told by a coach that you "played like a girl" was even worse. To be told you were "soft"—a term that suggested you were feminine or possibly gay—was worst of all. This kind of talk was reflexive. Zirin doesn't believe all his childhood coaches understood the connection between it and sexism.

A memory stands out for him, an episode in the locker room, when he was a freshman in high school. The quietest boy on the team interrupted the chatter to ask the other guys to stop using gay slurs like "fag" and "punk." His dad was gay, the boy said, and he wanted his teammates to respect that. "You could have heard a pin drop," Zirin tells me. Teams demand cohesion; to speak out of turn and to challenge the attitudes of the other guys was unheard of, he says. It was also incredibly courageous. "We were all ashamed. And we were kind of in awe of his bravery. Sensitivity like his wasn't typically valorized, but we understood how brave it was for him to say what he did. After that, we stopped using homophobic language."

A few weeks before we spoke, Zirin had tackled the question of locker-room culture on his podcast. Having zero experience myself in the goings-on in boys' and men's dressing rooms, I asked him to describe the atmosphere. I was especially curious about the athletes rushing to defend locker rooms and male behavior in them. Were these spaces as high-minded and sacred as the players made them out to be? Wasn't there also a tradition of sexist and homophobic trash talk and of hazing and bullying?

Locker rooms, Zirin explains, are defined by their intimacy and vulnerability. Sports are a rare space where boys and men are encouraged to express emotion and where they can freely express physical affection toward other men. In locker rooms, there's a lot of nudity, and with that a lot of curiosity, confusion, and competition. Alongside genuine friendship and connection among teammates, Zirin says, "you can hear a lot of bullshit in locker rooms." Often it's used to compensate for the vulnerability, affection, and emotion—bragging about exploits with women, for instance, and jockeying for dominance. As much as team sports can foster a sense of family and community, it can also be a mercenary culture. Players are aware they might be cut or traded and that the guy next to them is vying for their spot on the lineup. Still, that intimacy, Zirin says, holds a lot of possibility, especially when the players are in middle or high school and impressionable. He points to examples of student activism, like high school students taking a knee during the national anthem or speaking out against sexual violence, as being crucial to changing the culture of sports, much like the brave kid with the gay father who shifted the consciousness of Zirin's high school basketball team.

———

The mission of the US nonprofit group You Can Play is to support kids like Zirin's old teammate. Through diversity training workshops for coaches and players and public awareness campaigns, You Can Play aims to reduce sexist, racist, and homophobic bullying by using the positive qualities of sports—teamwork, discipline, winning on merit— and extending them to other aspects of kids' lives. A study done by the Boston Children's Hospital in 2014 found that sexual minority youth (kids who identified as lesbian, gay, bisexual, or transgender) were far less likely than straight kids to participate in team sports.[33] Gay boys reported substantially less positive views of their own athletic ability and cited low self-esteem and fears of being bullied as reasons they didn't participate in team sports. That lack of participation has serious consequences. Not only are LGBTQ kids missing out on the social benefits of being part of a team, but their physical inactivity puts them at a higher risk for stress and depression.

Wade Davis is an activist, public speaker, and the director of professional sports outreach for You Can Play. He's also a former NFL defensive back and one of the few openly gay men to have played pro sports.[34] For him, football provided a sense of "brotherhood and camaraderie." And when he became aware as a teenager that he was gay, football also provided a cover. His athleticism and the privilege he received for being a jock cut short any questions about his masculinity. As an example, he tells me about a friend he had at the time who was not among the school's football elite. In fact, the boy was probably gay too, but, unlike Davis, not able to disguise it. Davis liked the boy, but when his football friends were around, he'd call him a "faggot." He still regrets his unkindness but explains that it was driven by his own fears of being outed: "Like so many other boys, I intuitively knew that I couldn't been seen being nice to a boy who was thought to be gay or perceived to be weak, because that would have been a reflection on me."

He acknowledges that sport has a troubling culture of sexism and homophobia but also says that athletes are rarely given credit for their intelligence and open-mindedness. Davis left the NFL in 2004 due to injuries and didn't come out to his former teammates until several years later. When he did, they embraced him. Not a single one had a negative reaction, he tells me. That response helped shape his approach when he talks to high schools and colleges. "There is a pervasive narrative about homophobia and athletes, African American athletes in particular, that they are less accepting and less tolerant. It's so pervasive that we never hear the stories of love and acceptance and support that exist in black communities and in locker rooms." Slurs such as "faggot" are used to enforce a culture of masculine conformity in sports, but that conformity can also, sometimes, work in a positive way. Davis's teammates supported him, because the brotherhood of the team came above all else. And it's that loyalty and solidarity that You Can Play aims to tap into: your teammate is your teammate whatever their race, gender, or sexuality.

Davis distinguishes between intent and impact in the kind of language athletes use. Many players make jokes about women and gay men less out of actual hatred and disdain than because they think it's expected of them. A 2016 report from the University of Alberta, supported by You Can Play, came to a similar finding. Sports sociologist Cheryl MacDonald spoke to nearly a hundred elite male hockey players, aged fifteen to eighteen, about their attitudes on gender, homosexuality, and masculinity.[35] What she found was a more complicated picture than she had anticipated. Boys made antigay and sexist comments because that's what they had learned from the entrenched, rough, and rugged rules of hockey; those comments weren't necessarily a reflection of their own beliefs. These kids were also products of the broader culture who were growing up in the twenty-first century, in a world of feminist pop stars, gay marriage, and gender-neutral bathrooms. "They'd never had a gay teammate, at least not an openly gay one," MacDonald noted, "but they knew that whether they liked it or not, it would eventually become normal, and everyone would get along."

That shrugging I-guess-we'll-all-figure-it-out-because-it's-really-not-that-big-a-deal, *that's* the possibility that Zirin identified. It lies in coaches like Randy Jackson using their locker rooms to ask boys to challenge their biases, to be brave and speak out. As a former professional athlete who is also openly gay, Davis is often asked what it will mean when—if ever—a superstar with the fame and talent of a LeBron James comes out. He says there's been far too much anticipation and expectation that one famous player will rid sports of its biases. "People imagine that if Tom Brady came out, it would change everything. It wouldn't," he says. "What would be truly revolutionary, what would truly change the culture of sexism and homophobia in sports, is for parents to start talking to their sons and for coaches to start talking to their young players about inclusion and justice and love. And for all of us to give young men permission to show their weaknesses and be vulnerable and not say that makes them any less masculine or strong."

6

GAME BOYS

Young Men and Popular Culture

———

Dressed in his white undershirt and an owl mask, Carl "C. J." Johnson, the protagonist of *Grand Theft Auto: San Andreas*, tears up the foothills outside the fictional city of Los Santos on a motorcycle. The player controlling C. J. is a quiet ten-year-old boy with an impish face and a faux hawk. He leads C. J. through various jumps, several wipeouts, and then into Los Santos, where he carjacks a woman, trading his beaten-up bike for a fancier set of wheels. The plot of the game, first released for PlayStation 2 in 2004 as part of the global best-selling *GTA* franchise, revolves around C. J., a black man who, having left his old neighborhood to escape its violence, returns to attend his mother's funeral. Once there, he's framed for a crime he didn't commit and reconnects with his old gang, which is attempting to return to power.

Elements of this fictionalized story are based on real events, including the 1980s crack epidemic and the 1992 LA riots. That's where any similarity to reality ends. The franchise was created by a group of Scottish developers[1] whose knowledge of American life comes primarily from movies, and *GTA: San Andreas*'s main influences and references are 1990s hip-hop videos and "hood films" such as *Menace II Society* and *Boyz n the Hood*. Graphically violent, technically complex, and visually stunning, *GTA: San Andreas* is considered by fans and game critics to be one of the greatest video games ever made. The franchise, which has sales in the tens of millions, deliberately draws on racial stereotypes of African Americans, Latinos, and Italian Americans and traffics in outrageously sexualized images of women.[2] And each new installment has sparked renewed criticisms about its violence and misogyny and its impact on young male players.[3]

Nick, the ten-year-old wielding the controller, seems oblivious to all this. He's mostly in it for the cars (and the masks). I'm in the attic playroom of his Toronto home—its walls covered in Transformer and Spider-Man decals, as well as a mounted cache of Nerf weapons—observing him at the invitation of his parents. This is the first time I've watched the game being played, and this is both a reporting trip and a personal mission. Up until our son was thirteen, my wife and I had limited his PlayStation repertoire to teen-rated games. For months, he'd begged to get a *GTA* game, and we'd refused, because of what we've read about its violence and racial and gender stereotypes. At home he played *Minecraft* and sports video games, mainly NBA and NHL, though undoubtedly he'd tried first-person-shooter games at friends' places. Like many kids, he wanted what was most forbidden.

Watching Nick and talking to his parents is my chance to see *GTA* in action, and so far it's a bit of a snooze. Nick stays on the fringes of action, more interested in vehicles and stunts than in gang activity (it's possible that he might be opting to play a more G-rated game for my benefit). Nick's father is an occasional gamer—he was just slaughtered by his son in a round of *Call of Duty*—but his mother, like me, doesn't play. She doesn't place many restrictions on Nick's gaming, however. She sees games as a way for him to socialize with his friends, online or in real life, and believes that the complex worlds and the immersive play he's engaged in are teaching him problem-solving skills and fluency in technology. For his upcoming birthday, she's taking Nick to a virtual-reality arcade with some friends. (For their privacy, Nick's mother asked that the family not be identified.)

When I tell her about my own reluctance to let my son play *GTA*, she suggests, diplomatically, that I might be overly cautious and over-reacting. She's a scientist and thoughtful in her parenting choices. She's read the research on video games and harm. And despite the hand-wringing that has occurred over violent video games, no causal relationship to real-life violence has been proven.[4] (It also bears mentioning that in the United States, as gaming has increased exponentially, re-ports of youth violence have dropped precipitously: according to a 2014 survey by the National Center for Juvenile Justice, juvenile arrests for violent crime and the number of killings committed by youth under eighteen are at a thirty-year low.)[5] Yet like so many impulses that influence how we parent, evidence isn't always required—especially when it comes to technology and popular culture that is unfamiliar. It *feels* as though games are making children more violent and antisocial in real life, and so they become a source of worry or a scapegoat.

"When we were kids, we played cops and robbers and fought with sticks and toy guns. Now our kids do this," she says, pointing to the screen. "The technology is just more advanced. It's the newness of the technology that's frightening."

Still, I'm not fully convinced. My childhood experiences of cops and robbers didn't include drive-by shootings, visits to strip clubs, and the murder of sex workers—all of which are player options in various *GTA* games. (To be fair, players have a great degree of choice in how violent they wish to be within the world of the games. Like Nick, you can play it for the vehicles.) These weren't options I felt my son was ready to contend with—even within the imaginary world of a game. But after talking with Nick's mom, I softened a little, recognizing that I've let myself become swept up in the video game panic. Mediating our son's consumption of popular culture and trying to filter the images and stories he takes in is an ongoing negotiation in which we've learned to pick our battles, especially as he gets older and more independent. At home later, I tell my son that *GTA* is still forbidden, but we make a compromise on another game. He can buy *Call of Duty*, provided he plays with the parental controls that limit the gore and cursing. Yet, as he now happily racks up kills on *CoD*, I'm aware that our compromise may still be irrational and more about my creating an illusory sense of control than about my son's safety—but in this approach to parenting, I know I'm not alone.

Over the years, my wife and I have had more and more conversations with our son about gender and racial stereotypes in pop culture—why female characters in movies tend to be victims and sidekicks and why so few male heroes are Asian, black, or Latino. When he couldn't create an avatar that looked like him in a game he liked, a protagonist who combined facial features and skin tone similar to his, we talked about why there weren't many indigenous characters in mainstream games. We discuss the violence in the action movies he loves and asked him why he thinks men in those movies take so much joy in, or at least seem undisturbed by, killing people. And we ask him why he thinks so many boys refused to see the girl-centric movie *Frozen*. We make a point of watching TV shows together that feature LGBTQ characters; *The Fosters, Brooklyn Nine-Nine*, the reboot of *One Day at a Time*, and the Degrassi franchise are among his favorites. We talk about the lyrics in the music he listens to and about who can and can't use the *n*-word and the word *bitch*.

I know. We sound like a pair of killjoys. Our son would probably agree. However, popular media plays a crucial role in shaping our collective attitudes about boys, and how boys define themselves, as well as molding and informing how we view gender and conceive of gender roles. The consequences of pop culture on girls' self-esteem and identity have been well examined and critiqued—from the cloying helplessness of *Sleeping Beauty* to the girl-power resourcefulness of *Moana*, from mean-girl bullying on social media to feminist pop song lyrics. Nearly every one of my feminist friends with daughters, for instance, worries about their girls' weakness for anything to do with princesses and instead encourages a fondness for Wonder Woman and soccer.

But what is boys' relationship to popular culture? How do they engage and respond to it? Setting aside the alarmist reaction to the extremes, such as hyperviolent games, how do pop culture and popular media affect boys' emotional and social selves, their attitudes about masculinity, and their self-esteem? It's curious that we don't take up these questions more, because boys, particularly white and straight ones, are overwhelmingly the target audience for so much media—hence, the never-ending stream of comic book and sci-fi movie franchises—and because they are so often at the core of the storytelling. Since their views and interests—or at least their perceived views and interests—are front and center, the impact on them of messages about gender and masculinity often go unexamined. Or else, when popular culture's effects on boys are raised, it's in the form of a moral panic.

This isn't new. In 1895 a woman named Emily Coombes was found stabbed to death in her home in London. Police charged her two sons, Robert, thirteen, and Nattie, twelve, for her murder. During their search of the Coombes house, investigators had found the children's stash of "penny dreadfuls," cheap magazines for working-class boys featuring lurid, serialized stories, which they seized upon as proof of the boys' guilt. In their heyday, more than a million boys' periodicals were being sold a week in Britain, making penny dreadfuls the video games and YouTube channels of their era. The publications were blamed for everything from theft to murder to, as an 1886 newspaper editorial put it, "threatening to destroy the manhood of the democracy." When the coroner's jury gave its verdict in the Coombes case, it advised that "the Legislature should take some steps to put a stop to the inflammable and shocking literature that is sold, which in our opinion leads to many a dreadful crime being carried out."[6]

Later generations of legislators and parents were just as concerned about the perilous influence of movies, television, and music. In 1985 in the United States, a powerful advocacy group called the Parents Music Resource Center created a playlist it dubbed the "Filthy 15," which included songs by Madonna, Prince, Twisted Sister, and Judas Priest that it considered the most offensive music of the time (gangsta rap was also a target for censure). Ultimately, the PMRC successfully lobbied the music industry to put parental advisory warning stickers on albums and CDs. Fourteen years later, in the days following the mass shooting at Columbine High School in 1999, media outlets reported that shooters Dylan Klebold and Eric Harris had been inspired by the music of Marilyn Manson.[7]

A central failing of these arguments about boys and popular culture is that they tend to assume a standard singular experience of boyhood, as though all boys listen to the same music and admire the same celebrities, play the same video games, and favor the same fashions. They assume that all boys are equally susceptible to the influences of popular media and experience pop culture in the same way consistently over time. What's more, boys are thought to be passive participants, incapable of critically thinking about the images they consume.

Instead of generalizing boys' experiences and instead of panicking, it's worth looking at how boys themselves interpret and use pop culture, what they embrace, and what they reject. Do blockbuster movies and video games and other media created for boys reflect who boys are, or is it more about who adults imagine, fear, or wish them to be?

——

The idea of the twentieth-century boyhood was invented out of concern for twentieth-century boys. As I discuss in Chapter 5 on boys and sports, the social and economic transformations of the early 1900s incited a great deal of anxiety about the state of manliness. Robert Baden-Powell, a career soldier in the British army, returned to England in 1910 after serving in India and Africa for three decades. Immediately he found himself disgusted by the state of British boys. The upper-class ones were lazy and flabby, the lower-class ones degenerate and weak. He was certain a great war was on the horizon and feared that these boys would be unable to defend the British Empire. He formed the Boy Scouts Association as a quasi-military training group to put a little steel back into his nation's spine.

For his Scouts, Baden-Powell drew deeply romanticized inspiration from American frontier stories, traveling cowboy shows, and Rudyard Kipling's *The Jungle Book*. And his image of his Scouts and the younger cohort of Cubs was shaped out of two contradictory impulses: the reverence for the "purity" of the frontier and free spirits (as represented by "noble savages" and the feral boy Mowgli) up against a desire to civilize, tame, and conquer. That vision struck a chord with the imperial, colonizing forces of the era in places where original peoples were being forced off their lands and forbidden from practicing their cultures and speaking their languages. Scouts quickly spread to Australia, Canada, the United States, Chile, Argentina, and Brazil.

The Boy Scouts, like the sporting movement, promoted the prevailing belief about the essence of boyhood. Boys' path to manhood is a process of taming their inherent wildness through discipline and manly activities like camping, hunting, farming, and sports.[8] Boyhood was understood as a microcosm of human enlightenment—the forward march from childish beast to reasonable, rational adult man. Throughout early popular culture about and for boys, this theme shows up again and again: in the early 1900s, with J. M. Barrie's character Peter Pan, a Lost Boy who refuses to grow up, and again a few decades later, in William Golding's 1954 novel, *Lord of the Flies*, in which a group of well-bred young boys quickly turn brutish when left to their own devices on a remote island. Nonwhite boys, however, were portrayed as permanently wild and degenerate—as exotic and noble or else as dangerously savage. And the tensions between these two states of male development—the wild versus the civilized—played out in early boys' adventure novels and radio serials and later in western movies.

Jesse Wente, an Ojibwe film producer and programmer in Toronto, says westerns were nostalgic for the very worlds they were attempting to annihilate. Manifest Destiny—the widely held nineteenth-century belief that American settlers were destined to expand westward and take over indigenous territories—is central to the Hollywood western, he says. "It's about the white male American hero man who triumphs over nature and conquers the land," he explains to me. "In those stories, Native men are either an evil warrior or a sage philosophical elder who is on his way out." These roles were not heroic, he says, "because in order for the cowboy to be the hero, the Indian is required to disappear." In his 2009 documentary, *Reel Injun*, about Hollywood's portrayal of indigenous people, Cree filmmaker Neil Diamond reveals the psychic toll of these stories, of seeing people like him being vilified or slaughtered. In the film's narration, reflecting on the old western movies he watched in his local church basement on Saturday nights when he was a little boy, he says, "We cheered for the cowboys, never realizing that we were the Indians."

Even now, positive, fleshed-out portrayals of indigenous people are scarce in popular culture. Coverage in mainstream media is often confined to stories of current-day suffering or historical trauma. My son learned traditional teachings in his elementary school and participated in powwows, ceremonies, and sweats, but what he rarely gets to see in the video games, action movies, and comedies he loves are people who look like him and share his cultural history. New Zealand filmmaker Taika Waititi, who is Māori and Jewish, has made two terrific, funny films about contemporary Māori young men, *Boy* (2010) and *Hunt for the Wilderpeople* (2016). The latter, about an endearing Tupac Shakur–loving foster kid, became New Zealand's highest-grossing film. Waititi went on to direct 2017's *Thor: Ragnarok*, in which he included a strong cast of indigenous actors in supporting roles. Aside from those films, however, there's not much else in mainstream media that presents indigenous boys in ways that aren't simplistic, tragic, or solely historical.

That limited representation was, in part, what inspired Vancouver-based Cree filmmaker Jules Koostachin to create a reality series called *AskiBOYZ* for Canada's Aboriginal Peoples Television Network (*aski* is Cree for "land") in 2014. The series stars her two oldest sons, Asivak and Mahiigan—urban-raised boys with skateboards and shaggy haircuts—who travel to a different First Nations community in each episode under the guidance of their mentor, Cassius Spears (Narragansett), where they are taught traditional skills, such as hunting, trapping, and making medicine from plants. The series is charming and sweet, and my son, another urban-raised boy with a skateboard and a shaggy haircut, connected with it instantly. It was accessible, it reflected a world similar to his own, and it offered an image of indigenous masculinity that felt contemporary and relevant.

Over the phone, Koostachin tells me it was important for her to create an image of indigenous young men to counter the limited and negative stereotypes that appear in most media. "I wanted to create a show that celebrates learning and resilience," she says. "I was tired of nonstop images that only showed young Cree people struggling or depressed." Asivak and Mahiigan are unfailingly cheerful, even when they falter—much of the humor in the series is in watching how difficult it is to master traditional skills.

Koostachin wanted the series to show the value in connecting young people to elders and knowledge keepers as well as to the land. "My sons could identify corporate logos, but not birds or trees," she says. Critical of "the colonial masculine BS," Koostachin says that for

Cree, gender roles aren't as rigidly defined. But there were lessons about being a Cree man that she felt she couldn't teach her boys. The series became a proxy, in a way, for her own grandfather, a trapper/hunter and community leader who died when the boys were young, before he could pass along his teachings. Later I speak to Asivak, who tells me that several years after the series wrapped up, he's still digesting what he learned. Most profound, he said, was understanding how to be a strong indigenous man through connection to his cultural practices and teachings. "I learned that masculinity is not about having power over your environment," he says, "but learning the skill set that allows you to navigate and live in harmony with your environment."

———

In Hollywood the American western helped establish the template for the contemporary male protagonist: a stoic, often brooding, all-powerful, self-reliant loner. From comic book superheroes, like the invincible Superman and ultimate soldier Captain America, to sci-fi characters like the legendary Jedi Luke Skywalker and space cowboy Han Solo, the hero presented to boys and young men conforms to a dominant idea of masculinity.

There are variations on this theme, of course. Harry Potter is a more complicated young male hero than most. Alongside his prophe-sized mission to vanquish Lord Voldemort are the usual schoolboy thrills of crushes and team sports. And unlike the many male heroes who are solo actors, Harry is surrounded by a team of friends and mentors. Likewise, *Lord of the Rings'* Frodo shares his quest with a gang of Middle-Earthers and has a deep bond with his best friend, Samwise. Yet these are still stories with a male protagonist and a male perspective at their heart. What's more, they're globally dominant cultural touchstones, making them heroes not just for boys but heroes full stop.

Women and girls in these tales play secondary roles; in the case of *Lord of the Rings*, female characters barely exist at all. Princess Leia and Hermione are badasses, to be sure, but they primarily exist to support Luke and Harry on their quests. Little is shown of their lives and motivations outside of what furthers the plot for the male protagonist. It was only in 2015 that *Star Wars* introduced a lead female character, the Jedi Rey, played by Daisy Ridley. In the DC Comics and Marvel Comics worlds, groups of heroes, such as the Justice League and the Avengers, typically allot a spot to just one exceptional female member, like Wonder Woman and Black Widow, as if the creators are afraid that the presence of two powerful women might be too emasculating.

In early 2018, *Black Panther* made history as the first of the current Marvel movies to feature a black hero and an almost entirely black cast—and it became the top-grossing superhero movie of all time in the United States. And *Aquaman* starring Jason Momoa, who is of mixed Native Hawaiian, Native American, and European ancestry, also out in 2018, is the first DC movie to have a nonwhite hero at its center. Up until now, when it came to imaginary heroes, the matter of inclusion has been, for the most part, relegated to supporting roles. *Spider-Man: Homecoming* (2017), which stars white English actor Tom Holland, is set in a realistically diverse New York. Peter Parker's classmates are a multicultural mix; his best friend, Ned, is played by Filipino American Jacob Batalon; and his two love interests are black girls played by Zendaya and Laura Harrier. The 2017 reboot of *Power Rangers*, based on the 1990s live-action TV series about a group of high school students who are endowed with superpowers, featured an Asian boy, a possibly lesbian Latina girl, and a black autistic boy—an encouraging nod to inclusion. But in the lead role as the red Power Ranger was, as usual, a white, straight guy.

Despite the success of *Black Panther* and the female-centered *Hunger Games* franchise, the persistence of the white male hero in mainstream movies helps enforce the commonly held belief that boys won't go see a female-driven movie and that white audiences won't see a movie featuring people of color. That coupled with a lack of diversity among Hollywood directors and producers, and it's not surprising, Jesse Wente says, that so many mainstream movies still reflect the concerns and experiences of white males. A 2018 Hollywood Diversity Report from UCLA noted that people of color are significantly underrepresented as film writers, directors, and leads. Ana-Christina Ramón, one of the report's coauthors, wrote, "Our reports have continually shown that diversity sells, but the TV and film product continues to fall short. So audiences are left starved for more representation on screen that reflects the world they see in their daily lives."[9]

The same holds in children's literature. A 2011 survey of almost six thousand children's books published between 1900 and 2000 found that males were central characters in 57 percent of the books published each year, with just 31 percent having central female characters. Even critter protagonists reflected this disparity: in 23 percent of books, the central characters were male animals, compared to just 7.5 percent that featured female animals. According to the researchers, the message this sends to children is that "women and girls occupy a less important role in society than men or boys."[10]

Kids' lit is no more diverse when it comes to race. Since 1985 the University of Wisconsin–Madison's Cooperative Children's Book Center has collected data on diversity and racial representation in children's books. Among books published in 2015, 73.3 percent of characters were white. In fact, you could add up all the black characters (7.6 percent), the Asian ones (3.3 percent), and the Native American and indigenous ones (fewer than 1 percent), and they'd still be outnumbered by nonhumans. A full 12.5 percent of books featured characters like animals and talking trucks.[11]

Looking at how much children's popular culture skews toward white and male characters, it's worth asking why so little imagination is expected of white boys. White girls and boys and girls of color have long had to read themselves into stories that don't reflect them. And millions of kids from every race, ethnicity, and gender legitimately love and connect to characters like Harry Potter. But white boys are rarely expected to stretch themselves to see the world from a perspective unlike their own and to root for someone who isn't like them. Literature plays a role in teaching children to relate to characters' motivations and feelings and in revealing to them new possibilities and unfamiliar worlds. If boys aren't exposed to stories featuring people from different backgrounds and experiences, and instead see only heroes who mirror them, they lose an opportunity to develop their capacity for empathy, humility, and imagination. Theirs is a boringly narrow window on the world.

And that window is getting narrower. As it turns out, the image of the superhero savior has an oppressive flipside: it's a standard of manliness that few men can live up to. Take the recent resurgence of comic book movie franchises. Not that long ago, comic book culture was geeky and "outside" and often a haven for kids who didn't fit a certain standard of cool. Now it's mainstream. And as the superhero has become the ubiquitous image of masculinity in popular culture, the characters are more muscle bound, beefy, and invulnerable. Adam West's Batman had a dad bod; Ben Affleck's version has a granite chest. Christopher Reeve's Superman was fit; Henry Cavill's is chiseled.

Psychologists and doctors are now connecting these images of extreme male bodies to a surge of eating disorders among men and boys. Britain's National Health Service reported that the number of adult men being admitted to the hospital with eating disorders rose by 70 percent between 2010 and 2016—the same rate of increase as among women. And a 2012 US study of more than twenty-five hundred students at twenty urban middle and high schools found that more than two-thirds of the boys reported changing their eating to increase their muscle size or tone, 34.7 percent used protein powders or shakes, 5.9 percent used steroids, and 10.5 percent used some other muscle-enhancing substance.[12]

The allure of superheroes wasn't always located in their super-invincibility but rather in their more down-to-earth humanity. Superman could leap tall buildings in a single bound, but Lois Lane made him weak in the knees—while his alter ego, Clark Kent, was a nebbish in glasses. Without Bruce Wayne's tragic childhood backstory, Batman is nothing more than an insufferable, rich vigilante. Spider-Man, traditionally one of the most fun superheroes, is, at heart, a goofball teenager thrilled with his unexpected powers. But with their increasing emphasis on rock-hard abs and indestructibility, the buff, brooding modern comic book heroes are so hypermasculine that even men can no longer relate.

———

PewDiePie is one of the most famous people in the world least known to most people over thirty. Swedish-born Felix Kjellberg has grown rich creating Let's Play videos on his phenomenally popular YouTube channel. (For newbs: Let's Play are videos showing a video game being played with commentary by the gamer. LPs dominate YouTube's top earner charts, and Twitch, a platform that streams live game play, has more than 100 million unique viewers per month.)

While he's playing, he's animated and loud, whooping to underscore a joke or to celebrate nailing a feat. This sophomoric shtick is seriously lucrative. In 2011 PewDiePie was a college dropout selling hot dogs to support his gaming and video-making habit; four years later, his YouTube channel was the first ever to surpass 10 billion views, making him, arguably, one of the biggest stars on the Internet. His projected earnings for 2017 are $15 million (from ad revenue, merchandise, and brand deals), and his subscriber base is currently 57 million strong.[13]

PewDiePie's celebrity represents a confluence of social and cultural trends: the vast and ever-growing popularity of gaming and online video platforms such as YouTube and Twitch, the global fluidity of modern fame, and the predominantly male and often hostile and anti-PC culture of certain corners of the Internet. PewDiePie's persona is emblematic of this. He calls his fan base his "Bro Army," trolls his haters with jokes about rape, and unapologetically deploys the *n*-word and slurs such as "retard." In early 2017, his anti-Semitic jokes led to his losing a contract with Disney.

The spirit of antiauthoritarianism is a great draw of online culture, creating freewheeling, uncensored pockets of connection and creativity. YouTube allows odd talents to be transformed into flourishing enterprises. Another prime example is Dude Perfect, a clique of five sporty Christian bros from Texas with more than 24 million subscribers, who have made a mint from their goofy videos of trick shots and stunts.[14] Unfortunately, for many boys and men, parts of the Internet—especially gaming spheres—have also reinforced the worst aspects of masculinity. In this realm, they have the authority and a vast platform to rebel against what they see as sourpuss feminists and humorless women who want to spoil guys' fun.

Gaming offers what's been called an "escapist masculinity"—worlds in which most of the protagonists are men, or else exaggeratedly curvy babes—a fantasyland where geeks rule. Gamer Arthur Chu has written that many geeks have a sense of "nerd entitlement." These are guys who weren't popular growing up, who weren't seen as cool or attractive. They may have been bullied and rejected for their nerdy interests in computers and gaming. But online, they've found a place where they have power. "We [male] nerds grow up force-fed this script," Chu wrote in the *Daily Beast*. "Lusting after women 'out of our league' was what we did. And those unattainable hot girls would always inevitably reject us because they didn't understand our intellectual interest in science fiction and comic books and would instead date asshole jocks."[15]

Which is why when some of those "hot girls" decided to design, play, or critique games, they were targeted by the Gamergate mobs, a torrent of harassment that includes being doxxed and threatened with murder and rape. Take the experience of Anita Sarkeesian, the games theorist and critic behind the website Feminist Frequency. In 2012 she created a series looking at female tropes in video games, from the damsel in distress to the sinister seductress to the lady sidekick. For many girls and women, she says, these tired female stereotypes, coupled with the predominance of male protagonists, make gaming an alienating experience.

As with sports, there is a belief that gaming is a natural realm for boys and that males have a stronger aptitude and interest in technology—one only needs to look at the predominance of men in Silicon Valley. But the male domination in tech is relatively recent. The numbers of women and men studying computer science in the 1970s and '80s were fairly equal, but then female enrollment in science, technology, engineering, and mathematics began to drop precipitously. One compelling reason that's been offered as an explanation for this decline is the rise in personal computers in the 1980s and the fact that they were marketed almost exclusively to boys and young men. And the more boys were targeted as tech whizzes, the more the notion took hold that gaming and coding belonged to boys and that girls weren't welcome.[16]

The desire of women designers, gamers, and academics, like Sarkeesian, to see girls and women represented in gaming culture and portrayed in games in complicated and powerful ways thwarts the male-centered gamer narrative. "The overall problem is one of a culture where instead of seeing women as, you know, people, protagonists of their own stories just like we are of ours, men are taught that women are things to 'earn,' to 'win,'" Chu writes. "That if we try hard enough and persist long enough, we'll get the girl in the end. Like life is a video game and women, like money and status, are just part of the reward we get for doing well."

This hostility and misogyny don't reflect the whole of gaming culture, however. In fact, gaming has tremendous potential for liberation and expansiveness. *Wired* contributor and author Clive Thompson has been a gamer since the days of *Atari* and arcades. Now the father of two game-playing boys, he's written extensively on how games and other new technologies provide rich, powerful, and unprecedented platforms to connect and create. In his 2013 book, *Smarter than You Think: How Technology Is Changing Our Minds for the Better*, he argues that our devices aren't turning us—or our kids—into mindless addicts but creating new opportunities for political and social engagement. Over breakfast at a diner near his home in Brooklyn, he explains that gaming is a social experience for many kids. "Whether in person or online, kids play together, frequently talking nonstop about what they're doing and giving each other pointers," he says.[17] Rather than viewing games as harming or isolating kids, he observes that the opportunity for global, borderless collaboration enables kids to create meaningful bonds.

One example he points to is the incredibly popular *Minecraft*—with more than 100 million users, it's one of the best-selling video games of all time. With its old-school blocky graphics, *Minecraft* is a little like a souped-up version of Lego. The point of the game is to build worlds. Players create tools and weapons, dig for precious metals, build homes and other structures, tame or kill the roaming creatures in the landscape. But that's just the basics: players can also design games and puzzles within the game and collaborate with others around the world. People have re-created cities both real and fictional (*Game of Thrones* and *Star Wars* locations figure prominently). My son's class built a replica of its school as an orientation tool for new students to help them find their way around. Significantly, Thompson points out that the game is popular with both boys *and* girls, and its focus is more on creation than killing (though the game can also be played in survival mode, in which players must fend off hunger and hostile mobs).

And when it comes to the impact of violence and games, it appears that Nick's mom is right. In their 2017 book, *Moral Combat: Why the War on Violent Video Games Is Wrong*, psychologists Patrick Markey and Christopher Ferguson examine the research and reveal there's little evidence of a causal link between playing violent video games (or watching violent movies, listening to violent music, and so forth) and behaving violently in real life. Markey and Ferguson use the phrase *Grand Theft Fallacy* to describe how people attempt to connect high-profile violent crimes, particularly by young men, to video games. It's a form of confirmation bias, where people are looking for information that supports their existing beliefs. One of the reasons for this disconnect, Ferguson said in an interview with *New York Magazine*, is that "too often older adults just don't 'get' gaming or see the appeal. Older adults mistake their own lack of value in a newer form of media or art with that new media sucking out their kids' souls."[18]

One of the important factors that adults don't get, Thompson says, is the simple fact that games are really fun to play. The allure isn't something toxic or pathological, but rather straight-up pleasure. Games are built to test players and keep them coming back. What scaremongers see as simply addictive, he views as brain and character building: "There's something philosophically profound about a situation that allows you to safely test the limits of your endurance and perseverance," he explains to me. "Our everyday lives don't give us those situations very often where we're pushed to the limit of our abilities and we see what we can really do." For a lot of boys, games may provide a thrill and a sense of purpose that are absent for them otherwise.

Which is why parents should play before they panic. Ottawa psychologist Jacques Legault, whose practice focuses on boys and men, advises worried parents to become gamers themselves. "It took me a while to master the gaming controls, but with a bit of perseverance, I was able to walk through a game-play without getting killed," he wrote in a 2017 post on *Medium*. "And then my brain started flooding me with the yummy feelings of mastery and accomplishment, and I got hooked. It was at that point that I entered my sons' world." Once in that world, Legault found that he was able to connect with his sons in ways he hadn't anticipated. "Engaging discussions around the dinner table about the best ways to master parkour, to roll and shoot, and the absurdity of the storylines replaced the top-down arguments we used to have. These conversations would open the door for more meaningful exchanges about what they thought the impact of too much gaming, virtual violence, misogyny, racism and so forth had on them and their generation. I was no longer lecturing; we were dialoguing about these important issues in a meaningful way. And they were much more insightful than I initially thought."[19]

———

Not only are boys more insightful than we think, but the relationship between boys and popular culture is not one-sided. What makes this generation distinct from those preceding it is the enormous potential for them to be visible to and to engage with massive audiences. Once kids age out of Pixar and Disney, the adult creators of pop culture aimed at young people are forever playing catch-up. Aside from blockbuster entertainment, such as mega pop acts and comic book movie franchises, tweens and teenagers are now making much of their own popular culture. In the United States, for example, more than 90 percent of teenagers are online, and 24 percent describe themselves as being online almost constantly.[20]

With a relatively cheap investment in a few pieces of technology, kids and teenagers can record themselves dancing, cracking jokes, performing stunts and pranks, doing celebrity impressions, lip syncing, offering makeup and grooming advice, coming out as queer or transgender, and playing video games, and then post it to YouTube, Instagram, and Snapchat. Visual, kinetic, mobile, and supernimble, these platforms seem purpose-built for kids and teenagers, who've exploited them for their entertainment and self-expression.

The now-defunct video app Vine was fertile for the creation of memes and teenage slang. Launched in 2013 and owned by Twitter, Vine was a video-hosting service that allowed users to post six-second-long looping video clips. At its peak it had more than 200 million active users. (Twitter disabled uploads in 2016.) The app was a near-perfect social media invention, as the clips were easily shared via text, email, and Facebook.

Not surprisingly, the ability to create their own media has allowed for the visibility of boys who either don't see themselves represented in mainstream media or don't fit norms of traditional masculinity. Jay Versace, a black, queer boy from New Jersey, began making Vine videos in 2014 when he was sixteen. He shot short, flamboyantly funny skits, often impersonating his mom and female celebrities like Kylie Jenner and Erykah Badu, and eventually racked up 3 million followers on social media. Meanwhile, on Instagram, young men count among the most prominent beauty industry influencers, posting images of themselves in full makeup to show off their Kardashian-level contour technique. Some have upward of a million followers and fans; one of the youngest is a ten-year-old British boy named Jack Bennett (@makeuupbyjack) who has garnered more than 300,000 followers for his killer pout and winged eyeliner. Just a decade ago, boys publicly sharing makeup tips was unfathomable. Now, *Marie Claire* refers to them glowingly as the "beauty boys of Instagram."

This more open and expansive interactive world is echoed in more open and expansive displays of masculinity in other parts of popular culture. Even within the mainstream, masculinity is ever shifting. While comic book movie stars are buffer with each installment, pop music has welcomed a crop of young male artists who are thoughtful, politically conscious, and emotive. Civil rights activist and artist Chance the Rapper sings about his love for his grandma and baby daughter. Frank Ocean shares intimacies about his same-sex attractions. Bruno Mars and Ed Sheeran work a boy-next-door vibe. And then, of course, there was One Direction. Writing about the group's 2016 breakup and its legacy of showing off a softer, gentler masculinity, essayist Alana Massey observed that the boy band challenged the notion that bringing together a group of young men "transforms them into buffoons or barbarians." Instead, One Direction, with their coiffed hair, abundant affection, and support for gay rights, was "an amplifier of the best that boys have to offer." The band's fans adored them, "not just for the love they professed for girls in their pop songs, but for how deeply they appeared to love *each other*."[21] And though One Direction has broken up, a wave of swoony-cute Korean pop (or K-pop) boy bands such as BTS are filling the gap 1D left behind in the West, bringing with them a fascinating take on male style and presentation. Cultural studies professor and author Sun Jung calls it a "hybrid masculinity," or a "global metrosexual masculinity,"[22] that marries a tough-guy Western physique (think six-pack abs) with a softer, more androgynous style (think guy-liner and highlights).

Back at the diner, Clive Thompson steers the conversation to the more general dilemma of raising boys at this moment in history. Young men are at once more fluid, more exposed to different expressions of self and of gender, and also more anxious about their identity as males. Popular culture will, of course, shape their worldview. The flourishing of positive self-expression exists alongside the more traditional and pervasive gender extremes of hypersexualized women in video games and the muscle-bound superheroes. But he cautions against freaking out and suggests more thoughtful engagement. Play games with boys, watch the movies they like, show them you respect their world. If you want to speak to your child with authority, you better have some authority on the subject. "We're not going to fix the problems in pop culture overnight, and we're not going to fix it by being preachy and dogmatic and telling boys that the things they care about are bad," he says. "The only way to raise a kid to navigate this stuff without being screwed up by it is by talking with them about it."

7

DROPPING THE
MASCULINITY MASK

How to Talk to Boys About Sex

═══

First there was Rehtaeh Parsons. In November 2011, the fifteen-year-old girl, a student at Cole Harbour District High School near Halifax, Nova Scotia, went to a party where she drank until she was woozy. Without her consent, four boys had sex with her in her intoxicated state and took pictures. In one image, Rehtaeh is vomiting out a window while a boy is penetrating her and flashing a thumbs-up to the camera. The image was texted to her classmates and soon spread throughout her school. Rehtaeh was ridiculed, bullied, and harassed by strangers. Transfers to two different schools and six weeks of residential treatment at a children's hospital couldn't heal her depression and humiliation. Nearly two years after the assault, she hanged herself in her mother's home and died several days later, after being taken off life support.

One night a few months later, in January 2012, a fourteen-year-old girl in Maryville, Missouri, named Daisy Coleman sneaked out of her house with a friend to visit a seventeen-year-old football player named Matt Barnett, who was hanging out with his friends. According to witnesses, Coleman twice went alone to a room with Barnett, and after the second time, she wasn't able to walk on her own. She had been drinking alcohol and said later that she didn't consent to sex with Barnett. Meanwhile, her thirteen-year-old friend went to another room with a fifteen-year-old boy, who later admitted to having sex with her even though she said no. Later, the boys drove Coleman and her friend back home, where Coleman's mom later found her daughter outside in the cold, barely conscious and wearing sweatpants and a T-shirt. In the days following, a sexually explicit video of Coleman and Barnett shot by another boy at the party surfaced. Coleman was harassed at school and bullied on social media.[1]

That fall, another girl, fifteen-year-old Audrie Pott of Saratoga, California, went to a party, where she was sexually assaulted by three boys. Pictures of the attack were posted on social media, and Pott was bullied by classmates. Like Parsons, she killed herself by hanging.[2]

The following August, in Steubenville, Ohio, two high school football players, Ma'Lik Richmond and Trent Mays, sexually assaulted a sixteen-year-old girl, who was incapacitated by alcohol, at a series of parties. The next morning, text messages, social media posts, photos, and videos emerged revealing the events of the night. In one video, a boy is heard laughing and saying, "She is so raped," before comparing her, in her unconscious state, to "JFK, O. J.'s wife, Trayvon Martin."[3]

In the summer of 2014, Jada, a sixteen-year-old girl from Houston, Texas, went to a house party hosted by a teenage boy, who Jada says spiked her drink. She blacked out and was stripped naked and allegedly raped. Photos of her unconscious, missing her pants and underwear and sprawled on the floor, went viral. Other teenagers mocked the girl by imitating her in selfies and circulating them with the hashtag #jadapose.[4]

Collectively, all these cases, with their similar tales of drinking and abuse and humiliation, coming as they did in rapid succession and from towns and cities across North America, suggested an epidemic of teenage sexual assault. They play into long-standing parental worries about unsupervised adolescents, drinking, and sex. Fears about the impact of technology on the lives of young people are magnified: social media is helping to turn them into rapists or unwilling porn stars.

The images of the vulnerable female victims, made helpless by alcohol, and the smirking boys preying on them hewed to stereotypes about gender, as did the bullying from their peers that suggested these girls were sluts who had it coming, while the boys were just being, well, boys. The Man Box rules demand that boys be sexually aggressive and in charge, just as the rules of femininity require passivity and purity. At Parsons's funeral, the minister said in his eulogy, "How can our society provide a safe haven for young girls? Why do young men feel that young girls are but objects for their sexual fantasies and pleasure?"[5]

Many parents are desperate for answers to these questions. Hearing stories of harassment and assault, it's impossible not to feel terribly worried for girls and boys both. If you're the parent or caregiver of a preteen or teenage boy, like me you've probably had to fight the urge to ground them preemptively, so they can't do damage. It's daunting to raise a boy while hearing endless reports of the violence young men are capable of.

Statistics on teenagers and sexual assault are disturbing. Forty-six percent of girls reported that they had experienced sexual assault, from unwanted kissing to rape, in a 2008 study of nearly two thousand Ontario high school students.[6] In 2014, according to the annual school crime report from the US Department of Justice and the Department of Education, about forty-four hundred rapes and twenty-three hundred fondling incidents were reported on public school campuses in the United States; overall, the number of reported forcible sex crimes on campus increased by 205 percent between 2001 and 2014.[7] A two-year longitudinal study of nearly a thousand middle school students in the

American Midwest found a link between early homophobic and sexist bullying and later incidents of sexual harassment. Boys who teased
peers with "gender-based epithets"—calling them "gay" or "fag"—
were more likely to sexually harass girls when they were older.[8]

About a decade ago, a group of educators at the Calgary Sexual
Health Centre in Alberta were poring over the results of a recent cli-
ent survey and were surprised to find that although the number of unwanted pregnancies among teen girls was dropping, there was a surge
in incidences of sexually transmitted infections among adolescent boys.
This was consistent with national figures: teenage pregnancy in Canada has declined steadily since the 1990s, but the transmission of STIs
is climbing. According to a report from Health Canada, people aged
fifteen to twenty-nine made up nearly 80 percent of chlamydia cases
reported in 2014. And among males between fifteen and nineteen,
rates of infectious syphilis increased by 300 percent between 2005 and
2014.[9] This suggests that while girls are using contraception to prevent
pregnancies, boys, who have more control over the use of condoms,
aren't using them consistently to prevent the spread of STIs.

Reflecting on this, the staff at the clinic realized that after more
than thirty years working in sexual health education, the center didn't
have a single program targeted specifically at young men. This imbalance isn't unusual. Sex educators report that heterosexual young men
are the demographic most ignored when it comes to sexual health. Out
of necessity, since girls and women overwhelmingly bear the consequences of unwanted pregnancies, violence, and discrimination, sexual
health initiatives around the world focus most heavily on their needs.
(One significant exception is AIDS awareness campaigns for gay men.)
The result is that teenage boys often find these female-slanted sex-ed
programs irrelevant. Even worse, this oversight has led many young
men to believe that they are off the hook when it comes to caring for
their sexual health and their partners'.

The basement-level expectations we have set for boys seem peculiarly irresponsible given how often they are the source of problems when it comes to sex and sexuality: as the bullies of gay classmates or the perpetrators of coercion or violence. Young men also visit considerable harm upon themselves. They're the group most prone to taking risks with their own health—using drugs and alcohol during sex, having multiple partners, and engaging in unprotected sex. They are also reluctant to report their experiences of abuse. (In the United States, the most commonly cited statistic regarding male victims is that one in six men and boys have had unwanted sexual experiences, including abuse and assault.) Since boys are socialized to believe that real men are powerful and straight, fears of appearing weak or gay make them less likely to seek treatment or help for abuse. Studies also indicate that boys are less likely than girls to seek clinical sexual health care, because they are embarrassed and afraid to look stupid or unmanly. When boys do receive medical attention, doctors are less likely to raise the issue of sexual health with them than they are with girls.

To correct this, the Calgary Sexual Health Centre set about developing a new, elective sexual health curriculum for boys in ninth grade called WiseGuyz. Over the course of a full school year, boys meet once a week to discuss everything from anatomy to ethics to self-awareness. Or, as one boy who went through WiseGuyz put it to me, "It's a program where you learn how not to be a jerk."[10]

And, so, in the late fall of 2013, I found myself in suburban Calgary in a classroom at George P. Vanier School, eavesdropping on a dozen fourteen-year-old boys in a heated conversation about breasts. "But what about boobs?" asks a boy grappling to understand the mechanics of being intersex. "Does a person still get boobs?" For the past fifteen minutes, the boys had been discussing sexual diversity and accommodation. The conversation eventually found its way to the subject of people who consider themselves as something other than "male" or "female."

Tristan Abbott, one of the WiseGuyz facilitators, cheerfully cor-
rects him: "You mean 'breasts,' right?" (Facilitators make a point of
using the appropriate names for body parts.) Then he unfolds himself
from his chair and sketches a picture on a whiteboard at the front of
the room: a gingerbread-man-shaped figure with a smiley face, a heart,
and a starburst at the crotch.

Abbott points to the head and explains that's where gender identity
lies (whether you define yourself as a man, woman, or something in between), the heart represents orientation (whom you're attracted to), the
starburst connotes sex (your physical characteristics), and the outline,
the external shape of the figure, stands for gender expression (how you
dress, talk, walk, and so on). These various aspects don't line up in the
same way for every person, he says.

A few boys nod, but the rest look baffled. Stafford Perry, a second
facilitator, speaks up. "It helps if you understand that for lots of people, gender is not just two possibilities but many," he says. "For a lot of
people, being a man or a woman exists on a scale, so it's not either-or;
you don't have to be one thing or the other."

A moment of silence while this sinks in. Then the kid who asked
the "boobs" question, a tall, athletic alpha-dog type, calls out, "So how
do you pee if you don't have a penis?" Several boys snicker.

Blake Spence, who oversees the WiseGuyz program, answers him,
straight-faced, with a brief explanation of the functions of the urinary
tract.

The kid was probably just angling for a laugh. He'd spent much of the
session ping-ponging between peeks at his phone, friendly trash-talking
with a couple of the other boys, and testing how far he could lean back
in his chair, balancing on its rear legs. But as Spence had explained to
me earlier, their policy is to answer every question put to them, even if
they know it's a joke. It builds trust with the group, it preempts unkind

comments, and—you never know—the answer may be useful to someone. At the end of the anatomy lesson, the joker, conceding defeat, flashes a smile at Spence and lets his chair thump forward onto all four legs.

A little earlier, Spence had asked the group members what they thought of when they heard the term *human rights*. One boy, who had been nearly silent to this point, mentioned that Vanier has a Gay-Straight Alliance group and that a gay kid would have no problem at their school. "Everyone is cool with that here," he said.

"I guess," piped up another boy across the room, sitting near the alpha-dog kid. "I mean, I'm okay with a guy being gay, but I wouldn't want him to look at me in the locker room when I'm changing or something."

Spence leaned against a table at the front of the room. The sleeves of his denim shirt were rolled up, revealing the tattoos on his forearms. "Okay, so what you're saying," he said to the boy, "is that what makes you uncomfortable about gay guys is that they might look at you in a way that's sexual."

"Yeah," the boy said, scanning the room to gauge the other boys' response.

When it was clear no one was going to say more, Spence nodded at the boy and then moved on to a slight kid with shaggy dark hair, who said he wanted to know why all the members of the school's branch of the Gay-Straight Alliance were girls.

"Why do you think it's that way?" Spence asked him.

"Um, I don't know. Maybe because guys are scared that if they join the group, maybe people will think they're gay?"

"Yeah?" Spence said. "And why would guys not want people to think they're gay?"

"Uh, because even though some people are okay with it," the kid ventured, "a lot of guys don't think it's okay to be gay, and they're afraid they'll be made fun of. I think maybe it's harder for guys to be gay or something."

Spence nodded again and then sent the group off for a short break; he told me later that he had mentally filed away this conversation for the upcoming months.

It usually takes the first half of the program for the boys to become comfortable enough to open up and "set the masculine bravado aside," Spence says. Initially, the boys clam up or make dumb jokes. They'll refer to a girl they don't like as a "bitch," call each other "fags," or dismiss something as "being so gay." Often they say things they think will impress the other guys, even if it's not really what they believe. "They might not be particularly homophobic or sexist," Spence says. "They just think that's how guys are supposed to talk to each other." This dynamic is at the very heart of the WiseGuyz program: underlying the lessons about condoms and chlamydia is a much more radical project. It's not enough to just teach boys the mechanics of sex and sexuality. What WiseGuyz does instead is teach them how to question all they have been told about what it means to be a man and then help them figure out how to become a good one.

Adults are lousy at talking to children about sex. A 2016 British study examined a range of international research from the past twenty-five years on young people's opinions about their school-based sex and relationship education.[11] The survey tracked students ages four to nineteen, in the United Kingdom, Ireland, the United States, Australia, New Zealand, Canada, Japan, Iran, Brazil, and Sweden. Despite social and cultural differences among these countries, and disparities in the content of their sex-ed curricula, the students were startlingly consistent in their assessments: sex education is terrible.

Students felt that sex was often portrayed as negative or danger-ous and that the content was "out of touch" with the reality of their lives. It didn't acknowledge that some young people were sexually ac-tive, and it narrowed in on the biology of sex, without discussing the social and emotional aspects of sexuality. Information on LGBTQ sex and relationships was limited or nonexistent, and female pleasure was routinely ignored. The content was laden with gender stereotypes. Girls and women were viewed as both passive participants in heterosexual sex and as "gatekeepers" required to either acquiesce or forbid sexual contact. (French sexual and relationship education was not included in this study, but a separate research paper from France published around the same time revealed the nation's sex ed was premised on the stereo-type that boys are focused on genital sexuality, while girls attach more importance to love.)[12]

Young men reported feeling anxious during sex-ed classes. They said that because men are expected to be sexually knowledgeable and competent, they were afraid of appearing ignorant or inexperienced. That led to their being disruptive in sex-ed lessons and, in some cases, to verbally harassing girls about their sexual reputations. Both boys and girls said they often felt embarrassed and that they didn't sense teachers were capable of delivering the lessons in ways that acknowl-edged and mitigated their vulnerability and discomfort.

In the United States, sex ed has become an increasingly divisive ex-ercise, with an influential conservative religious lobby curtailing access to information about birth control. Comprehensive sex-ed programs ex-ist in pockets—in 2012, for example, New York City mandated that sexual health be taught in its public schools—but elsewhere, compre-hensive sex ed appears to be on the decline. Between 2006–2010 and 2011–2013, the number of teenagers in the United States aged fifteen to nineteen who were taught about abstinence but who had received no in-structions about birth control increased from 22 percent to 26 percent for girls and from 29 percent to 35 percent for boys.[13] Only twenty states have a requirement that information offered in sex and HIV/AIDS education classes be medically, factually, or technically accurate. In many cases, lessons are outsourced to abstinence-education consultants, like Pam Stenzel, a Christian conservative, who claims to reach up to five hundred thousand young people annually at lectures she gives with titles like "The High Cost of Free Love." Stenzel, who considers condoms to be unsafe and useless against sexually transmitted infections, is known for offering teenagers such gems as "If you take birth control, your mother probably hates you."

Abstinence programs have turned out to be major failures in influencing teenage behavior—which should come as a surprise only to those who have never been, or encountered, a seventeen-year-old with a crush. Also not a surprise: the teenage birthrate in the United States is nearly eight times higher than in the Netherlands, which offers extensive sexual health education that normalizes teenage sexuality.[14] In addition to having one of the lowest teen fertility rates in the developed world, that country also has one of the lowest rates of teen abortion, suggesting that Dutch teens are more vigilant about contraception or are having less intercourse—but more on the Dutch later.

Outside of abstinence education, one of the biggest shortcomings in sexual education in the United States, Canada, and much of Europe is that it's premised on what progressive sex educators refer to as the "disaster model"—teachings that concentrate on all the negative consequences of sex, like disease, unwanted pregnancy, and rape. Rather than talking about pleasure and intimacy, the emphasis is on preparing for the worst. Ultimately, this model isn't that much different from abstinence teachings.

Jonathan Zimmerman, a historian at New York University and the author of the 2015 book *Too Hot to Handle: A Global History* of *Sex Education*, says that "sex is so tied to our deepest values and faith systems, that teaching it will always be a source of conflict." In the United States, sex ed began to be taught in the early twentieth century, sparked by panic over the rise of sexually transmitted infections. Its aim was to promote sexual continence and abstinence. Even now, in the more comprehensive sexual education classes he's sat in on, he witnesses an undercurrent of prudishness. "Morality is dressed up in the science of biology and reproduction," he tells me. "Teachers want to educate young people about sex without sparking their interest in it. I've observed so many sex-ed classes in the US where, at some point, the teacher will list the reasons young people have sex, and it's always things like 'low self-esteem,' 'peer pressure,' and 'wanting to be cool.' I always want to raise my hand and say, 'Um, also, because it feels really good.'"

About a decade ago, when researchers at Planned Parenthood's office in Toronto wanted to update their services to youth, the organization spoke to twelve hundred teenagers and young adults in the Toronto area, asking them what was missing from their sexual health knowledge. The top three issues that young people cited were healthy relationships, HIV/AIDS, and sexual pleasure. It's that latter topic—pleasure—that's so important when it comes to engaging young men, Michele Chai explains to me, because sexual pleasure and living up to the stud stereotype is deeply embedded in beliefs about masculinity. Chai facilitates and runs the agency's programs for young men. She says that the assumption that boys are always "on" makes them feel like they are less of a man if they need sexual advice on pleasing themselves or their partner. "People tend to think that the swagger young men display is because they have confidence about sex.... But do you want to know the three things about sex that young guys report lying about most often?" she asks. Before I can offer an answer, she ticks them off on her fingers. "One, how often they have sex. Two, how much they enjoy the sex they actually have. And three, whether or not they use condoms." This adds up, she says, to less pleasurable and potentially unsafe encounters.

Giving young men the opportunity to talk about what they enjoy, or the room to admit they might not want to have sex, also opens the door to respecting and considering the desires of others. Chai says compassion for boys is imperative. "If they don't feel safe to connect with their feelings and be vulnerable, they will likely struggle to be compassionate with others." That's why she avoids an antagonistic approach. "If you only talk to young men as though they are predators, monsters and potential rapists, they'll shut down," she says. Instead, Chai focuses on examining masculinity and the pressures and expectations that boys experience—as well as recognizing that boys' attitudes about sex are influenced by their specific life histories, race, ethnicity, class, and faith, as well as by their sexual and gender identities. "What I want young men to consider are questions like, 'How am I perceived in the world because of my race and sexuality? How do I perceive myself and others? How do I benefit from the Man Box, and how am I hurt by it? When do I feel vulnerable? *Can* I be vulnerable as a young man? And how do these experiences impact my ability to communicate in my relationships and to negotiate consent and safer sex?' "

The goal, she says, is for young men to be able to be authentic, within themselves and within their relationships. But fear of vulnerability can hinder them from doing so. School is a place where many boys feel unsafe, afraid they won't live up to the rules of the Man Box; they won't be cool enough, or popular enough, or tough enough. Underneath all that is the very real fear of becoming a target. Acting out by bringing another boy's manliness into question by calling him a homophobic slur, or by harassing and sexualizing a girl with a catcall, is a way to fortify their masculine image. (It's not just the perpetrators who cause harm—it's also the boys who are bystanders to this behavior, who ignore or enable it.)

As the ubiquity of sexual harassment and assault among young people has been revealed over the past several years, there are growing calls to address sexual violence by teaching boys and young men about consent. The trouble is that few educators know how to do it well. Conversations about consent rely on simple semantics: the difference between yes and no. But they don't typically take into account all the social dynamics and gender expectations at work. They often don't confront broader power disparities or teach boys skills such as empathy, self-awareness, and communication. And these conversations about consent typically don't address that boys, too, experience sexual abuse.

Rarely do boys have the opportunity to talk about the pressure they feel to live up to social expectations about masculinity and sex. Sometimes this pressure leads young men to harass, bully, and assault girls. Other times it leads them to deny their own discomfort and pursue sex when they don't want it. Cisgender- and heterosexual-identified young men have told Chai that they've been judged by male peers, and in some cases female peers, for not being sexually assertive. Girlfriends question their fidelity ("If you don't want sex with me, you must be getting it elsewhere"), friends question their manhood ("Real men are always eager to have sex, so there must be something wrong with you"), and everyone questions their sexual orientation ("What are you, gay?").

There isn't a lot of support for boys trying to navigate this terrain. Progressive school-based sex-ed programs like WiseGuyz are a rarity. In 2011 the *New York Times Magazine* profiled a popular and highly regarded educator named Al Vernacchio, who teaches an inclusive, in-depth elective course called Sexuality and Society at an affluent private school in Philadelphia. The story quoted Leslie Kantor, vice president of education for Planned Parenthood Federation of America, saying the options for high-quality sex ed in public schools were bleak: "There is abstinence-only sex education, and there's abstinence-based sex-ed. There's almost nothing else left in public schools."[15]

Other children and young people might find useful and nonjudgmental information on Planned Parenthood's website. Or they could download Real Talk, an app that uses real teenagers' stories to answer middle schoolers questions about sex, puberty, gender, and relationships. Or they might turn to Sex, Etc., a website written and edited by teenagers and covering subjects from relationships and sexual orientation to STDs and contraception. It's published by Answer, an organization based out of Rutgers University in New Jersey, which advocates for better and more comprehensive sexual health education.

Over the phone, Answer executive director Nicole Cushman and director of training Dan Rice explain that by the time young people turn eighteen or nineteen, they've internalized all kinds of unhelpful and even harmful messages about sex. And when it comes to comprehensive sexual education that teaches communication skills, emotional literacy, and healthy relationship practices alongside reproductive health, there is little available to American students. As for educating LGBTQ students about sex, Cushman says there's barely any information and even less willingness. "How are LGBTQ students' emotional needs being addressed in terms of healthy relationships, having a crush, and falling in love? The honest answer is not much at all."

The only exception, Cushman notes, are some frank and explicit sex-ed programs in poor schools and schools with a high percentage of children of color. But she says these intervention programs have built-in biases about sexuality and use the disaster-model approach. "They presume sexual activity and sexual violence," she says, "playing on pervasive negative stereotypes. These sorts of programs are solely about preventing sexually transmitted infections and pregnancies and rarely focus on emotional health, communication, and building healthy and loving relationships."

And it's exactly these kinds of broad conversations and lessons about sex, relationships, love, and respect that boys and young men of all races, sexualities, and class backgrounds most desperately need. Dan Rice says it's crucial to challenge the social messages boys receive about sex, masculinity, and dominance. "In the 'boy code' or the 'man code,' the only emotions acceptable for a boy to express are anger and frustration," he says. "They don't have social permission, or haven't even been taught, to express their feelings. And so when it comes to our current conversations about consent and sexual bullying, boys are in a bind. They are getting so much pressure from their peers, from media, and from society to prove their manhood by acting tough, sexually confident, and sexually aggressive." At the same time, he says, when it comes to violence prevention, the message is to be sensitive and caring. But "sensitive and caring" aren't part of the "boy code."

This tension explains why it can be so difficult, once boys reach high school, to address issues of consent, sexual assault, and sexual bullying. What they've been told about being "a real man" doesn't necessarily square with being a good one. There's a sharp comedy sketch from the TV series *Inside Amy Schumer*, in 2015, that spoofs the football drama *Friday Night Lights* to make this very point. In the parody, a new coach shows up in town and lays down the law with his players: "No raping." The boys protest this new rule with a series of questions, looking for an exception: *Can we rape at away games? What if she thinks it's rape, but I don't? What if my mom is the DA and won't prosecute? What if she's drunk, has a slight reputation, and no one's going to believe her?* But the coach persists: No raping. Then, after a big win, he turns to his triumphant team and says: "How can I get through to you boys that football is not about rape? It's about violently dominating anyone who stands between you and what you want. You've got to get it in your heads that you are gods, and you are entitled to this." The sketch perfectly illustrates the mixed messages we send to young men about power, control, manliness, and sex. If we tell boys competition and domination are everything, why are we surprised when they apply this thinking to sex?

———

If schools aren't teaching kids about sex, where are they learning about it? Pornography. The ubiquity of porn in young men's lives is so much a given that every sex educator I spoke to raised it without prompting. As Tristan Abbott from Calgary's WiseGuyz explains, "Adults may want teens to have information about sex, but most of them don't want to give teens permission to actually have sex. Porn gives teens permission."

Most of those sex educators, however, don't indulge in the widespread cultural pearl-clutching about the influence porn may have in shaping boys' attitudes and behaviors about sex. In part, that's because there's not enough research on the subject, and what little there is isn't conclusive. In 2013, for example, Middlesex University London, at the request of England's Office of the Children's Commissioner, released a report titled *Basically...Porn Is Everywhere*, an exhaustive overview of studies from around the world on the impact of porn on young people.

Many of the findings were predictable: kids look at porn out of curiosity and use it to masturbate, and boys use it more often and have a more positive view of it than girls do. Young people have far more exposure and access to porn than ever before, and consumption of pornography has been linked to unrealistic attitudes about sex and regressive attitudes about gender. Still, researchers had difficulty establishing a direct, causal relationship between porn use and harm. It's a difficult connection to measure. Not all porn is created alike, nor is it consumed in the same way and to the same degree by all young people. Those audiences come to pornography with a range of personal temperaments, sexual experiences, sexual knowledge, parental support, and guidance around sex. Compared to previous generations, modern adolescents are also far more sophisticated in interpreting and criticizing media. And another reason it's hard to understand the impact of pornography is that popular culture in general is much more explicitly sexual now. There are graphic imagery and language in music and video games and on TV series, blurring the boundaries between porn and other forms of popular media.

What may be more important than trying to measure the impact of pornography is addressing why adolescents look at so much of it. On this point, the British researchers seem convinced: "There is growing evidence...that young people are unhappy with the sex education they are receiving and that they increasingly use pornography, expecting it to educate and give information regarding sexual practices and norms."[16] This is especially true of boys: one study found that young men wanted porn to be included in sex-ed classes, because issues around sex and sexuality weren't covered sufficiently; another noted that young gay men relied on porn to teach them about sex, because they weren't learning about it elsewhere. Researchers concluded that their findings suggest "not only that children and young people want more education and opportunity to discuss sex and relationships but also that many parents feel poorly equipped to help their children."[17]

———

This is where the Dutch come in. The Netherlands is the undisputed world leader of comprehensive sexual and relationship education, which builds abilities like communication, negotiation, and self-awareness, while teaching matter-of-factly about reproduction, sexual orientation, and sexual health. Every spring, starting in kindergarten, Dutch children in primary school spend a week in focused sex-ed classes, the youngest children exploring topics such as gender stereotypes and the older ones moving on to crushes and contraception. Even in its modern candor, the approach is grounded in old-fashioned ideals of love, respect, intimacy, and common decency. A 2015 *PBS NewsHour* story about the Dutch sex-ed curricula includes a clip of four-year-olds talking about hugging, kissing, and getting married. Another video features eleven-year-olds discussing what it feels like to fall in love ("You become shy," says a girl. "Nervousness," a boy says. "You blush."). The teacher then explains what to do when you fall out of it: don't text or send a friend to break up for you; do it in person and be kind.[18] The demise of a relationship can be hard, she tells the children, but you can do your best not to be hurtful or cruel.

These lessons are built on the belief that sexuality education should be taken seriously by parents and teachers and that a healthy, positive, and pleasurable sex life is a basic human right. This attitude has led to impressive results. Most Dutch young people report that their first sexual experiences were "well-timed, wanted and fun," unlike most American teenagers, who said that they wished they had waited longer to lose their virginity. Nine out of ten Dutch teenagers used contraception the first time they had sex, and the country has very low rates of teen pregnancy, HIV infections, and sexually transmitted diseases. Amy T. Schalet, a sociologist at the University of Massachusetts–Amherst who studies cross-cultural differences in teenage development, has written that "adult acceptance of adolescent sexuality [in the Netherlands] makes it easier for teens to recognize that they are sexual beings, plan sexual acts, negotiate sexual interactions, and ask for assistance when they need it."[19]

The advantages for young women are obvious: fewer assaults and unwanted encounters, fewer STIs, fewer undesired pregnancies, more sexual and romantic agency. The benefits for boys are also very real. Schalet notes that in the United States, teenage boys are viewed as horny and predatory, driven by their hormones and solely interested in sex. American parents assume that boys and girls are fundamentally dissimilar when it comes to sex and that this opposition is the basis for a kind of natural antagonism, a "battle of the sexes." American parents also treat boys and girls differently, with fathers admitting that they are protective of their daughters but lenient with their sons. The implication for heterosexual teenagers is that men and women can't be equal partners in sex and romance.

In the Netherlands, by contrast, boys' desire for love and intimacy is emphasized, acknowledged, and normalized. According to one national survey, 90 percent of twelve- to fourteen-year-old boys reported that they had been in love. Dutch parents don't talk much about gender differences, nor do they anticipate conflict between boys and girls. "Instead of the metaphor of battle," Schalet observes, "[the] Dutch use a language of relationships and loves, and they apply such a language of love equally to girls and boys."[20] What this creates for boys is the expectation that enjoyable sex and healthy relationships are based on respect and mutual satisfaction, not on domination and control.

Imagine that: a model of sex ed that teaches boys about sex and relationships while cherishing their tenderness and acknowledging their fears, a model that emphasizes responsibility, decency, and accountability and doesn't reduce their feelings and desires to a punch line. "American boys end up paying a price for a culture that does not support their needs for intimacy," Schalet writes. (I'd expand that to Canadian and British boys, and boys in so many other nations, too.) "While boys crave closeness, they are expected to act as if they are emotionally invulnerable. With less practice sustaining intimacy, boys enter romantic relationships less confident and less skilled."[21]

———

When the Calgary Sexual Health Centre first decided to create its WiseGuyz program, it commissioned a team of social workers from the University of Calgary to help. Given that there weren't many existing models to draw on, the social workers looked for what was missing in the field. They put together a small focus group of guys in their late teens and early twenties and asked them how they learned about sex and what they wished they had been taught.

Almost to a man, the group said school-based sex ed started too late and seemed abstract and unrelated to what people really did in bed. They thought the classes should be frank and fun. One said that he suspected that his teachers had focused on anatomy in order to "shy away from actually having to talk about [sex]." The group said that birth control and disease prevention are left entirely up to girls; guys, they said, were often ignorant about risks and felt they were invincible. They stressed the importance of teaching boys "the right attitude" toward sex, including being more sensitive to women and more responsible for their actions.

When asked who should deliver this kind of information, they were unanimous: other guys, not too old or out of touch, engaging, smart, and with a sense of humor. No awkward academic types. No middle-aged ladies. As one participant said, "If some fifty-five-year-old woman tried to teach me all this stuff...I'd just be like, 'You're just like my mom, I'm not going to listen to you.'"

Ideas raised in that focus group are evident in the WiseGuyz program today, right down to the profile of the facilitators. When I visit, all three whom I meet are thirty-ish with well-groomed beards, dark denim jeans, white T-shirts peeping out from under fitted flannel shirts. The trio are undeniably cool, and the boys, even the ones who give them a hard time, regard them with awe.

In a conversation with one of boys, he tells me the best thing about the facilitators is that they're relatable and nonjudgmental. "Sometimes it feels like adults think that teenaged guys are nothing but trouble," he says. When I ask him if he talks to his parents about sex and relationships, he says he'd like to, but he's afraid they'll overreact. "It's just easier to talk to Blake and Stafford and Tristan, because they don't force you to tell them every detail of what's going on." When he asks his parents about sex, he says, "I get the third degree. Then I say to them, 'This is why I didn't want to talk to you in the first place.'"

WiseGuyz regularly evaluates its work,[22] and "emotionality" is consistently one of the most significant areas of growth for the boys who do the program. When they start, boys report that throughout their lives, they have been told by adults to "be tough" or that "you have to hide your fear inside sometimes." The boys come into the program conscious that these stereotypes of masculinity increase their feelings of disconnection and loneliness, but they also feel that it would be shameful to express their sadness and isolation. When asked what has been most useful to them in WiseGuyz, the boys point to their new awareness of the Man Box, as well as learning to sustain healthy relationships. They say they are more comfortable with expressions of emotions, such as vulnerability, and having a greater capacity to practice safer sex and to maintain healthy romantic and sexual relationships.

Evaluators also see positive changes in attitudes and language about homosexuality, or what they refer to as a disruption of "the fag discourse." At the beginning of the program, WiseGuyz participants routinely say that put-downs such as "fag" and "queer" and "you're so gay" don't necessarily reflect their feelings about gay people—it's just stuff guys say. But after talking about the power of language and the impact of homophobia, the boys become more conscious of the weight of the words they use and more empathetic about how those words might wound others. One told evaluators that he'd challenged his own father on this subject, drawing on what he learned from WiseGuyz. "It's like you can't just say those words, cuz if you think about it, there are gay people, and like why do we dis them like that?" the boy said. "Like even my dad, he says, 'Oh, that's gay'...I was like, 'Why, why is that gay? What does that have to do with gay people?' He said, 'What do you mean?' I talked to him, and I haven't heard him say it since."

Similarly, boys who've done the WiseGuyz program say they have more empathy for girls. They describe a lesson on media portrayals of women and girls as "opening their eyes" to the realities that girls experience. Boys become more understanding of the ways girls are sexualized and sexually harassed. They also think about the language they use to talk about their female classmates and friends: no more "sluts" or "bitches."

To get to this point, the program follows a strictly plotted schedule, beginning with the subject of healthy relationships, before moving on to sexual health; then to gender, sex, and media; and finally to advocacy and leadership. That last unit is key. "The whole point of Wise-Guyz," Spence says, "is how they apply what they learned, how they intend to stay woke. What we really want is to have them recognize their ability to create change and influence other boys in positive ways."

That mission is serious, but in the classroom, facilitators keep the tone light. Take the standard sex-ed lesson in rolling a condom on a banana. It's a useful exercise, technically, but one that doesn't take into account the nerves and pressure of the moment. The most common reasons young men give for not using condoms are that they reduce pleasure and ruin the mood. They also want to be seen as skilled and suave and worry that if they start fumbling with a condom, they'll look stupid—the ultimate buzz kill. One practice session with a banana is not going to cut it. In WiseGuyz, the boys are allowed to get silly. They blow up condoms and bat them around like balloons or fill them with water and fling them at each other. The more times they practice opening the packages, examining what different varieties feel and look like, the better—the aim is to demystify condoms, make them seem fun and normal, not scary or humiliating.

After a short break in the morning session I attend, the facilitators divide the boys into small groups and give them an activity: create a map of an imaginary island and establish a charter of human rights for it. I've been warned that one group in a previous course created an island that looked like a huge pair of breasts, while another championed the right "for girls to be naked all the time." Today, the results are tamer. One nation is divided evenly into the regions of "Dopest" and "Least Dope" and has a constitution that forbids killing and currency. ("If no one has money, then there's less corruption," one boy in the group explains.)

The discussion is half goofy, half serious. There's enthusiastic agreement when the right to free speech is raised (not surprising for a demographic that gets told to shut up a lot) and whoops at the suggestion that people should be given free rein when it comes to eating cookies. Crayons in hand, immersed in drawing their island utopias and slurping juice boxes, the group resembles a pack of third graders more than adolescents in the throes of puberty.

Up until about the age of ten, children hang out mainly in single-sex friendship groups, where there are distinct patterns of interaction; while girls talk to each other, boys do activities together. As kids move into middle school, they begin to have mixed-gender friendships and to develop crushes. By the time kids reach thirteen or fourteen—the age of the boys in the WiseGuyz group—dating begins. Many of the boys in the group are dating or have some sort of romantic involvement, and about 20 percent report they are sexually active. Only a few boys who have gone through the program have identified as something other than straight. Younger teens typically date within large, mixed peer groups, but same-sex friendships are still the most important ones during this time. As Niobe Way's work on boys' friendships shows in Chapter 3, this is the period right before boys begin to lose their intimate friendships.

That's one of the reasons the WiseGuyz program targets this age group, to catch boys when they're still willing to be open and when they're still connected to other boys. "The guys set the bar for each other," Spence says. "At the beginning, the popular guys have the most power in the group, and the other guys look to them for approval. But as we progress, they start to challenge each other in different ways." To illustrate how WiseGuyz facilitates this evolution, he tells me about a recent class in which all the boys vocally condemned sexual assault and sexual bullying. But then Spence pushed them a little further. What would they do about these kinds of incidents if they witnessed them or heard about them? he asked. "I said, 'You might not identify with boys who do things like that, but if you do nothing about it when it happens, then you're contributing to it. You don't have to passively accept it. You don't have to forward that text message, you don't have to laugh when someone makes a rape joke.' "

This has become the standard approach in antibullying campaigns, but it's much easier preached than practiced. It's noble to tell a kid to stand up for what's right, but children, particularly those in the peer-dependent middle school and early teenage years, are pack animals who find it difficult to set themselves apart. So WiseGuyz doesn't just target individual boys; it tries to reshape the dynamics of boy culture: the popular boys are encouraged to cede some power, the shy kids to become more vocal.

The fundamental skill at work here is establishing and respecting boundaries. Later in the program, the boys will be paired up for a role-playing exercise to negotiate a hypothetical trip to a water park by asking each other a series of questions. Do you like waterslides? Do you want to go on a ride just once or repeatedly? Do you want to dive in the deep end? Do you know how to swim? The idea is to help the boys learn to define what they want and to work through the tension created when their friend wants something else. And, of course, the lesson applies equally to platonic relationships and romantic ones. If boys can't figure out how to plan a fun and safe trip to a water park with a friend, then they won't be able to enjoy a fun and safe sex life with a partner. Success requires a degree of self-knowledge—the boys must know what they want, and they must know how to respect what other people want. But they also have to know how to communicate and listen.

——

The afternoon session of the WiseGuyz program at Vanier school is quieter than the morning one. During check-in, the boys leisurely share the events of their past week: basketball practice, guitar lessons, marathon sessions of *Dr. Who* on Netflix and *Last of Us* on PlayStation. One kid is frustrated because his hockey team sucks and hasn't won a game in ages. ("Been there, man," the guy beside him says.) Another boy announces he just passed his Bronze Cross exam, bringing him closer to being certified as a lifeguard. ("That's sweet, dude!" says Stafford Perry, ever enthusiastic.) It's typical, nothing-special teenage guy stuff, but the boys seem to savor the conversation.

As much as WiseGuyz teaches boys about romance and sex, the facilitators have come to see the development of intimacy in platonic male friendships as being a significant part of the course. In this group, the boys don't feel like they have to disguise or disassociate from their feelings. It's that disengagement that research has shown can lead to depression, violence, and suicide. The boys talk about the pressure to be good at things and keep up appearances and how WiseGuyz is "a stress relief," one place where they could speak freely and let down their guard. Facilitators call this "dropping the masculinity mask," which allows "boys to return to themselves, and to recover their emotional interior lives."

Four years after I visit the program, I speak with Blake Spence over the phone. Three hundred boys have graduated from WiseGuyz; another three hundred are enrolled this year. There are eight facilitators now, and the program is being run in ten schools in Calgary, three in rural areas outside the city, as well as in a group for indigenous boys, at a recreation center, and in a residential diversionary program for young men who have behaved in ways that are sexually inappropriate. Spence says there have been requests for WiseGuyz from across the country.

The program has a decidedly progressive bent, but provided the participants aren't hateful or abusive, facilitators allow the boys to talk through sensitive political and social issues. The past few years have given them no shortage of subject matter. Spence says the boys have had questions about Milo Yiannopoulos, the alt-right blogger who was a ringleader in the Gamergate campaign. Some of the boys in WiseGuyz are susceptible to Yiannopoulos's style of angry, antiwoman posturing. Conversations about male power and male privilege can be bewildering or frustrating to them, since many don't feel very powerful themselves. When boys express their confusion or resentment, facilitators don't cut them off or talk down to them, but instead help them work through their feelings and questions. One kid liked to be provocative and constantly challenged Spence about his "feminist agenda." But he later came to Spence with a concern about a sexual assault that had happened between two classmates. The boy told Spence that he didn't think the assault was being taken seriously and that the young woman involved didn't feel safe at school. With Spence's encouragement, the boy went to the principal and helped push for more school supports for her.

"I think the success of the program is that we take young men and their feelings seriously," Spence says. "And we teach them how to look at the world and themselves in a different way. We don't tell them what to think, but we teach them critical thinking, and I think that's really a gift." During my earlier visit, Spence had told me how as a kid he had wrestled with the demands placed on him by his father. He was the eldest son and was expected to play sports and "man up." Spence, who is gay, says that ultramacho way of being a guy didn't suit him. "I would have loved to have been in WiseGuyz when I was fourteen. It might have spared me a lot of struggle."

He adds that, for each kid, the process of becoming a man is different—and he doesn't want the program to take traditional ideas of masculinity or manliness off the table. "Being that kind of a manly man is really meaningful to a lot of guys. We just want to let boys know that you can't expect everyone to fit into that box all the time, or even at all." Ultimately, he says, he wants the boys to worry less about acting like a man and think more about acting like themselves.

8

CONCLUSION

Beyond the Boy Box

———

As I write this, at the end of 2017, the news continues to be filled with stories of sexual abuse and harassment. Every day brings new allegations against some powerful man: a Hollywood producer, a celebrity chef, a movie star, a respected journalist, a politician, a Grammy-winning singer, an acclaimed editor, a beloved comedian. These gropers and predators are known as such now because they're famous and because hundreds of women, and a handful of men as well, have bravely come forward with their painful and raw stories. But each abuser represents thousands of other nonfamous men who have crossed lines, who have attempted to control other people's bodies, largely girls' and women's, and then intimidated them into silence.

Raising a boy at a time like this is sobering. We cannot deny the costs of harmful constructions of masculinity, the gendered imbalance in power, and the violence boys and men visit upon girls and women. Just as critically, we can't ignore the degree to which these beliefs and behaviors harm boys and men too. Among young men, the endorsement of stereotypical masculinity, and the expression of male dominance and toughness, is associated with depression, substance abuse, bullying and delinquency, unsafe sex practices, lower rates of sexual pleasure, and intimate-partner abuse. Boys who don't adhere to the rules of masculinity, or who can't or won't live up to them, are also at risk for being bullied, belittled, and ostracized. This extreme, some say toxic, version of manliness is the very definition of destructive. It's empty of empathy, vulnerability, and generosity. And the cruel joke is that the power it confers is fleeting. This sort of masculinity isn't secure or sustaining. It must constantly be buttressed by a simultaneous acting out and shutting down. As an outsider looking in, I see the Man Box as very lonely.

How, then, do we help boys and young men embrace a more inclusive and spacious form of masculinity? As long as the Man Box provides benefits and privilege—approbation, camaraderie, status, power—it will be tough to abandon. After all, if buying into traditional ideas of masculinity was overtly and wholly detrimental, men and boys wouldn't be so willing to conform in the first place. For girls and women, the disadvantages caused by feminine stereotypes are clearer, because they come attached to material inequity. Beliefs that women are weak, hysterical, superficial, manipulative, slutty, and so on are used to justify their continued subordination—from smaller salaries to the limits placed on reproductive choices to the violence they experience. And so, feminism, like other civil rights and social change movements, offers women and girls a tangible "more": more rights, more equality, more opportunities, more justice. Creating a movement to incite men and boys to relinquish their disproportionate power and privilege is a far trickier proposition. It will almost inevitably be perceived by some as a loss—hence the undercurrent of victimhood in so much of the rhetoric of the men's rights movement.

One of the biggest hurdles in this transformation is the ongoing framing of maleness in opposition to femaleness. If one is up, the other must be down. In reality, gender equality is not a zero-sum game. None of us can succeed, or reach our full potential, if we view each other as adversaries. When qualities associated with femaleness and femininity, such as tenderness and vulnerability, are denigrated, not only are women and girls devalued, but men and boys are discouraged from claiming those qualities as theirs too. As long as we perceive women and girls to be less worthy of respect and autonomy, men and boys will exert power over them. The liberation of girls and women from limiting, damaging gender stereotypes is inextricably tied to the liberation of boys and men from their own set of limiting, damaging gender stereotypes. We cannot move forward without each other.

And move forward we must. The social trends are clear. More women are working and becoming economically independent, and men must adapt or fall behind. In some arenas, this is already happening. Just consider how much fatherhood has changed in the past few decades. Modern dads are involved in their children's lives to a degree unimaginable a generation ago. My father loves my sister and me, but like most 1970s dads, he did little hands-on caregiving toward us when we were young. He rarely changed diapers or took us to doctors' appointments. Today, my male friends talk knowledgably about teething and diaper rash, they rearrange their work schedules to accommodate school drop-offs, and my local playground is packed with fathers pushing swings and building sandcastles. While they might not yet be the rule, these men are no longer the exception.

But what comes next? We can start by educating and encouraging boys the way we are educating and encouraging girls. The work of feminism is far from complete in eliminating structural bias, but it's already been transformative. Girls are now widely encouraged to strive for success in school, in sports, in the arts, and in the sciences.

More and more we are telling girls, and more girls now believe, that they can transcend traditional gender roles. They can be strong and emotional, tough and empathetic. While inequality persists (women are still shamefully underrepresented in politics and in tech, for example), there is also a well-articulated distrust of claims about girls' inferiority. Suggestions that girls are inherently incapable of excelling in math, or that their menstrual cycles prevent them from being effective leaders, are met with criticism and a wealth of evidence to prove otherwise.

With boys and men, however, we cling to the idea that the problems and deficits they express, as well as their advantages, must be the result of their biology. Femininity is created, this suggests, but masculinity is a given. By now I hope that I've presented convincing evidence that the social forces and structural inequalities that affect women are the same ones that shape men's status and conditions. By treating boys' troubling behavior as normal and innate, by validating the idea that "boys will be boys," whether it's risk taking or sexual violence, failing grades or social isolation, we fail to address the role that the ideology of masculinity plays in boys' struggles and failings. And crucially in our conversations about the state of boys, we also overlook the ways in which racial and class bias, homophobia and transphobia, ableism and other forms of discrimination influence how adults perceive and treat certain boys—and how that shapes their prospects and self-esteem.

Therefore, just as we have encouraged girls to challenge gender norms and limits, we need to encourage boys to do the same, particularly before adolescence when these attitudes begin to solidify. We need to teach them how to talk about their feelings and give them permission to ask for help. We need to create opportunities for them to be tender and nurturing, expressive and vulnerable. We need to talk to them about sex, love, and communication, but even more than that, we also need to listen and learn from them. We need to look at boys not as a homogenous mass, but rather in all their complexity, individuality, and humanity.

There are plenty of boys and young men already leading this charge. You've met some in these pages. Here's one more example. In October 2017, Erica Brown, a high school student in Guelph, Ontario, wore a T-shirt to school that read "The Future Is Female." The design is deliberately retro. First created in 1975 and sold at Labyris Books, a feminist bookstore in New York City, the shirt was revived and popularized a few years back, and it's been spotted on celebrities such as British model Cara Delevingne and at feminist marches and rallies. It's a cheeky nod to an optimistic moment in feminist herstory at a time when the future feels uncertain and when dystopian stories like *The Handmaid's Tale* cut close to home. For her part, Brown didn't see the shirt as a putdown of men; it was a gift from a feminist cousin, as a positive encouragement to support other women. When she wore the shirt at school, however, she was stopped by a teacher in the hallway and reprimanded. The teacher told her the slogan was inappropriate and could make boys uncomfortable. She asked Brown how she'd feel if a boy wore a shirt that said "The Future Is Male." When a friend of Brown's tried to jump in to protest, the teacher reportedly told her to "stop being sassy."

Like any social-media savvy postmillennial, Brown took her grievance to social media. "Just because the slogan empowers females does not mean that it tears down males," Brown wrote in an open letter to the teacher on Facebook. "The feminist movement aims to bring equality between men and women, not to make women more powerful than men." Brown's response—thoughtful, passionate, and, yes, a little sassy—was a delight. Here was a young woman who had found her voice.

Equally delightful was the response of some of Brown's male classmates. They jumped in to defend her. One told a CBC reporter, "I love the T-shirt. I honestly believe that the future is female. I thought it was really inspiring even to myself, as a guy. I found it empowering." Another boy said, "I don't think it's offensive at all to male students. I think it's a great shirt personally because there is such a need for female representation in a lot of high-ranking positions. It's not demoting males at all. I think it's an awesome shirt." He'd already placed an order for a "The Future Is Female" T-shirt of his own.[1]

This is what the future can look like. One of the most moving aspects of working on this book was talking to so many men and women as well as boys and girls committed to gender equality. They are black, indigenous, Asian, South Asian, white, and Latino; queer, straight, cisgender, and trans; young and old; conservative and liberal; religious and secular. The work of a football coach in Texas in teaching his players about consent and respect for women might not be the same as that of a mom of a transgender boy advocating for the rights of gender-nonconforming children, or that of a sexual health educator in Calgary teaching boys about healthy relationships, or a Cree mother and filmmaker connecting her sons to their culture and traditions, or a yoga teacher in Baltimore mentoring boys of color through mindfulness, but there's much in common in what they do. Each is carving out more space in the gender landscape, and each is helping to raise emotionally healthy and compassionate young men. If we want a world that's better for everyone—safer, more just, more fair and equitable, happier, and less restrictive—then all the rest of us need to do is join them.

ACKNOWLEDGMENTS

Several years ago, Samantha Haywood took me to lunch and told me she thought I had a book in me. At the time, I wasn't sure I agreed, but now, here we are. Such are Sam's superpowers as an agent and a friend: she can charm you into believing you're capable of doing the very thing that scares you most. May all writers have someone as fierce and loyal in their corner.

The unflagging enthusiasm and patience of my Canadian editor Patrick Crean kept this sometimes unruly book (and its sometimes unruly author) on track. I am indebted to him for his faith in *Boys* and to the rest of the terrific team at HarperCollins Canada, especially Allyson Latta, Melissa Nowakowski, and Noelle Zitzer. I am exceedingly grateful to Laura Mazer at Seal Press for bringing me on board. I can't think of a more fitting home for the US version of *Boys* than this venerable feminist press.

As editors and friends, Danielle Groen and Amy Macfarlane have long made my writing better and my thinking sharper. Their feedback on the manuscript, as well as their loving support, was invaluable.

Boys grew out of a story I wrote for the *Walrus* in 2014 about the Calgary Sexual Health Centre's WiseGuyz program, and some of that reporting is featured in Chapter 7. I'm grateful to Blake Spence and the rest of the Wise-Guyz crew, as well as to the wonderful young men in the group, for their early inspiration.

Thank you to all the people who spoke with me for my reporting of *Boys*, who patiently and generously answered my questions, and to the researchers, thinkers, and writers whose work on gender, boys, and masculinity was so critical in shaping my own thoughts. Special thanks for their time to Jermal Alleyne, Michele Chai, Andres Gonzalez, Shaka Licorish and Laura Sygrove, Todd Minerson, Jeff Perera, Jake Pyne, and Richard Van Camp.

Some research and reporting in the chapters on biology, sports, and schooling were drawn from stories of mine that appeared in *Toronto Life*, *Today's Parent*, and *NewYorker.com*, where I was skillfully edited by Mark Pupo, Sarah Fulford, Leah Rumack, Kathryn Hayward, and Jeremy Keehn. As well, much love and gratitude to the smart, funny, and big-hearted sisterhood at *Chatelaine* for giving my writing a regular home.

For emotional sustenance and cheerleading, I am grateful to Tori Allen, Garvia Bailey, Gordon Bowness, Nana aba Duncan, Stacey May Fowles, Lianne George, Christine Giese, Lyndon Goveas, Teva Harrison, Rachel Harry, David Hill, Vandana Kattar-Miller, Joshua Knelman, David Leonard, Lynda Manser, Ioyan Manser-Goveas, Rachel Matlow, Michael Miller, Lyndsay Moffatt, Alexandra Molotkow, Andrea Ridgley, Lori Smith, Angelina Vaz, and Maurice Vellekoop.

This book would not exist at all if not for the enormous love and unwavering confidence of my favorite reader and fabulous wife, Jenn. She talked me through half-baked ideas and messy drafts, kept the bills paid and our son occupied when I needed to devote my attention to writing, and trusted me to share our family's story in these pages. *Boys* is every bit hers as much as it is mine. And finally, to my son, heart of this book and joy of my life: I'm infinitely proud of the boy you are and man you are becoming.

NOTES

A note on sources: Some subjects asked for anonymity to protect their privacy. In these cases, I've stated where pseudonyms, or only first names, are used. Unless otherwise noted, quotes from experts come from interviews I conducted with them in person or on the phone.

PREFACE

1. LaMont Hamilton, "*Five on the Black Hand Side*: Origins and Evolutions of the Dap."
2. Nicky Woolf, "'PUAHate' and 'ForeverAlone': Inside Elliot Rodger's Online Life," *Guardian*, May 30, 2014, http://www.theguardian.com /world/2014/may/30/elliot-rodger-puahate-forever-alone-reddit-forums.
3. Kate Mather and Richard Winton, "Isla Vista Shooting Suspect Vowed 'War on Women,' Sorority," *Los Angeles Times*, May 24, 2014, http:// beta.latimes.com/local/lanow/la-me-ln-isla-vista-shooting-suspect-vowed -war-on-women-sorority-20140524-story.html.
4. Kate Manne, *Down Girl: The Logic of Misogyny*, 77.
5. "Facebook Post Linked to Toronto Van Attack Points to Insular, Misogynistic World of 'Incels.'"
6. Megan Garber, "When *Newsweek* 'Struck Terror in the Hearts of Single Women.'"
7. Catherine Porter, "No Improvement 25 Years After Montreal Massacre," *Toronto Star*, December 6, 2014, http://www.thestar.com/news /insight/2014/12/06/porter_no_improvement_25_years_after_montreal _massacre.html.

8. Kimberlé Crenshaw, "Why Intersectionality Can't Wait," *Washington Post*, September 24, 2015, https://spcs.stanford.edu/sites/default/files/intersectionality_crenshaw.pdf.

9. bell hooks, *The Will to Change: Men, Masculinity, and Love*, 35–39.

10. Hanna Rosin, *The End of Men and the Rise of Women*, 3.

11. *MTV's "Look Different" Gender Bias Survey*, 11.

CHAPTER 1. THE BOY BOX

1. Audrey Smedley and Brian D. Smedley, "Race as Biology Is Fiction, Racism as a Social Problem Is Real: Anthropological and Historical Perspectives on the Social Construction of Race," 16.

2. Haeyoun Park and Iaryna Mykhyalyshyn, "L.G.B.T. People Are More Likely to Be Targets of Hate Crimes than Any Other Minority Group," *New York Times*, June 16, 2016, http://www.nytimes.com/interactive/2016/06/16/us/hate-crimes-against-lgbt.html. See also *Latest Hate Crime Statistics Available*.

3. C. J. Pascoe, *Dude, You're a Fag: Masculinity and Sexuality in High School*, 55.

4. Ibid., 54.

5. Alexander Lu, "How Are the Experiences of Asian American Men Stressful?"; Alexander Lu and Y. Joel Wong, "Stressful Experiences of Masculinity Among U.S.-Born and Immigrant Asian American Men."

6. Oliver S. Wang, "Lin Takes the Weight."

7. Jessica Contrera, "A Year Ago, Ahmed Mohamed Became 'Clock Boy.' Now, He Can't Escape That Moment," *Washington Post*, August 2, 2016, http://www.washingtonpost.com/lifestyle/style/a-year-ago-ahmed-mohamed-became-clock-boy-now-he-cant-escape-that-moment/2016/08/02/2b8650be-484b-11e6-bdb9-701687974517_story.html.

8. Michael Kimmel, "Almost All Violent Extremists Share One Thing: Their Gender," *Guardian*, April 8, 2018, http://www.theguardian.com/world/2018/apr/08/violent-extremists-share-one-thing-gender-michael-kimmel.

9. *Millennials in Adulthood: Detached from Institutions, Networked with Friends*.

10. B. Heilman, G. Barker, and A. Harrison, *The Man Box: A Study on Being a Young Man in the US, UK, and Mexico*, 28.

11. Kim Parker, Juliana Menasce Horowitz, and Renee Stepler, *On Gender Differences, No Consensus on Nature vs. Nurture.*

12. Heilman, Barker, and Harrison, *Man Box*, 28.

13. Ibid., 26.

14. Janelle Jones, "African American and Hispanic Unemployment Rates Are Higher than White Unemployment Rates in Every State at the End of 2017."

15. *Trends in U.S. Corrections.*

16. Christopher Greig, Canadian gender historian at the University of Windsor, in discussion with the author, April 2016.

17. Katie Reilly, "Hillary Clinton Apologizes for 'Superpredator' Remark."

18. Candace Cortiella and Sheldon H. Horowitz, *The State of Learning Disabilities: Facts, Trends and Emerging Issues*, 12.

19. Jelani Cobb, "Between the World and Ferguson."

20. *Children Behind Bars: The Global Overuse of Detention of Children.*

CHAPTER 2. BORN THAT WAY?

1. Thomas D. Shipp et al., "What Factors Are Associated with Parents' Desire to Know the Sex of Their Unborn Child?"

2. Angelique J. A. Kooper et al., "Why Do Parents Prefer to Know the Fetal Sex as Part of Invasive Prenatal Testing?"

3. "This Military Couple's Gender Reveal Blows All Others Away!"

4. Wesley Morris, "The Year We Obsessed over Identity."

5. Annie Murphy Paul, *Origins: How the Nine Months Before Birth Shape the Rest of Our Lives*, 112.

6. Gordon B. Dahl and Enrico Moretti, "The Demand for Sons."

7. Marcelo L. Urquia et al., "Variations in Male-Female Infant Ratios Among Births to Canadian- and Indian-Born Mothers, 1990–2011: A Population-Based Register Study."

8. Mariagiovanna Baccara et al., "Child-Adoption Matching: Preferences for Gender and Race." See also Aarefa Johari, "When It Comes to Adoption, Indian Parents Prefer Girls over Boys."

9. Alexei Quintero Gonzalez and Richard Koestner, "Parental Preference for Sex of Newborn as Reflected in Positive Affect in Birth Announcements."

10. Peggy Orenstein, "What's Wrong with Cinderella?"

11. Emanuella Grinberg, "Target to Move Away from Gender-Based Signs."

12. David Crouch, "Toys R Us's Stockholm Superstore Goes Gender Neutral," *Guardian*, December 23, 2013, https://www.theguardian.com /world/2013/dec/23/toys-r-us-stockholm-gender-neutral.

13. Elizabeth Sweet, "Toys Are More Divided by Gender Now than They Were 50 Years Ago."

14. Elizabeth Sweet, "Guys and Dolls No More?," *New York Times*, December 21, 2012, http://www.nytimes.com/2012/12/23/opinion/sunday /gender-based-toy-marketing-returns.html.

15. Louann Brizendine, *The Female Brain*, 8; Simon Baron-Cohen, *The Essential Difference: The Truth About the Male and Female Brain*, 1.

16. Cordelia Fine, *Delusions of Gender: How Our Minds, Society, and Neurosexism Create Difference*, 178.

17. Lise Eliot, *Pink Brain, Blue Brain: How Small Differences Grow into Troublesome Gaps—and What We Can Do About It*, 14.

18. Jake Pyne, "Gender Independent Kids: A Paradigm Shift in Approaches to Gender Non-conforming Children," 1.

19. Kate Lyons, "Gender Identity Clinic Services Under Strain as Referral Rates Soar," *Guardian*, July 10, 2016, https://www.theguardian.com /society/2016/jul/10/transgender-clinic-waiting-times-patient-numbers -soar-gender-identity-services.

20. S. L. Reisner et al., "Mental Health of Transgender Youth in Care at an Adolescent Urban Community Health Center: A Matched Retrospective Cohort Study."

21. Sheryl Gay Stolberg, "Bathroom Case Puts Transgender Student on National Stage," *New York Times*, February 23, 2017, https://www .nytimes.com/2017/02/23/us/gavin-grimm-transgender-rights-bathroom .html.

22. Camila Domonoske, "17-Year-Old Transgender Boy Wins Texas Girls' Wrestling Championship."

23. Rachel Giese, "What Life Is Like for Transgender Children Now."

24. Jessica Botelho-Urbanski, "Baby Storm Five Years Later: Preschooler on Top of the World," *Toronto Star*, July 11, 2016, https://www.thestar.com /news/gta/2016/07/11/baby-storm-five-years-later-preschooler-on-top -of-the-world.html.

CHAPTER 3. NO HOMO

1. "12-Year-Old Couldn't Begin to Guess Name of Friend Whose House He Visits to Play Xbox."
2. W. M. Bukowski, B. Laursen, and B. Hoza, "The Snowball Effect: Friendship Moderates Escalations in Depressed Affect Among Avoidant and Excluded Children."
3. Richard Brookhiser, "Was Lincoln Gay?," *New York Times*, January 9, 2005, http://www.nytimes.com/2005/01/09/books/review/was-lincoln-gay.html.
4. Vivek Murthy, "Work and the Loneliness Epidemic."
5. Niobe Way, *Deep Secrets: Boys' Friendships and the Crisis of Connection*, 1.
6. Ibid., 97.
7. Ibid., 3.
8. Ibid., 110.
9. Judy Y. Chu, *When Boys Become Boys: Development, Relationships, and Masculinity*, 66.
10. Christopher Ingraham, "Toddlers Have Shot at Least 23 People This Year," *Washington Post*, May 1, 2016, https://www.washingtonpost.com/news/wonk/wp/2016/05/01/toddlers-have-shot-at-least-23-people-this-year.
11. Chu, *When Boys Become Boys*, 143.
12. Eliot, *Pink Brain, Blue Brain*, 84.
13. Way, *Deep Secrets*, 11.

CHAPTER 4. THE BOY CRISIS

1. *From Strengths to Solutions: An Asset-Based Approach to Meeting Community Needs in Brownsville*, 10–11.
2. Winnie Hu and Jonah Bromwich, "A Boy Praises the Principal of His Brooklyn School, and a Fund-Raising Campaign Takes Off," *New York Times*, January 29, 2015, https://www.nytimes.com/2015/02/01/nyregion/a-boy-praises-the-principal-of-his-brooklyn-school-and-a-fund-raising-campaign-takes-off.html.
3. Wendy Sawyer, "Youth Confinement: The Whole Pie."
4. *Honouring the Truth, Reconciling for the Future: Summary of the Final Report of the Truth and Reconciliation Commission of Canada*, 4.

5. Nikole Hannah-Jones, "Choosing a School for My Daughter in a Segregated City."

6. Seth Gershenson et al., "The Long-Run Impacts of Same-Race Teachers," 33–35.

7. Katy Reckdahl, "Training More Black Men to Become Teachers."

8. Walter S. Gilliam et al., *Do Early Educators' Implicit Biases Regarding Sex and Race Relate to Behavior Expectations and Recommendations of Preschool Expulsions and Suspensions? A Research Study Brief*, 3.

9. Daniel McGraw, "How Should Tamir Rice Be Remembered?"

10. Gilliam, *Early Educators' Implicit Biases*, 15.

11. Ibid., 7.

12. "Ethnicity Facts and Figures."

13. Lisa Naccarato, "Almost Half of TDSB Students Expelled over Last 5 Years Are Black, Report Says."

14. Eyal Press, "Do Immigrants Make Us Safer?"

15. Emma Brown, "DC Charter Schools Expel Students at Far Higher Rates than Traditional Public Schools," *Washington Post*, January 5, 2013, https://www.washingtonpost.com/local/education/dc-charter -schools-expel-students-at-far-higher-rates-than-traditional-public -schools/2013/01/05/e155e4bc-44a9-11e2-8061-253bccfc7532_story .html.

16. Elizabeth Green, "The Charter School Crusader."

17. Emily Bazelon, *Sticks and Stones: Defeating the Culture of Bullying and Rediscovering the Power of Character and Empathy*, 299.

18. Jim Rankin and Sandro Contenta, "Suspended Sentences: Forging a School-to-Prison Pipeline?," *Toronto Star*, June 6, 2009, https://www .thestar.com/news/gta/2009/06/06/suspended_sentences_forging_a _schooltoprison_pipeline.html.

19. "Attention Deficit Hyperactivity Disorder (ADHD): Data & Statistics." See also National Center for Health Statistics, "Health, United States, 2016: With Chartbook on Long-Term Trends in Health."

20. "Autism Spectrum Disorder (ASD): Data & Statistics."

21. S. Sandin et al., "Autism Risk Associated with Parental Age and with Increasing Difference in Age Between the Parents."

22. Ryan D'Agostino, "The Drugging of the American Boy."

23. *Civil Rights Data Collection: Data Snapshot (School Discipline)*.

24. Rachel Giese, "Is There a Better Way to Integrate Kids with Special Needs into Classrooms?"

25. Christina Hoff Sommers, "The War on Boys."

26. Christina Hoff Sommers, "School Has Become Too Hostile to Boys."

27. Claire Cain Miller, "A Disadvantaged Start Hurts Boys More than Girls," *New York Times*, October 22, 2015, https://www.nytimes.com /2015/10/22/upshot/a-disadvantaged-start-hurts-boys-more-than-girls .html.

28. Raj Chetty et al., "Race and Opportunity in the United States."

29. Cara Okopny, "Why Jimmy Isn't Failing: The Myth of the Boy Crisis." See also Sara Mead, *The Evidence Suggests Otherwise: The Truth About Boys and Girls*.

30. Amie Presley and Robert S. Brown, *Portuguese-Speaking Students in the TDSB: An Overview*. See also Louise Brown, "Fight Portuguese Dropout Rate, School Trustees Say," *Toronto Star,* March 8, 2011, https://www .thestar.com/news/world/2011/03/08/fight_portuguese_dropout_rate _school_trustees_say.html.

31. David Pereira, "Dropping Out or Opting Out? A Qualitative Study on How Young Men of Portuguese Ancestry in Toronto Perceive Masculinity and How This Informs Educational Attainment," 67–81.

32. Ibid., 78.

33. Donna Martinez, "School Culture and American Indian Educational Outcomes."

34. Doris F. Chang and Amy Demyan, "Teachers' Stereotypes of Asian, Black, and White Students."

35. Carolyn Chen, "Asians: Too Smart for Their Own Good?," *New York Times*, December 19, 2012, http://www.nytimes.com/2012/12/20 /opinion/asians-too-smart-for-their-own-good.html. See also Kat Chow, "'Model Minority' Myth Again Used as a Racial Wedge Between Asians and Blacks."

36. Donna St. George, "How Mindfulness Practices Are Changing an Inner-City School," *Washington Post*, November 13, 2016, https://www .washingtonpost.com/local/education/how-mindfulness-practices-are

-changing-an-inner-city-school/2016/11/13/7b4a274a-a833-11e6-ba59
-a7d93165c6d4_story.html.

CHAPTER 5. MAN UP

1. "Extinct Hockey."
2. Rachel Giese, "Puckheads: Inside the Crazed Arenas of the GTHL."
3. *How Many ER Visits for Sport-Related Brain Injuries Receive a Concussion Diagnosis?*
4. "Traumatic Brain Injury & Concussions."
5. Patrick Hruby, "The Choice."
6. Bruce Kelley and Carl Carchia, "Hey Data Data—Swing!"
7. Michael S. Kimmel, *Guyland: The Perilous World Where Boys Become Men*, 125.
8. Bruce Kidd, "Sports and Masculinity." See also Bruce Kidd, "Muscular Christianity and Value-Centred Sport: The Legacy of Tom Brown in Canada."
9. Richard Holt, *Sport and the British: A Modern History*, 76.
10. Ken McLeod, *We Are the Champions: The Politics of Sport and Popular Music*, 46.
11. Arnaldo Testi, "The Gender of Reform Politics: Theodore Roosevelt and the Culture of Masculinity."
12. "American Football."
13. Sally Jenkins, *The Real All Americans*, 2.
14. "Ending the Legacy of Racism in Sports & the Era of Harmful 'Indian' Sports Mascots."
15. Kathleen E. Miller, "Sport-Related Identities and the 'Toxic Jock.'"
16. Rachel Giese, "How Energy Drink Companies Prey on Male Insecurities."
17. R. F. Levant et al., "Moderated Mediation of the Relationships Between Masculinity Ideology, Outcome Expectations, and Energy Drink Use."
18. Hilary Stout, "Selling the Young on 'Gaming Fuel,'" *New York Times*, May 19, 2015, https://www.nytimes.com/2015/05/20/business/energy -drink-industry-under-scrutiny-looks-to-gamers-to-keep-sales-surging .html.
19. Ken Belson, "Not Safe for Children? Football's Leaders Make Drastic Changes to Youth Game," *New York Times*, January 31, 2017, https://

www.nytimes.com/2017/01/31/sports/youth-football-wants-to-save-the -game-by-shrinking-it.html.

20. Sean Gregory, "Donald Trump Dismisses His 'Locker-Room Talk' as Normal. Athletes Say It's Not," *Time*, October 11, 2016, http://time.com /4526039/donald-trump-locker-room-athletes/. See also: Mahita Gajanan, "Melania Trump Says Donald's Comments in Leaked Video Were 'Boy Talk'," *Time*, October 17, 2016, http://time.com/4534216/melania -donald-trump-billy-bush-boy-talk/.

21. "Not in My Locker Room: DeAndre Levy of the Detroit Lions Speaks Out," *Edge of Sports*, episode 63, October 15, 2016, http://www .edgeofsportspodcast.com/post/151838004210/not-in-my-locker-room -deandre-levy-of-the-detroit.

22. DeAndre Levy, "Man Up," *The Players' Tribune*, April 27, 2016, http:// www.theplayerstribune.com/deandre-levy-sexual-assault-awareness.

23. Nancy Kaffer, "8 Years into Tests of Abandoned Rape Kits, Worthy Works for Justice," *Detroit Free Press*, December 17, 2017, https://www.freep .com/story/opinion/columnists/nancy-kaffer/2017/12/17/rape-kit-detroit /953083001/.

24. Sarah Kogod, "Ohio State LB Jerome Baker Wants to Change How Athletes Talk about Sexual Violence," *SB Nation*, September 17, 2015, http://www.sbnation.com/2015/9/17/9105829/ohio-state-jerome-baker -is-changing-athletes-sexual-assault-2015.

25. Michael Sokolove, "For Trump, a Different Kind of 'Locker Room Talk,'" *New York Times*, September 29, 2017, https://www.nytimes.com/2017/09 /29/opinion/trump-nfl-protest.html.

26. Julie Turkewitz, "Protest Started by Colin Kaepernick Spreads to High School Students," *New York Times*, October 3, 2016, https://www .nytimes.com/2016/10/04/us/national-anthem-protests-high-schools.html.

27. Sarah Mervosh, "New Baylor Lawsuit Alleges 52 Rapes by Football Players in 4 Years, 'Show 'Em a Good Time' Culture," *Dallas News*, January 27, 2017, https://www.dallasnews.com/news/baylor/2017/01/27 /new-baylor-lawsuit-describes-show-em-good-time-culture-cites-52-rapes -football-players-4-years.

28. Matthias Gafni, "De La Salle Sex Assault Case: Suspect's Father, a Registered Sex Offender, Defends Son," *East Bay Times*, December 1,

2016, http://www.eastbaytimes.com/2016/12/01/victim-of-alleged
-de-la-salle-sex-assault-speaks-out.

29. Michael E. Miller, "'A Steep Price to Pay for 20 Minutes of Action':
Dad Defends Stanford Sex Offender," *Washington Post*, June 6, 2016,
https://www.washingtonpost.com/news/morning-mix/wp/2016/06/06
/a-steep-price-to-pay-for-20-minutes-of-action-dad-defends-stanford-sex
-offender.

30. Juliet Macur and Nate Schweber, "Rape Case Unfolds on Web and
Splits City," *New York Times*, December 16, 2012, http://nytimes.com
/2012/12/17/sports/high-school-football-rape-case-unfolds-online
-and-divides-steubenville-ohio.html.

31. Charles Scudder, "Not in My Locker Room: Texas HS Football Coaches
Give Players the Trump Talk," *Dallas News*, October 2016, https://www
.dallasnews.com/life/life/2016/10/11/locker-room-texas-hs-football
-coaches-give-players-trump-talk.

32. Cassandra Pollock, "Study: A Quarter of Texas Public Schools No Longer
Teach Sex Ed," *Texas Tribune*, February 14, 2017, https://www.texastribune
.org/2017/02/14/texas-public-schools-largely-teach-abstinence-only-sex
-education-repor/.

33. J. P. Calzo et al., "Physical Activity Disparities in Heterosexual and
Sexual Minority Youth Ages 12–22 Years Old: Roles of Childhood
Gender Nonconformity and Athletic Self-Esteem."

34. Jessica Taff and Joseph Auriemma, "Out on the Field: Former NFL Player
Wade Davis Opens Up."

35. Wallis Snowdon, "Ending Homophobia in Hockey Starts in the Locker
Room, Edmonton Researcher Says."

CHAPTER 6. GAME BOYS

1. Dave Lee, "*Grand Theft Auto*: One of Britain's Finest Cultural Exports?"

2. Andre Mayer, "*GTA5*: How *Grand Theft Auto* Has Changed the Gaming
World."

3. Ben DeVane and Kurt D. Squire, "The Meaning of Race and Violence in
Grand Theft Auto: San Andreas."

4. Greg Toppo, "Do Video Games Inspire Violent Behavior?"

5. Melissa Sickmund and Charles Puzzanchera, eds., *Juvenile Offenders and Victims: 2014 National Report.*

6. Kate Summerscale, "Penny Dreadfuls: The Victorian Equivalent of Video Games," *Guardian*, April 30, 2016, https://www.theguardian.com/books /2016/apr/30/penny-dreadfuls-victorian-equivalent-video-games-kate -summerscale-wicked-boy.

7. Marilyn Manson, "Columbine: Whose Fault Is It?"

8. Kenneth B. Kidd, *Making American Boys: Boyology and the Feral Tale*, 7.

9. Darnell Hunt et al., "The Hollywood Diversity Report, 2018." See also Marina Fang, "Audiences Want Diversity in Hollywood. Hollywood's Been Slow to Get the Message."

10. Janice McCabe et al., "Gender in Twentieth-Century Children's Books: Patterns of Disparity in Titles and Central Characters."

11. Kristian Wilson, "How Diverse Is Children's Literature?"

12. Marla E. Eisenberg, Melanie Wall, and Dianne Neumark-Sztainer, "Muscle-Enhancing Behaviors Among Adolescent Girls and Boys."

13. Laura A. Parker, "The Cult of PewDiePie: How a Swedish Gamer Became YouTube's Biggest Star."

14. Chris O'Connell, "How Dude Perfect Makes Child's Play Hard Work."

15. Arthur Chu, "Your Princess Is in Another Castle: Misogyny, Entitlement, and Nerds," *Daily Beast*, May 27, 2014. https://www.thedailybeast .com/your-princess-is-in-another-castle-misogyny-entitlement-and -nerds-1.

16. T. L. Andrews, "Silicon Valley's Gender Gap Is the Result of Computer-Game Marketing 20 Years Ago."

17. Clive Thompson, *Wired* contributor and author, in discussion with the author, December 2016.

18. Jesse Singal, "A New Book Argues That the Concerns over Violent Video Games Are a Moral Panic."

19. Jacques Legault, "Why Parents Need to Become Gamers."

20. Amanda Lenhart, *Teens, Social Media & Technology Overview, 2015.*

21. Alana Massey, "Hold Your Laughter: Men Could Learn Something from One Direction."

22. Sun Jung, *Korean Masculinities and Transcultural Consumption.*

CHAPTER 7. DROPPING THE MASCULINITY MASK

1. Dugan Arnett, "Daisy Coleman, Teen at Center of Maryville Sexual Assault Case, Is Recovering After Suicide Attempt," *Kansas City Star*, January 7, 2014, http://www.kansascity.com/news/special-reports /maryville/article335557/Daisy-Coleman-teen-at-center-of-Maryville -sexual-assault-case-is-recovering-after-suicide-attempt.html.

2. Nina Burleigh, "Sexting, Shame and Suicide."

3. Rosie Swash, "Is Hacktivism on Behalf of Rehtaeh Parsons a Revolution in Rape Campaigning?," *Guardian*, April 13, 2017, https://www.theguardian .com/lifeandstyle/2013/apr/15/hacktivism-rehtaeh-parsons-rape.

4. Alicia W. Stewart, "#IamJada: When Abuse Becomes a Teen Meme."

5. Wendy Gillis, "Rehtaeh Parsons: Halifax Community Mourns Bullied Teen," *Toronto Star*, April 13, 2013, https://www.thestar.com/news /canada/2013/04/13/rehtaeh_parsons_halifax_community_mourns _bullied_teen.html.

6. Kristin Rushowy, "Sexual Harassment Common in High Schools, Study Finds," *Toronto Star*, February 7, 2008, https://www.thestar.com/news /gta/2008/02/07/sexual_harassment_common_in_high_schools_study _finds.html.

7. L. Musu-Gillette et al., *Indicators of School Crime and Safety, 2016*, 122.

8. Dorothy L. Espalage et al., "Longitudinal Associations Among Bullying, Homophobic Teasing and Sexual Violence Perpetration Among Middle School Students."

9. *Report on Sexually Transmitted Infections in Canada, 2013–2014.*

10. Rachel Giese, "The Talk."

11. Pandora Pound, Rebecca Langford, and Rona Campbell, "What Do Young People Think About Their School-Based Sex and Relationship Education? A Qualitative Synthesis of Young People's Views and Experiences."

12. *Remise du rapport relatif à l'éducation à la sexualité aux ministres Najat Vallaud-Belkacem et Laurence Rossignol.*

13. L. D. Lindberg, I. Maddow-Zimet, and H. Boonstra, "Changes in Adolescents' Receipt of Sex Education, 2006–2013."

14. Ammie Feijoo, *Adolescent Sexual Health in Europe and the United States.*

15. Laurie Abraham, "Teaching Good Sex."

16. Miranda A. H. Horvath et al., *Basically...Porn Is Everywhere*, 39.
17. Ibid., 67.
18. Saskia de Melker, "The Case for Starting Sex Education in Kindergarten."
19. Amy T. Schalet, "Beyond Abstinence and Risk: A New Paradigm for Adolescent Sexual Health."
20. Amy T. Schalet, "Must We Fear Adolescent Sexuality?"
21. Amy T. Schalet, "Why Boys Need to Have Conversations About Emotional Intimacy in Classrooms."
22. *Boys Returning to Themselves: Healthy Masculinities and Adolescent Boys.*

CHAPTER 8. CONCLUSION

1. Marisa Meltzer, "A Feminist T-Shirt Resurfaces from the '70s," *New York Times*, November 18, 2015, https://www.nytimes.com/2015/11/19/fashion/a-feminist-t-shirt-resurfaces-from-the-70s.html. See also Muriel Draaisma, "'The Future Is Female': T-shirt Worn by Student Sparks Discussion at Guelph High School."

BIBLIOGRAPHY

Abraham, Laurie. "Teaching Good Sex." *New York Times Magazine*, November 16, 2011. http://www.nytimes.com/2011/11/20/magazine /teaching-good-sex.html.

"American Football." Season 13, episode 4, of *Radiolab*. http://www.radiolab .org/story/football.

Andrews, T. L. "Silicon Valley's Gender Gap Is the Result of Computer-Game Marketing 20 Years Ago." Quartz, February 16, 2017. https://qz.com /911737/silicon-valleys-gender-gap-is-the-result-of-computer-game -marketing-20-years-ago/.

Assembly of First Nations. *2011 AFN School Survey Results*. Ottawa: Assembly of First Nations, 2012. http://www.afn.ca/uploads/files/events /afn-survey-results.pdf.

"Attention Deficit Hyperactivity Disorder (ADHD): FastStats." National Center for Health Statistics, Centers for Disease Control and Prevention. https://www.cdc.gov/nchs/fastats/adhd.htm.

"Autism Spectrum Disorder (ASD): Data & Statistics." Centers for Disease Control and Prevention. https://www.cdc.gov/ncbddd/autism/data.html.

Baccara, Mariagiovanna, Allan Collard-Wexler, Leonardo Felli, and Leeat Yariv. "Child-Adoption Matching: Preferences for Gender and Race." *American Economic Journal: Applied Economics* 6, no. 3 (2014). http:// people.hss.caltech.edu/~lyariv/papers/Adoption.pdf.

Baron-Cohen, Simon. *The Essential Difference: The Truth About the Male and Female Brain*. New York: Basic Books, 2003.

Bazelon, Emily. *Sticks and Stones: Defeating the Culture of Bullying and Rediscovering the Power of Character and Empathy*. New York: Random House, 2013.

Boys Returning to Themselves: Healthy Masculinities and Adolescent Boys. WiseGuyz Research Report 3. Calgary: Calgary Sexual Health Centre, May 2016. https://www.calgarysexualhealth.ca/media/WiseGuyz-Research -Report-3-Boys-Returning-to-Themselves.pdf.

Bradlow, Josh, Fay Bartram, April Guasp, and Vasanti Jadva. *School Report: The Experiences of Lesbian, Gay, Bi and Trans Young People in Britain's Schools in 2017.* Cambridge: Stonewall and the Centre for Family Research at the University of Cambridge, 2017. http://www.stonewall.org .uk/sites/default/files/the_school_report_2017.pdf.

Brizendine, Louann. *The Female Brain.* New York: Morgan Road Books, 2006.

Brown, R., L. Newton, and G. Tam. "The Toronto District School Board's Student Group Overviews: Aboriginal Heritage, Afghan, Portuguese- Speaking, Somali-Speaking, and Spanish-Speaking Students." Research Report, no. 14/15-31. Toronto: Toronto District School Board, 2015.

Bukowski, W., B. Laursen, and B. Hoza. "The Snowball Effect: Friendship Moderates Escalations in Depressed Affect Among Avoidant and Excluded Children." *Development and Psychopathology* 22, no. 4 (2010): 749–757.

Burleigh, Nina. "Sexting, Shame and Suicide." *Rolling Stone*, September 17, 2013. https://www.rollingstone.com/culture/news/sexting-shame-and -suicide-20130917.

Calzo, J. P., A. L. Roberts, H. L. Corliss, E. A. Blood, E. Kroshus, and S. B. Austin. "Physical Activity Disparities in Heterosexual and Sexual Minority Youth Ages 12–22 Years Old: Roles of Childhood Gender Nonconformity and Athletic Self-Esteem." *Annals of Behavioral Medicine* 47, no. 1 (2014): 17–27.

Canada, Geoffrey. *Reaching Up for Manhood: Transforming the Lives of Boys in America.* Boston: Beacon Press, 1998.

Chang, Doris F., and Amy Demyan. "Teachers' Stereotypes of Asian, Black, and White Students." *School Psychology Quarterly* 22, no. 2 (2007): 91–114.

Chetty, Raj, Nathaniel Hendren, Maggie R. Jones, and Sonya R. Porter. "Race and Opportunity in the United States." Equality of Opportunity Project, March 2018. http://www.equality-of-opportunity.org/assets/documents /race_paper.pdf.

Children Behind Bars: The Global Overuse of Detention of Children. New York: Human Rights Watch World Report, 2016. https://www.hrw.org /world-report/2016/children-behind-bars.

Chow, Kat. "'Model Minority' Myth Again Used as a Racial Wedge Between Asians and Blacks." On *Code Switch: Race and Identity, Remixed*. NPR, April 19, 2017. http://www.npr.org/sections/codeswitch/2017/04/19 /524571669/model-minority-myth-again-used-as-a-racial-wedge -between-asians-and-blacks.

Chu, Judy Y. *When Boys Become Boys: Development, Relationships, and Masculinity*. New York: New York University Press, 2014.

Civil Rights Data Collection: Data Snapshot (School Discipline). Washington, DC: US Department of Education Office for Civil Rights, March 21, 2014. https://www2.ed.gov/about/offices/list/ocr/docs/crdc-discipline -snapshot.pdf.

Cobb, Jelani. "Between the World and Ferguson." *New Yorker*, August 26, 2014. https://www.newyorker.com/news/news-desk/world-ferguson.

Corbett, Ken. *Boyhoods: Rethinking Masculinities*. New Haven, CT: Yale University Press, 2009.

Cortiella, Candace, and Sheldon H. Horowitz. *The State of Learning Disabilities: Facts, Trends and Emerging Issues*. New York: National Center for Learning Disabilities, 2014.

Cross, Allison. "'Not a Time of Condemnation': Family Says Goodbye to Rehtaeh Parsons as Probe into Suicide Reopens." *National Post*, April 13, 2013. http://news.nationalpost.com/news/canada/not-a-time-of -condemnation-rehtaeh-parsons.

Cullen, Dave. *Columbine*. New York: Twelve, 2010.

D'Agostino, Ryan. "The Drugging of the American Boy." *Esquire*, April 2014. http://www.esquire.com/news-politics/a32858/drugging-of-the-american -boy-0414.

Dahl, Gordon B., and Enrico Moretti. "The Demand for Sons." *Review of Economic Studies* 75 (2008): 1185–1120. http://eml.berkeley.edu/~moretti /sons.pdf.

de Melker, Saskia. "The Case for Starting Sex Education in Kindergarten." *PBS NewsHour*, May 27, 2015. https://www.pbs.org/newshour/health /spring-fever.

DeVane, Ben, and Kurt D. Squire. "The Meaning of Race and Violence in *Grand Theft Auto: San Andreas*." *Games and Culture* 3, nos. 3–4 (2008): 264–285. https://doi.org/10.1177/1555412008317308.

Domonoske, Camila. "17-Year-Old Transgender Boy Wins Texas Girls' Wrestling Championship." NPR, February 27, 2017. https://www.npr.org /sections/thetwo-way/2017/02/27/517491492/17-year-old-transgender -boy-wins-texas-girls-wrestling-championship.

Draaisma, Muriel. "'The Future Is Female': T-Shirt Worn by Student Sparks Discussion at Guelph High School." *CBC News*, October 20, 2017, http:// www.cbc.ca/news/canada/kitchener-waterloo/the-future-is-female-shirt -controversy-guelph-high-school-1.4364618.

Eisenberg, Marla E., Melanie Wall, and Dianne Neumark-Sztainer. "Muscle-Enhancing Behaviors Among Adolescent Girls and Boys." *Pediatrics* 130, no. 6 (2012): 1019–1026. https://doi.org/10.1542/peds.2012-0095.

Eliot, Lise. *Pink Brain, Blue Brain: How Small Differences Grow into Troublesome Gaps—and What We Can Do About It*. New York: Houghton Mifflin Harcourt, 2009.

"Ending the Legacy of Racism in Sports & the Era of Harmful 'Indian' Sports Mascots." National Congress of American Indians, October 2013. http:// www.ncai.org/resources/ncai-publications/Ending_the_Legacy_of_Racism .pdf.

EQAO's Provincial Elementary School Report, 2016. Toronto: Education Quality and Accountability Office, September 21, 2016. http://www.eqao .com/en/assessments/results/assessment-docs-elementary/provincial-report -elementary-2016.pdf.

Espalage, D. L., K. C. Basile, L. De La Rue, and M. E. Hamburger. "Longitudinal Associations Among Bullying, Homophobic Teasing and Sexual Violence Perpetration Among Middle School Students." *Journal of Interpersonal Violence* 30, no. 14 (2015): 2541–2561.

"Ethnicity Facts and Figures." UK government, October 10, 2017. https:// www.ethnicity-facts-figures.service.gov.uk/education-skills-and-training /absence-and-exclusions/pupil-exclusions/latest.

"Extinct Hockey." Episode 15 of *Surprisingly Awesome*, Gimlet Media, June 14, 2016. https://gimletmedia.com/episode/15-extinct-hockey.

"Facebook Post Linked to Toronto Van Attack Points to Insular, Misogynistic World of 'Incels.'" *CBC News*, April 25, 2018. http://www.cbc.ca/news /canada/toronto/what-is-an-incel-toronto-van-attack-explainer-alek -minassian-1.4633893.

Faludi, Susan. *Backlash: The Undeclared War Against American Women*. New York: Broadway Books, 1991.

Fang, Marina. "Audiences Want Diversity In Hollywood. Hollywood's Been Slow to Get the Message." *HuffPost*, February 27, 2018. https://www .huffingtonpost.ca/entry/hollywood-diversity-study-black-panther_us _5a954898e4b0699553cc3cc8.

Feijoo, Ammie. *Adolescent Sexual Health in Europe and the United States*. 4th ed. Updated by Sue Alford and Deb Hauser. Washington, DC: Advocates for Youth, March 2011. http://www.advocatesforyouth.org /storage/advfy/documents/adolescent_sexual_health_in_europe_and_the _united_states.pdf.

Ferguson, Ann Arnett. *Bad Boys: Public Schools in the Making of Black Masculinity*. Ann Arbor: University of Michigan Press, 2000.

Fields, Errol Lamont, Laura M. Bogart, Katherine C. Smith, David J. Malebranche, Jonathan Ellen, and Mark A. Schuster. "I Always Felt I Had to Prove My Manhood: Homosexuality, Masculinity, Gender Role Strain, and HIV Risk Among Young Black Men Who Have Sex with Men." *American Journal of Public Health* 105, no. 1 (2015): 122–131. https:// www.ncbi.nlm.nih.gov/pmc/articles/PMC4265897.

Fine, Cordelia. *Delusions of Gender: How Our Minds, Society, and Neurosexism Create Difference*. New York: W. W. Norton, 2010.

Flicker, Sarah, Susan Flynn, June Larkin, Robb Travers, Adrian Guta, Jason Pole, and Crystal Layne. *Sexpress: The Toronto Teen Survey Report*. Toronto: Planned Parenthood Toronto, 2009.

From Strengths to Solutions: An Asset-Based Approach to Meeting Community Needs in Brownsville. New York: Citizens' Committee for Children of New York, 2017. https://www.cccnewyork.org/wp-content/uploads/2017 /03/CCC-Brownsville_5_8_A.pdf.

Gajanan, Mahita. "Melania Trump Says Donald's Comments in Leaked Video Were 'Boy Talk.'" *Time*, October 17, 2016. http://time.com/4534216 /melania-donald-trump-billy-bush-boy-talk.

Garber, Megan. "When *Newsweek* 'Struck Terror in the Hearts of Single Women.'" *Atlantic*, June 2, 2016. https://www.theatlantic.com /entertainment/archive/2016/06/more-likely-to-be-killed-by-a-terrorist -than-to-get-married/485171.

Bibliography

Gershenson, Seth, Cassandra M. D. Hart, Constance A. Lindsay, and Nicholas W. Papageorge. "The Long-Run Impacts of Same-Race Teachers." Bonn, Germany: Institute of Labor Economics, March 2017. http://ftp.iza.org /dp10630.pdf.

Giese, Rachel. "How Energy Drink Companies Prey on Male Insecurities." NewYorker.com, November 28, 2015. http://www.newyorker.com/business /currency/how-energy-drink-companies-prey-on-male-insecurities.

———. "Is There a Better Way to Integrate Kids with Special Needs into Classrooms?" Today's Parent, April 12, 2017. https://www.todaysparent .com/family/special-needs/is-there-a-better-way-to-integrate-kids-with -special-needs-into-classrooms.

———. "Puckheads: Inside the Crazed Arenas of the GTHL." Toronto Life, February 4, 2015. https://torontolife.com/city/gthl-puckheads.

———. "The Talk." Walrus, April 30, 2014. https://thewalrus.ca/the-talk.

———. "What Life Is Like for Transgender Children Now." Today's Parent, August 19, 2015. https://www.todaysparent.com/family/parenting/what -life-is-like-for-transgender-children-now.

Gilliam, Walter S., Angela N. Maupin, Chin R. Reyes, Maria Accavitti, and Frederick Shic. Do Early Educators' Implicit Biases Regarding Sex and Race Relate to Behavior Expectations and Recommendations of Preschool Expulsions and Suspensions? A Research Study Brief. New Haven, CT: Yale Child Study Center, September 28, 2016.

Gladwell, Malcolm. Outliers: The Story of Success. New York: Back Bay Books, 2011.

Gonzalez, Alexei Quintero, and Richard Koestner. "Parental Preference for Sex of Newborn as Reflected in Positive Affect in Birth Announcements." Sex Roles 52 (2005): 407. https://doi.org/10.1007/s11199-005-2683-4.

Green, Elizabeth. "The Charter School Crusader." Atlantic, January–February 2018. https://www.theatlantic.com/magazine/archive/2018/01/success -academy-charter-schools-eva-moskowitz/546554.

Greig, Christopher J. Ontario Boys: Masculinity and the Idea of Boyhood in Postwar Ontario, 1945–1960. Waterloo: Wilfred Laurier University Press, 2014.

Gregory, Sean. "Donald Trump Dismisses His 'Locker-Room Talk' as Normal. Athletes Say It's Not." Time, October 11, 2016. http://time.com/4526039 /donald-trump-locker-room-athletes.

Grinberg, Emanuella. "Target to Move Away from Gender-Based Signs." CNN, August 8, 2015. http://www.cnn.com/2015/08/08/living/gender-based-signs-target-feat/index.html.

Gurian, Michael. *The Wonder of Boys: What Parents, Mentors and Educators Can Do to Shape Young Boys into Exceptional Men.* New York: TarcherPerigee, 2006.

Hallowell, Edward M. and John J. Ratey. *Delivered from Distraction: Getting the Most out of Life with Attention Deficit Disorder.* New York: Ballantine, 2005.

———. *Driven to Distraction (Revised): Recognizing and Coping with Attention Deficit Disorder.* New York: Anchor, 2011.

Hamilton, LaMont. "*Five on the Black Hand Side*: Origins and Evolutions of the Dap." *Folklife*, September 22, 2014. https://folklife.si.edu/talkstory/2014/five-on-the-black-hand-sideorigins-and-evolutions-of-the-dap.

Handelman, Kenny. *Attention Difference Disorder: How to Turn Your ADHD Child or Teen's Differences into Strengths in Seven Simple Steps.* New York: Morgan James, 2011.

Hannah-Jones, Nikole. "Choosing a School for My Daughter in a Segregated City." *New York Times Magazine*, June 9, 2016.

Heilman, B., G. Barker, and A. Harrison. *The Man Box: A Study on Being a Young Man in the US, UK, and Mexico.* Washington, DC, and London: Promundo-US and Unilever, 2017. https://promundoglobal.org/resources/man-box-study-young-man-us-uk-mexico.

Herman, Jody L., Andrew R. Flores, Taylor N. T. Brown, Bianca D. M. Wilson, and Kerith J. Conron. "Age of Individuals Who Identify as Transgender in the United States." Los Angeles: Williams Institute at the UCLA School of Law, January 2017. https://williamsinstitute.law.ucla.edu/wp-content/uploads/TransAgeReport.pdf.

Holt, Richard. *Sport and the British: A Modern History.* Oxford: Clarendon Press, 1990.

Honouring the Truth, Reconciling for the Future: Summary of the Final Report of the Truth and Reconciliation Commission of Canada. Winnipeg: Truth and Reconciliation Commission of Canada, 2015.

hooks, bell. *The Will to Change: Men, Masculinity, and Love.* New York: Washington Square Press, 2004.

Horvath, Miranda A. H., Llian Alys, Kristina Massey, Afroditi Pina, Mia Scally, and Joanna R. Adler. *Basically…Porn Is Everywhere*. London: Office of the Children's Commissioner, 2013. http://www.mdx.ac.uk/__data/assets /pdf_file/0026/48545/BasicallyporniseverywhereReport.pdf.

How Many ER Visits for Sport-Related Brain Injuries Receive a Concussion Diagnosis? Ottawa: Canadian Institute for Health Information, July 26, 2016. https://www.cihi.ca/en/how-many-er-visits-for-sport-related-brain -injuries-receive-a-concussion-diagnosis.

Hruby, Patrick. "The Choice." *Sports on Earth*, November 13, 2013. http:// www.sportsonearth.com/article/63895452.

Hunt, Darnell, Ana-Christina Ramón, Michael Tran, Amberia Sargent, and Debanjan Roychoudhury. "The Hollywood Diversity Report, 2018." UCLA College of Social Sciences, 2018. https://socialsciences.ucla.edu /wp-content/uploads/2018/02/UCLA-Hollywood-Diversity-Report-2018 -2-27-18.pdf.

Innes, Robert Alexander, and Kim Anderson, eds. *Indigenous Men and Masculinities: Legacies, Identities, Regeneration*. Winnipeg: University of Manitoba Press, 2015.

Jenkins, Sally. *The Real All Americans*. New York: Penguin Random House, 2008.

Johari, Aarefa. "When It Comes to Adoption, Indian Parents Prefer Girls over Boys." *Dawn*, August 4, 2015. http://www.dawn.com/news/1198361.

Jones, Janelle. "African American and Hispanic Unemployment Rates Are Higher than White Unemployment Rates in Every State at the End of 2017." Economic Policy Institute Report, February 20, 2018. https://www .epi.org/files/pdf/141486.pdf.

Jordan, Benjamin René. *Modern Manhood and the Boy Scouts of America: Citizenship, Race, and the Environment*. Chapel Hill: University of North Carolina Press, 2016.

Jung, Sun. *Korean Masculinities and Transcultural Consumption*. Hong Kong: Hong Kong University Press, 2011.

Kelley, Bruce, and Carl Carchia. "Hey Data Data—Swing!" *ESPN the Magazine*, July 11, 2013. http://www.espn.com/espn/story/_/id/9469252/hidden -demographics-youth-sports-espn-magazine.

Kidd, Bruce. "Muscular Christianity and Value-Centred Sport: The Legacy of Tom Brown in Canada." *Sport in Society: Cultures, Commerce, Media,*

Politics 16, no. 4 (2013): 405–415. https://doi.org/10.1080/17430437.201
3.785752.

———. "Sports and Masculinity." *Sport in Society: Cultures, Commerce, Media, Politics* 16, no. 4 (2013): 553–564. http://dx.doi.org/10.1080/1743
0437.2013.785757.

Kidd, Kenneth B. *Making American Boys: Boyology and the Feral Tale.* Minneapolis: University of Minnesota Press, 2004.

Kimmel, Michael S. *Angry White Men: American Masculinity at the End of an Era.* New York: Nation Books, 2013.

———. *Guyland: The Perilous World Where Boys Become Men.* New York: Harper, 2008.

Kogod, Sarah. "Ohio State LB Jerome Baker Wants to Change How Athletes Talk About Sexual Violence." *SB Nation*, September 17, 2015. http://www
.sbnation.com/2015/9/17/9105829/ohio-state-jerome-baker-is-changing
-athletes-sexual-assault-2015.

Kooper, Angelique J. A., Jacqueline J. P. M. Pieters, Alex J. Eggink, Ton B. Feuth, Ilse Feenstra, Lia D. E. Wijnberger, Robbert J. P. Rijnders, et al. "Why Do Parents Prefer to Know the Fetal Sex as Part of Invasive Prenatal Testing?" *ISRN Obstetrics and Gynecology* (2012). Article ID 524537, 2012. doi:10.5402/2012/524537.

Latest Hate Crime Statistics Available. Washington, DC: Federal Bureau of Investigation, November 16, 2015. https://www.fbi.gov/news/stories/latest
-hate-crime-statistics-available.

Lee, Dave. "*Grand Theft Auto*: One of Britain's Finest Cultural Exports?" *BBC News*, September 17, 2013. http://www.bbc.com/news/technology-24066068.

Legault, Jacques. "Why Parents Need to Become Gamers." *Medium*, August 20, 2017. https://medium.com/@jacquesrlegault/why-parents-need-to-become
-gamers-4074b3561b89.

Lenhart, Amanda. *Teens, Social Media & Technology Overview, 2015.* Washington, DC: Pew Research Center, April 9, 2015. http://www
.pewinternet.org/2015/04/09/teens-social-media-technology-2015.

Levant, R. F., M. D. Parent, E. R. McCurdy, and T. C. Bradstreet. "Moderated Mediation of the Relationships Between Masculinity Ideology, Outcome Expectations, and Energy Drink Use." *Health Psychology* 34, no. 11 (2015): 1100–1106. http://dx.doi.org/10.1037/hea0000214.

Levy, DeAndre. "Man Up." *Players' Tribune*, April 27, 2016. http://www
.theplayerstribune.com/deandre-levy-sexual-assault-awareness.

Lindberg, L. D., I. Maddow-Zimet, and H. Boonstra. "Changes in Adolescents'
Receipt of Sex Education, 2006–2013." *Journal of Adolescent Health* 58,
no. 6 (2016): 621–627. https://doi.org/10.1016/j.jadohealth.2016.02.004.

Lu, Alexander. "How Are the Experiences of Asian American Men Stressful?"
Gender & Society (blog), May 31, 2013. https://gendersociety.wordpress
.com/2013/05/31/how-are-the-experiences-of-asian-american-men-stressful.

Lu, Alexander, and Y. Joel Wong. "Stressful Experiences of Masculinity Among
U.S.-Born and Immigrant Asian American Men." *Gender & Society* 27,
no. 3 (2013): 345–371. https://doi.org/10.1177/0891243213479446.

Luther, Jessica W. *Unsportsmanlike Conduct: College Football and the Politics
of Rape*. New York: Akashic Books, 2016.

Manne, Kate. *Down Girl: The Logic of Misogyny*. New York: Oxford
University Press, 2017.

Manson, Marilyn. "Columbine: Whose Fault Is It?" *Rolling Stone*, June 24,
1999. https://www.rollingstone.com/culture/news/columbine-whose-fault
-is-it-19990624.

Markey, Patrick M., and Christopher J. Ferguson. *Moral Combat: Why the
War on Violent Video Games Is Wrong*. Dallas: BenBella Books, 2017.

Martinez, Donna. "School Culture and American Indian Educational
Outcomes." Fifth World Conference Educational Sciences—WCES 2013.
Procedia—Social and Behavioral Sciences 116 (2014): 199–205.

Massey, Alana. "Hold Your Laughter: Men Could Learn Something from One
Direction." *MEL Magazine*, May 3, 2017. https://melmagazine.com
/out-of-the-many-one-direction-70edbbf0d64.

Mayer, Andre. "*GTA5*: How *Grand Theft Auto* Has Changed the Gaming
World." *CBC News*, September 17, 2013. http://www.cbc.ca/news
/technology/gta5-how-grand-theft-auto-has-changed-the-gaming
-world-1.1857987.

McCabe, Janice, Emily Fairchild, Liz Grauerholz, Bernice A. Pescosolido, and
Daniel Tope. "Gender in Twentieth-Century Children's Books: Patterns of
Disparity in Titles and Central Characters." *Gender & Society* 25, no. 2
(2011): 197–226. https://doi.org/10.1177/0891243211398358.

McGraw, Daniel. "How Should Tamir Rice Be Remembered?" The Undefeated, August 23, 2016. https://theundefeated.com/features/how-should-tamir-rice-be-remembered.

McLeod, Ken. *We Are the Champions: The Politics of Sport and Popular Music*. London: Routledge, 2011.

Mead, Sara. *The Evidence Suggests Otherwise: The Truth About Boys and Girls*. Washington, DC: Education Sector, June 2006.

Millennials in Adulthood: Detached from Institutions, Networked with Friends. Washington, DC: Pew Research Center, March 7, 2014. http://www.pewsocialtrends.org/2014/03/07/millennials-in-adulthood.

Miller, Kathleen E. "Sport-Related Identities and the 'Toxic Jock.'" *Journal of Sport Behavior* 32, no. 1 (2009): 69–91.

Mintz, Steven. *Huck's Raft: A History of American Childhood*. Cambridge, MA: Harvard University Press, 2004.

Morris, Wesley. "The Year We Obsessed over Identity." *New York Times Magazine*, October 6, 2015. http://www.nytimes.com/2015/10/11/magazine/the-year-we-obsessed-over-identity.html.

MTV's "Look Different" Gender Bias Survey. New York: MTV Insights, 2015. http://www.lookdifferent.org/about-us/research-studies/2-mtv-s-2015-look-different-gender-bias-survey.

Murthy, Vivek. "Work and the Loneliness Epidemic." *Harvard Business Review*, September 27, 2017. https://hbr.org/cover-story/2017/09/work-and-the-loneliness-epidemic.

Musu-Gillette, L., A. Zhang, K. Wang, J. Zhang, and B. A. Oudekerk. *Indicators of School Crime and Safety, 2016*. NCES 2017-064/NCJ 250650. Washington, DC: National Center for Education Statistics, US Department of Education, and Bureau of Justice Statistics, Office of Justice Programs, US Department of Justice, 2017.

Naccarato, Lisa. "Almost Half of TDSB Students Expelled over Last 5 Years Are Black, Report Says." *CBC News*, April 11, 2017. http://www.cbc.ca/news/canada/toronto/almost-half-of-tdsb-students-expelled-over-last-5-years-are-black-report-says-1.4065088.

National Center for Health Statistics. "Health, United States, 2016: With Chartbook on Long-Term Trends in Health." Hyattsville, MD: National

Center for Health Statistics, 2017. https://www.cdc.gov/nchs/data/hus
/hus16.pdf#035.

"Not in My Locker Room: DeAndre Levy of the Detroit Lions Speaks Out."
Episode 63 of *Edge of Sports*, October 15, 2016. http://www
.edgeofsportspodcast.com/post/151838004210/not-in-my-locker
-room-deandre-levy-of-the-detroit.

O'Connell, Chris. "How Dude Perfect Makes Child's Play Hard Work." *Texas
Monthly*, August 2017. https://www.texasmonthly.com/the-culture/yes/.

Okopny, Cara. "Why Jimmy Isn't Failing: The Myth of the Boy Crisis."
Feminist Teacher 18, no. 3 (2008): 216–228.

Orenstein, Peggy. "What's Wrong with Cinderella?" *New York Times Magazine*,
December 24, 2006. http://www.nytimes.com/2006/12/24/magazine
/24princess.t.html.

Parker, Kim, Juliana Menasce Horowitz, and Renee Stepler. *On Gender
Differences, No Consensus on Nature vs. Nurture*. Washington, DC: Pew
Research Center, December 2017.

Parker, Laura A. "The Cult of PewDiePie: How a Swedish Gamer Became
YouTube's Biggest Star." *Rolling Stone*, December 16, 2015. http://www
.rollingstone.com/culture/news/the-cult-of-pewdiepie-how-a-swedish
-gamer-became-youtubes-biggest-star-20151216.

Pascoe, C. J. *Dude, You're a Fag: Masculinity and Sexuality in High School*.
Berkeley: University of California Press, 2012.

Paul, Annie Murphy. *Origins: How the Nine Months Before Birth Shape the
Rest of Our Lives*. New York: Free Press, 2010.

Pereira, David. "Dropping Out or Opting Out? A Qualitative Study on How
Young Men of Portuguese Ancestry in Toronto Perceive Masculinity and
How This Informs Educational Attainment." Master's thesis, Ontario
Institute for Studies in Education, University of Toronto, 2011.

Pound, Pandora, Rebecca Langford, and Rona Campbell. "What Do Young
People Think About Their School-Based Sex and Relationship Education?
A Qualitative Synthesis of Young People's Views and Experiences." *BMJ
Open* 6, no. 9 (2016). https://doi.org/10.1136/bmjopen-2016-011329.

Presley, Amie, and Robert S. Brown. *Portuguese-Speaking Students in the
TDSB: An Overview*. Toronto: Toronto District School Board, September

2011. http://www.tdsb.on.ca/Portals/research/docs/reports/Portuguese
-speakingStudentsInTheTDSBOverview.pdf.

Press, Eyal. "Do Immigrants Make Us Safer?" *New York Times Magazine*, December 3, 2006. http://www.nytimes.com/2006/12/03/magazine /03wwln_idealab.html.

Pyne, Jake. "Gender Independent Kids: A Paradigm Shift in Approaches to Gender Non-conforming Children." *Canadian Journal of Human Sexuality* 23, no. 1 (2014): 1–8. http://dx.doi.org/10.3138/cjhs.23.1.CO1.

Reckdahl, Katy. "Training More Black Men to Become Teachers." *Atlantic*, December 15, 2015. https://www.theatlantic.com/education/archive /2015/12/programs-teachers-african-american-men/420306/.

Reilly, Katie. "Hillary Clinton Apologizes for 'Superpredator' Remark." *Time*, February 26, 2016. http://time.com/4238230/hillary-clinton-black-lives -matter-superpredator.

Reisner, S. L., et al. "Mental Health of Transgender Youth in Care at an Adolescent Urban Community Health Center: A Matched Retrospective Cohort Study." *Journal of Adolescent Health* 56, no. 3 (2015): 274–279. http://www.ncbi.nlm.nih.gov/pmc/articles/PMC4339405/.

Remise du rapport relatif à l'éducation à la sexualité aux ministres Najat Vallaud-Belkacem et Laurence Rossignol. Paris: Haut Conseil à l'Egalité Entre les Femmes et les Hommes, République Française, June 15, 2016. http://www.haut-conseil-egalite.gouv.fr/sante-droits-sexuels-et/actualites -53/article/remise-du-rapport-relatif-a-l.

Report on Sexually Transmitted Infections in Canada, 2013–2014. Ottawa: Centre for Communicable Diseases and Infection Control, Infectious Disease Prevention and Control Branch, Public Health Agency of Canada, 2017.

Rosin, Hanna. *The End of Men and the Rise of Women*. New York: Riverhead, 2012.

Rothman, Barbara Katz. *The Tentative Pregnancy*. New York: W. W. Norton, 1993.

Sandin, S., D. Schendel, P. Magnusson, C. Hultman, P. Surén, and E. Susser. "Autism Risk Associated with Parental Age and with Increasing Difference in Age Between the Parents." *Molecular Psychiatry* 21 (2016): 693–700. http://www.nature.com/mp/journal/v21/n5/full/mp201570a.html.

Bibliography

Sawyer, Wendy. "Youth Confinement: The Whole Pie." Prison Policy Initiative, February 27, 2018. https://www.prisonpolicy.org/reports/youth2018.html.

Schalet, Amy T. "Beyond Abstinence and Risk: A New Paradigm for Adolescent Sexual Health." *Women's Health Issues* 21, no. 3 (2011): S5–S7. http://www.whijournal.com/article/S1049-3867(11)00008-9/fulltext.

———. "Must We Fear Adolescent Sexuality?" *Medscape General Medicine* 6, no. 4 (2004): 44. http://www.ncbi.nlm.nih.gov/pmc/articles/PMC1480590.

———. "Why Boys Need to Have Conversations About Emotional Intimacy in Classrooms." The Conversation, February 25, 2016. https://theconversation.com/why-boys-need-to-have-conversations-about-emotional-intimacy-in-classrooms-54693.

Sedgwick, Eve Kosofsky. *Between Men: English Literature and Male Homosocial Desire*. New York: Columbia University Press, 1985.

Semuels, Alana. "Poor Girls Are Leaving Their Brothers Behind." *Atlantic*, November 27, 2017. https://www.theatlantic.com/business/archive/2017/11/gender-education-gap/546677.

Shipp, Thomas D., Diane Z. Shipp, Bryann Bromley, Robert Sheahan, Amy Cohen, Ellice Lieberman, and Beryl Benacerraf. "What Factors Are Associated with Parents' Desire to Know the Sex of Their Unborn Child?" *Birth: Issues in Perinatal Care* 31, no. 4 (2004): 272–279.

Sickmund, Melissa, and Charles Puzzanchera, eds. *Juvenile Offenders and Victims: 2014 National Report*. Pittsburgh: National Center for Juvenile Justice, 2014.

Singal, Jesse. "A New Book Argues That the Concerns over Violent Video Games Are a Moral Panic." *New York Magazine*, March 17, 2017.

Smedley, Audrey, and Brian D. Smedley. "Race as Biology Is Fiction, Racism as a Social Problem Is Real: Anthropological and Historical Perspectives on the Social Construction of Race." *American Psychologist* 60, no. 1 (2005): 16–26.

Snowdon, Wallis. "Ending Homophobia in Hockey Starts in the Locker Room, Edmonton Researcher Says." *CBC News*, January 19, 2017. http://www.cbc.ca/news/canada/edmonton/ending-homophobia-in-hockey-starts-in-the-locker-room-edmonton-researcher-says-1.3942599.

Sommers, Christina Hoff. "School Has Become Too Hostile to Boys." *Time*, August 19, 2013. http://ideas.time.com/2013/08/19/school-has-become-too-hostile-to-boys.

———. "The War on Boys." *Atlantic*, May 2000. https://www.theatlantic.com
/magazine/archive/2000/05/the-war-against-boys/304659.

Stewart, Alicia W. "#IamJada: When Abuse Becomes a Teen Meme." CNN, July
18, 2014. http://www.cnn.com/2014/07/18/living/jada-iamjada-teen-social
-media/index.html.

Sweet, Elizabeth. "Toys Are More Divided by Gender Now than They Were
50 Years Ago." *Atlantic*, December 9, 2014. https://www.theatlantic.com
/business/archive/2014/12/toys-are-more-divided-by-gender-now-than
-they-were-50-years-ago/383556.

Taff, Jessica, and Joseph Auriemma. "Out on the Field: Former NFL Player
Wade Davis Opens Up." *Al Jazeera America*, May 12, 2014. http://america
.aljazeera.com/watch/shows/america-tonight/articles/2014/5/12/out-on-the
-fieldwadedavisonprosportsevolutionoverlgbtqplayers.html.

Talbot, Margaret. "Red Sex, Blue Sex." *New Yorker*, November 3, 2008.
https://www.newyorker.com/magazine/2008/11/03/red-sex-blue-sex.

Testi, Arnaldo. "The Gender of Reform Politics: Theodore Roosevelt and the
Culture of Masculinity." *Journal of American History* 81, no. 4 (1995):
1509–1533. https://doi.org/10.2307/2081647.

"This Military Couple's Gender Reveal Blows All Others Away!" Bearing Arms,
May 9, 2016. http://bearingarms.com/jenn-j/2016/05/09/this-military
-couples-gender-reveal-blows-all-others-away.

Thompson, Clive. *Smarter than You Think: How Technology Is Changing Our
Minds for the Better*. New York: Penguin Random House, 2013.

Toppo, Greg. "Do Video Games Inspire Violent Behavior?" *Scientific American*,
July 1, 2015. https://www.scientificamerican.com/article/do-video-games
-inspire-violent-behavior.

"Traumatic Brain Injury & Concussions." Centers for Disease Control and
Prevention. https://www.cdc.gov/traumaticbraininjury/get_the_facts.html.

Trends in U.S. Corrections. Washington, DC: Sentencing Project, June 26,
2017. http://sentencingproject.org/wp-content/uploads/2016/01/Trends-in
-US-Corrections.pdf.

"12-Year-Old Couldn't Begin to Guess Name of Friend Whose House He Visits
to Play Xbox." The Onion, May 3, 2014. https://local.theonion.com/12
-year-old-couldn-t-begin-to-guess-name-of-friend-whos-1819576239.

Urquia, Marcelo L., Joel G. Ray, Susitha Wanigaratne, Rahim Moineddin, and Patricia J. O'Campo. "Variations in Male-Female Infant Ratios Among Births to Canadian- and Indian-Born Mothers, 1990–2011: A Population-Based Register Study." *Canadian Medical Association Journal* (April 11, 2016). http://cmajopen.ca/content/4/2/E116.full.

Wang, Oliver S. "Lin Takes the Weight." *Atlantic*, March 1, 2012. https://www.theatlantic.com/entertainment/archive/2012/03/lin-takes-the-weight/253833.

Way, Niobe. *Deep Secrets: Boys' Friendships and the Crisis of Connection.* Cambridge, MA: Harvard University Press, 2011.

Wilson, Holly A., and Robert D. Hoge. "The Effect of Youth Diversion Programs on Recidivism: A Meta-analytic Review." *Criminal Justice and Behavior* 40, no. 5 (2013): 497–518. http://dx/doi.org/10.1177/0093854812451089.

Wilson, Kristian. "How Diverse Is Children's Literature?" Bustle, September 14, 2016. https://www.bustle.com/articles/183948-how-diverse-is-childrens-literature-this-infographic-tells-the-disturbing-truth.

Wiseman, Rosalind. *Masterminds & Wingmen: Helping Our Boys Cope with Schoolyard Power, Locker-Room Tests, Girlfriends, and the New Rules of Boy World.* New York: Harmony Books, 2013.

Zimmerman, Jonathan. *Too Hot to Handle: A Global History of Sex Education.* Princeton, NJ: Princeton University Press, 2015.

ABOUT THE AUTHOR

Rachel Giese is the editor at large at *Chatelaine*, Canada's preeminent women's magazine, and a regular contributor to CBC Radio. Her award-winning writing has appeared in the *Globe and Mail*, the *Toronto Star*, the *Hairpin*, *Real Life*, and *NewYorker.com*. She lives in Toronto with her wife and son.